A Bible-based Guide to Prophetic...

Parables, Riddles, and Mysteries of the Lord Revealed

Blessings as you unwrap mysteries from the Lord
Heidi?

Sandra L. Dawson

Printed in Canada

ISBN: 978-1-4866-1787-6

Word Alive Press
119 De Baets Street Winnipeg, MB R2J 3R9
www.wordalivepress.ca

Cataloguing in Publication information can be obtained from Library and Archives Canada.

DEDICATION

I DEDICATE THIS BOOK TO THE FOLLOWING SPECIAL PEOPLE IN MY Christian walk and life:

Charlotte Quist, Senior Pastor of Victory Church on the Rock in Grande Prairie, and Author of **Canada's Jesus Revolution.** I give thanks to her for the acknowledgement of my gifting in the prophetic vein, the acknowledgement of all the work that has gone into this book, and the giving of her time and the support for this book. She is an amazing preacher and teacher of the Word of God, who encourages the pursuit of one's calling.

As well, Paul and Janice Juss, the Founding Pastors of Victory Church on the Rock in Grande Prairie, for their many years of pastoral leadership, prayers, support and being an awesome spiritual father and mother, plus so much more. They truly shepherd the flock with great care.

Also, Erika Ocayo a long-time prayer partner, intercessor and friend. She is such a prayer warrior for so many people and receives dreams from the Lord for revelation and direction on what to pray and intercede for. Prayer and intersession is her life. We have often collaborated together with many dream symbols in context with each specific dream. She truly cares for those who she ministers to.

Finally, thanks to the many brothers and sisters in Christ for all their positive words on this book, their friendship, and prayers and support. And for those who have trusted in me to help with dreams they have dreamed, along with the then current circumstances or events in their lives, receive from me, help to tie these all together for what the Lord could be revealing to them. Thank you all for valuing my insight.

CONTENTS

SUMMARY   vii
ACKNOWLEDGEMENTS   ix
PREFACE   xi
FOREWORD   xiii
INTRODUCTION   xv

PART 1
A-Z ALPHABETICAL LIST   1

PART 2
COLORS   295

PART 3
NUMBERS   303

PART 4
DIRECTIONS   313

ABOUT THE AUTHOR   317
BIBLIOGRAPHY   319

SUMMARY

THIS IS A BIBLE-BASED PROPHETIC DREAM SYMBOLISM Interpretation book. It has an easy to read layout, including subtitles, with a few of the main titles of any given symbol. For example, under the title "Trees", are the different kinds of trees, which are included as subtitles. Another is with "Birds". I have included these subtitles, so the reader does not have to look up other titles throughout the book, to save them time and energy.

ACKNOWLEDGEMENTS

FIRST AND FOREMOST, I GIVE THANKS TO THE LORD FOR THE CALL and enablement and wisdom I needed for the writing of this book.

I also want to express my great appreciation to Les Bourassa, an amazing pastor from my home church Victory Church on the Rock in Grande Prairie, who is also a very gifted teacher in the Word of God, and every aspect of a believer's life. I am so thankful for all his knowledge with the ins and outs of writing a book, answering my many questions, the giving of his time and support throughout this whole process. I especially give thanks for his amazing editorial skills and for the proofreading of my manuscript, and the editing of this book. His support has been invaluable in the finished product being made possible. He is an amazing pastor so full of the joy of the Lord, a great sense of humor and fun to be around.

PREFACE

THE PURPOSE OF THIS BOOK IS TO SHARE THE LISTED PROPHETIC symbolisms but with a redemptive purpose in mind. As long as we, Spirit-filled believers, remain on this earth, there will always be redemption available. This book gives an all-encompassing description, the possible negative, which can be observed through dreams of warnings, as well as the positive and confirming aspects of such dreams. Dreams may also have double meanings and can often be for more than the one involved in a situation or circumstance; these may even apply to systems in the world. One may receive judgment, correction or exposure, while the other receives justice, repayment and restoration for the injustices they have endured. There are many double, positive and negative, meanings for these very reasons. What one feels in the dream can also be an indicator of whether there is something wrong, a call to prayer and spiritual warfare, direction, etc, or whether a solution, strategy, breakthrough, or confirmation in which direction to take is being offered. In some dreams the dreamer has an opportunity to change the outcome of the dream by taking action within the dream to change a natural situation, or an oncoming attack of the enemy of our souls. (Often times this can happen through people, other times these are literal or spiritual attacks). Intercessors dream dreams for those they are called to intercede for, counsel with, and sometimes to warn them of imminent disastrous circumstances. Another purpose may be to warn of a plotting, or a serious betrayal, etc. So, I give as detailed as possible, an all-encompassing description for any of the above possibilities. I and my intercessor friend have had similar experiences to the above dreams of warnings. I am a new author, this is my first book. Because I am unknown publically, I have made sure to check everything over for accuracy and most importantly keeping connected to the Source of all revelation. I have searched out Scriptures as much as possible to back up, Biblically, the definitions I have listed.

Another reason for which I wrote this book, is as a culmination of the experiences listed above, as well as the fact that there have been symbolisms we were not able to reference elsewhere.

I and a certain intercessor friend and prayer partner, have worked together for several years with all sorts of prophetic dreams and interpretations. We have had to seek the Lord at times, for some unusual symbolisms not found in other books. There are some books with very complete guides, this book is a culmination of my experiences, as well as a complete-as-possible listing as I have been able to include.

The part on Numbers can also be a reference to a particular Scripture the Lord is leading the reader to, as well as it can have the meanings listed with the numbers. It could be one or the other, or both.

So, I include my and my prophetic intercessor friends' experiences, along with more familiar symbolisms many have dreamt or have had visions of, as well as the other, more uncommon ones that I have searched out. This book has a different lay-out that I think will be easier to follow than most. There are, to be sure, a few double entries, as there are some different words or names for the same sorts of things, and I believe will keep the reader from having to keep flipping through the book to find what they are looking for, especially when referencing several books together.

FOREWORD

THE FOLLOWING BOOK IS AN EXCELLENT RESOURCE FOR PEOPLE who are trying to figure out what their dreams may be about. The symbols discussed, and their meanings are the common or known applications for what these usually mean. In many ways this resource is to be taken as a confirmation of what the Holy Spirit may be revealing to the visionary or dreamer. I know that Sandra has been working on this book for some time now and has been diligent in her research and study. It has been a pleasure to see her go through the process of compiling this anthology of vision and dream symbolism. I recommend it as a useful tool for illuminating some otherwise confusing dreams and/or visions. It's simple format and lay out make it a handy guide for the mysteries and riddles of life in the here and now, and for life in the Spirit.

Pastor Les Bourassa
Director, Victory Ministry Training Centre
(an affiliation with Victory Bible College International)
Grande Prairie, Alberta
Canada

INTRODUCTION

HAVE YOU EVER WONDERED WHAT YOUR DREAMS MEAN? HAVE you experienced repeated dreams and wondered what you should do about them. This is a Bible-based Prophetic Dream Symbolism Interpretation book. It has an easy to read layout, which includes subtitles with a few of the main titles of a symbol. For example, Birds has various kinds of birds listed just below that entry. The same format applies with Trees, Bugs, Vehicles, Aircraft, etc. This format saves the reader from having to search throughout the book for separate titles. This arrangement is meant to save the reader time and energy especially if consulting several references at once.

There are a lot of extras found in this book as well.... For example, the author has included a very detailed description of the Candlestick (Lamp stand), its relation to Jesus, its formation, its relation to the teaching of the Seven Spirits of God (Seven-fold Spirit of God) and its relation to some color's symbolisms. This sort of extra information is included to help demonstrate how it all originated and is all tied together. Scripture is used as much as possible, to show how they all relates to one another as well as for instance, the natural formation of the colors of the rainbow.

This book isn't meant to be read through from the first page to the last, it is more like a manual.

This is a quick reference, dictionary-like, guide to finding the prophetic symbolisms that the reader is looking for.

There are four parts to this book:

Part 1, is a complete **Alphabetical listing**, and is the main section of this book.

Part 2, is a listing on **Colors**.

Part 3, is a listing on **Numbers**.

Part 4, is a listing on **Directions**; which are in the alphabetical listing also as certain definitions can relate to other definitions, again to save the reader from having to turn to near the end of the book from where they are reading.

Under each symbol listing, are the Scriptures references for the reader to verify and check out for themselves.

The Scriptures are kept in the order of the description listings as much as possible. This is done so the reader can see the parts of the description that stand out according to their dream or vision, as well as to see, which Scriptures are related to the specific description.

Also, there are Sub Headings listed under some major Headings. Again, for example, in the Main Heading of Trees, are Sub Headings of the specific type of tree the dreamer may be looking for. The Main Heading gives the main general symbolic descriptions, and the Sub Headings give specific descriptions of the specific type of tree. This may give a fuller meaning that the reader may be looking for. Another example is the Major Heading of Birds. There are Sub Headings of different kinds of birds; along with different actions of the birds.

There are sections like this for several similar things, which should save the reader time and energy in their searching the information they are looking for.

PART 1

A – Z: ALPHABETICAL LIST

Aardvark - Enemy of the industrious and diligent; nosey; discernment; sniffs out and destroys hidden corruption. Proverbs 6:6-8, 2 Timothy 2:17, 1 Timothy 1:20, 2 Timothy 3:1-9.
Ant = Industrious; wise; diligent; prepared for the future; nuisance, stinging or angry.
Proverbs 6:6-8, Proverbs 30:25.
  Fire Ant = Fiery, angry words; attack of the enemy; volatile, dangerous situation.
  James 3:6, Proverbs 16:27.
Termites = Corruption; hidden destruction; secret sin; deception; demons; unclean spirits.
Psalm 11:3, Haggai 1:6.

Abominable Snowman - Cold-hearted abuser; abomination of the Lord; demonic deception.
Exodus 7:14, Exodus 1:22, Acts 7:19, Proverbs 11:20, Proverbs 6:16-19.

Abortion - Aborted project; cut off; failure; to kill promise (Herod spirit); seize ones' inheritance. See Miscarriage.
Matthew 2:16, Exodus 1:16, Revelation 12:4, Amos 1:13, 2 Kings 8:12, Hosea 13:16.

Acacia Tree - Symbolizes immortality, and the duality of life and death; thorny. See Trees.
Isaiah 41:19.

Accident, Vehicle, Ship, Train, Airplane etc. - Strife; contention; conflict; confrontation; calamity; offense; mistake or sin in ministry; failure; church split; personal disaster (failed marriage, business venture, ministry, project etc.); end of one

phase (for whatever reason unbeknownst to the dreamer). See Driver, Captain, Conductor, or Pilot, and associated means of transportation.
Nahum 2:3-4, 2 Corinthians 11:25-28, 1 Timothy 1:19-20.

Acid - Bitter; offense; carry a grudge; hatred; sarcasm. Acts 8:23, Hebrews 12:15.
Acid in a Container = Potentially dangerous situation, must handle with care. Jeremiah 4:18.
Acid on Skin = Extremely damaging and challenging situation; facing dangerous, corrosive scenario. Lamentations 3:19.

Acorn - Potential for greatness; small but significant. Judges 6:11-12.

Actor - Pretending; insincere; role-playing; idol worship; hypocrite.
Matthew 6:5, Matthew 23:13-14, & 23-29.

Addiction - Bondage; obsessed; demonized. See Drugs, Alcohol.
Hebrews 2:15.

Adultery - Sin; idolatry; pornography. See Sex.
Galatians 5:19-21, James 4:4, Ecclesiastes 7:26, Proverbs 30:20, Matthew 5:28.
Married Person Dreaming of Having an Affair = Unfaithful in the things of God; literal or tempting situation; divided loyalty; wavering between opinions.
1 Kings 18:21, Zephaniah 1:5, Matthew 6:24, 1 Corinthians 10:21, 2 Corinthians 6:14-16.
Married Man Dreams of Looking for a Person to Marry = Need to fully identify one's calling; not completely settled

into the marriage relationship; need to become more intimate with one's spouse.
Revelation 3:15-16, Matthew 24:12, Revelation 2:4-5.

The Dreamer Suspects their Spouse of Having an Affair = One's spouse is paying attention to business or profession, or even calling; spirit of jealousy.
Numbers 5:14- 31, Proverbs 6:34, Song of Solomon 8:6, 1 Corinthians 10:22.

Air Conditioner - Spiritual conditioning; ministering in the gifts of the Spirit; cooling off; calming down.
Galatians 3:5, 1 Corinthians 12:1-31, Genesis 27:44-45, Proverbs 15:1, Psalm 37:8.

Airline Pilot - One in control; self; Christ; pastor; teacher; Satan; emphasis may be on the nature of the pilot (Confident, kind, careful, frantic, careless, selfish, rude ...). See Captain.
2 Samuel 22:11, Psalm 18:10, Acts 8:39.

Airplane/Aircraft - Person or work; the Church; ministry; oversight.
Habakkuk 1:8, Judges 13:25.

PTO (Aircraft Power Take-off Systems) = Empowerment through the Word of God; divine boldness; impartation of anointing from one to another; given miraculous ability to further the kingdom of God; manifest presence of God.
Acts 4:29-31, Acts 10:37-38, Romans 15:19, Acts 1:8, Luke 9:1, John 20:21-23, Mark 9:1, 1 Corinthians 4:20, 1 Thessalonians 1:5.

Black Box = Record of conversations; to investigate; search out the answers; find evidence.
Genesis 18:21, Exodus 2:11-14, Mark 14:72, John 21:24-25, 1 Corinthians 2:9-10.

Flying near Electrical Power Lines = Caution; danger; need for prayer.

Flying Too Low = Insufficient power, prayer, preparation, or training; only partially operating in the spirit; not following, being led by the Spirit.

Flying High = Fully empowered by the Spirit.
2 Kings 2:9-11, Psalm 104:3-4.

Soaring Aircraft = Deep in the Spirit; moving in the deep things of God.

Supersonic Flight = Fast; powerful; soaring in the Spirit; fully empowered by the Spirit; deep in the Spirit; moving in the deep things of God; extreme acceleration into the new season and ministry.
2 Kings 2:9-11, Psalm 104:3-4.

Passenger Airplane = The Church.

Cargo Plane = Large ministry; bearer of large loads; apostolic ministry; releases international ministries.
Acts 13:1-5, 13-14, & 46-51, Romans 15:19, 2 Corinthians 10:13, Colossians 1:6, & 23-29.

Small Airplane = Small or personal ministry.

Helicopter = Ministry; individual; the Church; versatile, no forward movement; stationary; lack of progress.
2 Timothy 4:2a.

> **Military Helicopter** = Powerful prayer life; challenging enemy attack.

> **Military Helicopter Fighting for One** = Powerful intercession on one's behalf.

> **Attacking Military Helicopter** = Enemy forces coming against oneself.

Fighter Jet = A call to intercessory ministry; spiritual warfare.
Genesis 41:43, 2 Kings 10:16, Zechariah 6:1-8, Isaiah 5:26-28.

Stealth Bomber = Strategic powerful ministry; effective; attacking; does not attract attention; very difficult to intercept ministry's assignment; effortless flow in the Spirit; a call to regional or national intercessory ministry; heavy spiritual warfare; great angelic protection. See Bomb, Nuclear Bomb.

Genesis 41:43, 2 Kings 10:16, Zechariah 6:1-8, Isaiah 5:26-28, Joshua 8:2-7, Daniel 10:12-13, & 20-21, Ephesians 6:12.

Airplanes Flying in Formation = Working together in unity; keeping the unity of the Spirit; every part doing its share; communicating effectively; skilled; trained up in the things of God; trained up in the gifts; alert to the will of God; faithful.

Psalm 133:1-3, Ephesians 4:1-16, 1 Corinthians 12:4-28, Romans 12:1-10.

Various Kinds of Aircraft = All the parts working together; no partiality; multi-generational; humble; in covenant.

1 Corinthians 3:6-10, 1 Corinthians 12:4-28, Romans 15:20, Romans 12:1-16, 2 Corinthians 10:13-16.

All the Same Type of Jet Aircraft = Specialized ministry (like the Snow Birds, or Dog-fighters); very agile and powerful ministry; highly skilled; specially trained; fiercely loyal; highly efficient communicators; organized; completely unified; keeping one's position; Special Forces in spiritual warfare.

2 Samuel 23:8-39, 1 Chronicles 11:10-47.

All the Same Type of Domestic Aircraft = Associating only with ones' own kind ("Clique"); excluding others different than ones' group; partiality; fear; pride; selfishness; not willing to move out of comfort zone; familiar spirit; could be a smaller unified and specialised ministry.

James 2:1-9, Romans 12:9-16.

Airplanes Flying out of Formation = Disunity; going AWOL; low or no communication; careless; concerned only with worldly cares; in collision course; in danger of catastrophic failure; in danger of church split.

2 Timothy 4:3-4, 1 John 2:19, Matthew 22:1-10, 1 John 2:15-16.

Various Kinds of Aircraft = Compromise for the sake of unity; false unity; fear of man; sold out to the world system.
Romans 12:2a, James 4:4, Romans 1:21-32.

All the Same Type of Aircraft = Disloyal; covenant breakers; betrayers; out of the will of God; never were a part of the ministry; have developed their own little group ("Clique"); rejecting ones who are "different"; partiality; fear; pride; selfishness; not willing to move out of comfort zone; familiar spirit; offense; could be weaker members (newer believers) not properly equipped.
1 John 2:19, Acts 15:24, Acts 20:30, Matthew 26:21-25, 1 Timothy 1:19-20, Jude 1:19, Matthew 18:6.

Airplane Mechanical Failure - Problem; sickness; spirit of poverty; demonic attack; hindrance to one's life, ministry, career, livelihood.
1 Thessalonians 2:18, Acts 16:6-7.

Airplane Crash = Strife; contention; conflict; confrontation; calamity; offense; mistake or sin in ministry; failure; church split; apostasy; personal disaster (failed marriage, business venture, ministry, project etc.); end of one phase (for whatever reason unbeknownst to the dreamer).
Nahum 2:3-4, 2 Corinthians 11:25-27, 1 Timothy 1:19-20.

Airport - High powered spiritual church capable of equipping and sending out ministries; ministry that sends out missionaries; ministry in preparation; ministry capable of providing others to be made ready for service; a place of waiting on the Lord.
Zechariah 6:1-8, Ezekiel 10:9-22, Psalm 68:17, 1 Peter 3:20, Jeremiah 23:22, Isaiah 40:31.

Alcohol - Intoxicated emotions; spiritual dissipation; toxic; spirit of man; counterfeit spirit; witchcraft; delusion; mocker.
Ephesians 5:18, Genesis 9:21-24, Proverbs 23:29-32, Proverbs 31:6, Deuteronomy 32:32-33, Proverbs 4:17, Acts 2:13-17, Proverbs 20:1.
Wine = Spirit of joy; Spirit of God; revelation; teaching truth; blessing.
Proverbs 31:6, Luke 5:37-38, 1 Corinthians 10:16, Titus 2:3, Deuteronomy 11:14.
Drink Wine in Moderation = Representative of healing in certain circumstances; giving into temptation if one has had a previous bondage.
1 Timothy 5:23, Proverbs 23:29-32.
Drinking Wine with Another = Representative of communion; spiritual fellowship.
1 Corinthians 10:16.
Wineskins = Human body as a vessel; the church; believers.
Luke 5:37-38.
Winepress = True doctrine; spiritual birthplace.
Matthew 21:33, Isaiah 5:1-2, Mark 12:1.

Alien (Foreigner) - Unbeliever; demonic; not of God; of the flesh; outcast; foreigner; believer (pilgrim on the earth), not of this world. See Nation.
Lamentations 5:2, Proverbs 25:25, Ephesians 2:12, Job 19:15, Genesis 47:9, 1 Chronicles 29:15, Psalm 119:19, Hebrews 11:13-16, & 34, 1 Peter 2:11.
Illegal Alien = Intruder; false identity; liar; deceiver; fraud; thief; spirit of death.
Joshua 9:3-15, John 10:1, 5, 8, & 10.

Aliens - Demonic spirits; demonic powers; deception. See UFO.

Ephesians 6:12, 2 Corinthians 11:13-15, Revelation 13:2, & 13-15, Galatians 1:8, Romans 8:38-39.

Alligator - Ancient; evil out of the past from generational or personal sin; danger, destruction, evil spirit; large mouthed enemy; verbal attack. See Snake.
Job 41:1, & 10, Psalm 74:14, Isaiah 27:1.

Almond Tree - Symbol of God's early execution of His purpose (this tree buds earlier than the other trees). See Trees.
Jeremiah 1:11-12.

Almonds - Chosen; awakened; fruitful; acceleration into one's purpose.
Numbers 17:5-8.

Altar - Sacrifice; service; offering; prayer; incense; consecration; worship.
Genesis 8:20, Genesis 13:4, Genesis 35:7, Exodus 27:1, Isaiah 56:7, 1 Samuel 2:28.

Anaconda - Divination; familiar spirits; ancestral spirits; a regional spirit; a coiling spirit that squeezes out the breath of life (the Holy Spirit) and cuts off a believer's lifeline to God (prayer); puts believers in bondage; thwarts a believer's purpose; high level of spiritual warfare needed. See Snake.
Acts 16:16-18, Ephesians 6:12, Psalm 91:13, Daniel 10:13 & 20.

Anchor - Representation of security, safety and hope; Jesus the Anchor of our soul.
Hebrews 6:19-20.
> **Trying to Secure an Anchor** = Need to put things in order; need to make things more secure.
> **Broken Anchor** = Lost firmness; lost security.

Weak Shaking Anchor = Need to strengthen existing security.
Strong Firm Anchor = Security in place.
Acts 27:29.
Cutting off of an Anchor = Letting go of security, in self or in God.
Acts 27:40.
Harbor = Safe place; divine protection; a place of God's refuge; a place of anchor; comfort zone; no progress; complacency, no growth; low expectations; hides weak faith; harbors anger, resentment, bitterness.
Psalm 91:1-2, John 10:10-13, Matthew 10:16, 1 Corinthians 16:9, Ezekiel 3:14, Proverbs 10:1.

Angel - Messenger; encouragement; help; deliverance.
Daniel 8:16, Daniel 9:21, Hebrews 1:14, Luke 1:19, & 26, Psalm 34:7, 2 Kings 6:16-17, Psalm 91:11.

Ankles - Little faith; early stages; trial of faith.
Ezekiel 47:3, Isaiah 3:16, Psalm 105:17-19, Genesis 39:20, Acts 16:24.
Weak Ankles = Weak faith; unsupported; undependable.
Acts 3:2-7.
Wearing an Anklet = Haughty; vain; seduction; beautiful.
Isaiah 3:16-20.
Chains on ankles = Bondage; trial.
Acts 16:24, Job 13:27, Job 33:11, Psalm 105:17-19, Jeremiah 20:2, Jeremiah 29:26.

Anoint - Equipping with the Holy Spirit for service; consecration; healing.
1 Kings 19:16, 2 Samuel 2:4, Acts 10:38, James 5:14.

Ant - Industrious; wise; diligent; prepared for the future; nuisance, stinging or angry.
Proverbs 6:6-8, Proverbs 30:25.
Invasion of Large Numbers of Ants = Challenging or dangerous situation; overwhelming situation; onslaught of the enemy.
Fire Ant = Fiery, angry words; attack of the enemy; volatile, dangerous situation.
James 3:6, Proverbs 16:27.
Stung or Bitten by Ants = Attacking words; stinging words; dangerous situation; attack of the enemy; strife.
Proverbs 26:20-21.

Antelope - Sure-footed; graceful.
2 Samuel 2:18-19, Psalm 18:33, Habakkuk 3:19, 2 Samuel 2:18.

Antenna - Receptive; attentive; listening.
Proverbs 8:10, & 32-34, Proverbs 5:1-2, Luke 11:28.
Broken Antenna = Unable to hear or understand; not listening.
Luke 9:45, Matthew 13:13-15.

Antiques - Past; inherited from our forefathers, good or evil; potential from the bloodline; memories. See Attic.
Jeremiah 6:16.

Antlers - Power; authority; past authority, if shed. See Horns, Wild Game.
Genesis 22:13.

Ape - Stronghold; defiant; strong man; strength; valiant; affluence; mammon.
1 Samuel 17:4, & 23-25, Matthew 12:29, Luke 11:21-22, 1 Samuel 14:52, Psalm 19:5, 2 Chronicles 9:21, 1 Kings 10:22.

Apple - Fruit; words; sin; temptation; appreciation; precious; love; comfort; promises of God; fruit of the Spirit.
Proverbs 25:11, Matthew 12:33-34, Genesis 3:6, Song of Solomon 2:3-5, Psalm 17:8, Galatians 5:22-23.
Spoiled Apple = Corrupted wisdom; wasted giftedness.
Unripe Apple = Future time and season of the promise or gift; potential.
Enticing Apple = Tempting situation.
Genesis 3:6.
Difficulty Reaching an Apple = Not fully equipped to reach a fulfillment of a promise; if the apple is precious, it is something of value to the dreamer or the apple of God's eye.
Deuteronomy 32:10, Psalm 17:8, Proverbs 7:2, Zechariah 2:8.

Apple Tree - Young man; lover, Jesus; grace; mercy; bears fruit, good or bad. See Trees.
Song of Solomon 2:3, Song of Solomon 8:5, Matthew 7:17.

Ark - God's presence and protection; deliverance; salvation; preparedness (for a rainy day).
Exodus 25:21-22, Hebrews 11:7.

Arm - Strength; Savior; deliverer; helper; aid; reaching out (showing mercy); striker.
Isaiah 53:1, Genesis 49:24, Exodus 6:6, 2 Chronicles 32:8, Titus 1:7, 1 Timothy 3:3.
An Arm Displayed = Threatening situation; boastfulness; warning from a superior power.
Jeremiah 17:5.
An Arm Coming against the Dreamer = A dangerous approaching; need additional wisdom, strength, or prayer.
Titus 1:7, 1 Timothy 3:3.

Armadillo - Self-protective; prepared to destroy, swiftly; easily startled; can put up a barrier between oneself and others, or God; discerning; diligent; shields oneself from the enemy.
Proverbs 6:11, Proverbs 24:34, 2 Samuel 12:4.

Armour - A symbol of warfare; spiritual covering.
Ephesians 6:10-18.

Army - Warriors; spiritual force; spiritual warfare; the Lord's battle.
Ephesians 6:12, 2 Kings 6:15-17, 2 Chronicles 20:15, Psalm 27:3.

Army Tank - Powerful deliverance ministry; impacting ministry; spiritual warfare; weighty words.
Nahum 2:3, 1 Samuel 2:10, Deuteronomy 20:1, Joel 2:5, Matthew 17:18, Ephesians 6:11, Ecclesiastes 8:4, Luke 4:32.

Arrows - Words; accusations; slander; gossip; attacks of the enemy; children; prayers; deliverance. See Knife, Sword.
Psalm 64:3, Psalm 11:2, Ephesians 6:17, Isaiah 49:2, Deuteronomy 32:42, 2 Kings 13:17.

Ashes - Memories; repentance; sorrow; ruin; destruction; consumed by God.
Job 13:12, Job 42:5-6, 2 Samuel 13:19, Ezekiel 28:18, 2 Peter 2:6, Hebrews 12:29.

Atom Bomb - Power; Holy Spirit outpouring; miracle power; sudden destruction; destroying words; ultimate judgement; can have an apocalyptic meaning.
Acts 1:8, Acts 2:17 - 19, 2 Peter 3:7, & 10-12, 1 Thessalonians 5:3, Luke 17:27-29, Zechariah 14:12.

Attic - Mind; thought; attitude, good or bad; learning; spiritual realm; past; neglected; stored. See Dusty Relics. Acts 10:9-11, Philippians 3:13.

Attorney - Advocate; Christ; legal defense; accuser. See Courthouse. Isaiah 43:26, 1 John 2:1.

Aunt - Married sister in Christ; similar characteristics or behaviour; literal aunt. Leviticus 20:19.

Autograph - Fame; prominence; royalty; favor; approval. 2 Chronicles 9:1-12, Matthew 4:23-25, Luke 5:15.

Automobile - Life; person; ministry; if new, then new ministry or new way of life; if fast may mean a reckless, self-righteous, or unsaved person (living life in the fast lane). Genesis 41:43, 2 Kings 10:16, 1 Chronicles 13:7, Acts 16:6-7, Genesis 45:27, Nahum 2:3-4, Isaiah 37:24.

Air Conditioning = If in good condition, adequate comfort; if not working, faulty provision for comfort.

Brakes = Slowing down; compelled to stop; stopping; hindrance. 1 Thessalonians 2:18, Acts 16:6-7, 2 Peter 2:14.

Driver's Seat = Indicates leadership; taking control.

Engine = Holy Spirit power; supernatural empowerment.

Catalytic Converter = New anointing of fire; transformative power; yoke-destroying power; gains territory; destroys strongholds; bringer of change; pioneer of new beginnings. Acts 3:19, James 5:19-20, Ezekiel 18:30-32, Lamentations 5:21, Jeremiah 31:18-20, Isaiah 1:16-20, Psalm 51:13, Acts 15:3, Acts 26:16-18.

Rear-view Mirror = Looking back; focus on the past; warning to watch your back; warning to look ahead. Genesis 19:7, & 26, Luke 17:31-32.

Seatbelts = Security; safety; preparedness when fastened; assurance; careless when unfastened.

Steering Wheel = The controlling or leading part; the means by which leadership is affected.

Tires = Spirit; life; relates to the spiritual condition. Exodus 14:25, Ezekiel 1:16-21.

Fully Inflated Tires = Encouraged in the Lord; enabled in ministry; prayerful; going in the power of the Lord.

Deflated Tires = Discouragement; dismay; hindrance; lack of prayer; lack of covering; lack of power.

Tires with no Tread = Worn out; unsafe ministry; careless ministry. Exodus 18:18, 1 Timothy 1:19-20, Psalm 73:2.

Keys = Authority; power to bind or loose; lock or unlock; wisdom; knowledge; important. Matthew 16:19, Isaiah 22:22, Revelation 3:7, Luke 11:52, Proverbs 4:7.

To be Given Keys = Given power and authority. Isaiah 22:22.

To Lose One's Keys = Lose the power and authority one was given.

Trunk = Heart; baggage. Proverbs 14:14, Hebrews 13:9 (KJV), Luke 11:46, Matthew 23:4, Acts 15:28.

Being Given a Replacement Automobile for One's Current Automobile = New assignment or ministry is being given to one, possible change of ministry.

Difficulty or Inability to Find One's Automobile = Hindrance; subversion or distraction; interference; opposition; being hidden from the automobile owner; losing one's way.

Vandalized Automobile = Ministry being destroyed, could be from all sorts of wrong motives.
John 10:10, Matthew 23:14.

Stolen Automobile = Ministry being taken away through opposition; attack of the enemy to destroy one's purpose; trip one up from an assignment; over-reaching of boundaries; restraint from living out one's heritage.
John 10:10, Genesis 27:35-36, Matthew 16:22-23, Jeremiah 9:4, 2 Corinthians 10:13-16, Micah 2:2.

Junkyard = Abandoned ministries; ministries need repair.

Convertible = Capable of open heaven administration; indicative of revelatory ministry.

> **With the Top Up** = Covered; protected; closed heaven; closed to revelation.

> **With the Top Down** = Uncovered; exposed; vulnerable; open heaven; open to receive revelation.

Motorcycle = Personal ministry; independence; rebellion; selfish; pride; swift progress.
Acts 8:4-7, & 26-39, 1 Corinthians 3:4-5, 1 Corinthians 12:14-16, & 20-21, 1 Samuel 15:23a.

Trail Motor Bike = Independent ministry; pioneering spirit; trail blazer.
2 Samuel 22:34, Psalm 18:33, Habakkuk 3:19.

Indy Race Car = Acceleration into the new season and ministry.

All-wheel Drive = Powerful ministry; ground breaking; capable of global influence; personal ministry or work in the natural; dependable; hard work; rescue; solid Biblical and gospel foundation.
Nahum 2:4, Isaiah 37:24.

Station Wagon = Natural or spiritual family; family ministry; fellowship.
Ephesians 3:14-15, 1 John 1:7.

Van = Natural or spiritual family; family ministry; fellowship.
Ephesians 3:14-15, 1 John 1:7.

Moving Van = Geographical move, natural or spiritual, (house, area, church, including change of affiliations, denominations); relocation.
Ezekiel 12:2-3.

Stalled Automobile = Ministry on hold; operation in one's own strength; need to take authority; hindrance by Satan; opposition.
Isaiah 49:2, Exodus 14:13-16, Galatians 5:7-12, Nehemiah 4:1-18, 1 Thessalonians 2:18.

Automobile Breakdown - Problem; sickness; spirit of poverty; demonic attack; hindrance to one's life, ministry, career, livelihood.
1 Thessalonians 2:18, Acts 16:6-7.

Automobile Crash - Strife; contention; conflict; confrontation; calamity; offense; mistake or sin in ministry; failure; church split; personal disaster (failed marriage, business venture, ministry, project etc.); end of one phase (for whatever reason unbeknownst to the dreamer).
Nahum 2:3-4, 2 Corinthians 11:25-27, 1 Timothy 1:19-20.

Autumn - End; completion; change; transition; close of harvesting; entering difficult times; sin; repentance.
Isaiah 64:6, Jeremiah 5:24, Jeremiah 8:20.

Avalanche - Unstoppable Force; sudden destruction; judgement; overwhelmed.
Proverbs 29:1.

Awake - Alert; watchful; aroused; stirred to action.
Isaiah 52:1-2, Judges 5:12, Zechariah 13:7, Psalm 78:65.

Axe - The Word of God; gospel; preach; exhort others; rebuke; repentance.
Matthew 3:7-12, Proverbs 27:17, Ecclesiastes 10:10.
Axe at the Foot of a Tree = Time to give account; judgement.
Matthew 3:10.
Swing or Wield the Axe = Forceful determination of an outcome.
Ax-head = Cutting edge of something.
Proverbs 27:27, 1 Samuel 13:21, Ecclesiastes 10:10.
Ax-head Floating = Miraculous event coming.

B

Baby - New beginning; new idea; new invention; new work; new ministry; new gift; new believer; dependant; helpless; innocent; sin; natural baby. See Pregnancy.
1 Peter 2:2, 1 Corinthians 3:1-2, James 1:14-15.
Giving Birth to a Baby = Something new is about to break forth.
Stolen Baby = Hindrances or delay to the manifestation of gift or potentials.
Deformed Baby = Corrupted or perverted gift beginning; corrupt attitude of gift; corrupt motives operating in gift.
Leviticus 21:17-23 (See with 1 Timothy 3:2-12, & 1 Thessalonians 2:10).
Miscarriage = New ministry destroyed; promise lost or robbed; failure; judgment; injustice (miscarriage of justice); lacking spiritual strength; repentance.
Acts 7:19, Matthew 2:16-18, Hosea 9:11- 16, Job 21:10, Isaiah 59:4, Isaiah 37:3,
Hosea 13:13, 2 Kings 19:1-4.
Experiencing a Miscarriage = Termination of ministry, plan or promise; experiencing an injustice.

Premature Delivery = Supernatural intervention; divine acceleration; presumptuous situation running ahead of the scheduled time.

The baby is Big for its age or has Hair and Teeth Early = One will mature in this new thing quickly.
1 Samuel 2:21, & 26, Luke 1:15, &80, Luke 2:40, &52.

Caring for another's Baby = Helping to nurture the ministry of another; enabling or training up another in ministry gift; interceding for another.
Exodus 2:6-10, Acts 7:21-22.

Finding, or being Given a Baby = Something another was called to do but did not do, is being given to you to do.

Baby Elephant - Potential for greatness; the beginning of something large or great.
1 Samuel 2:21, & 26, Luke 1:15, &80.

Elephant = Invincible; hard to offend; powerful; immovable; strong; strong prophetic voice; the largest among others; retains the things of God; has great memory.
Philippians 4:13, 1 Corinthians 15:10, Acts 19:11, Amos 3:6-7, Luke 7:28, Hebrews 7:4.

Elephant Trunk = Voice; channel to the Spirit; brings cleansing; strength.
Isaiah 40:3, Matthew 3:1-3, Revelation 4:1; John 4:14, John 7:38-39, Isaiah 51:9, Isaiah 62:8-11.

Elephant Ears = Extra sensitive hearing.

Back - Past; previous event or experience, good or evil; unaware; unsuspecting; hidden; memory.
Genesis 22:13, Joshua 8:4.

Back Door - Past; previous event or experience, good or evil; unaware; unsuspecting; hidden; memory; entrance; Christ; new opportunity; way; avenue; mouth.
John 10:7, Colossians 4:3, Psalm 141:3.

Backyard - Past; play time.

Back Half of Horse - Last part of time or work; end; an offensive or obnoxious person. See Horse.

Badge - Authority; ordained; deputized. See Police. Mark 3:14, 1 Timothy 2:7.

Badger - Constant harassment and annoyance; controlling. Matthew 19:3-6 (MSG), Luke 18:5 (MSG).

Baker - Instigator; one who originates sin; anger; mischief in one's heart; Satan; minister; oneself.
Hosea 7:4-7, Genesis 40:1-2, & 16-19.
Oven = Heart; intense; fervency; passion; meditation; imagination; judgement.
Hosea 7:4-7, 1 Corinthians 7:9, Psalm 21:9.
Kitchen = Heart; intent; motive; plans; preparation; nourishment; passion; ambition; affliction.
Hosea 7:6, Hebrews 4:12.

Balances - Justice; judgement; business; falsehood; deceitful; divide; purchase; integrity; make judgement before hearing the matter; vanity. See Business, Merchant.
Proverbs 16:11, Ezekiel 45:10-12, Daniel 5:27, Proverbs 20:23, Proverbs 11:1, Deuteronomy 25:13-15, Leviticus 19:35-36, Hosea 12:7, Micah 6:10-11, Ezekiel 5:1, Jeremiah 32:9-10, Job 31:6, Job 6:2, Proverbs 18:13, John 7:51, Psalm 62:9.
Weighing of Oneself = Pondering truth; considering one's ways; looking at one's progress of ridding oneself of sins; natural concern for health; obsession of appearance.
2 Timothy 2:15, 1 Corinthians 14:29, 1 Thessalonians 5:21, Hebrews 12:1-3, 2 Corinthians 10:7, 12, & 17, 1 Corinthians 1:26-31, 1 John 2:16.

Balcony - Spiritual realm; spiritual oversight and viewpoint; prophetic vision; prophets' position.
Revelation 4:1, Numbers 22:41, 1 Samuel 9:19.

Bald - Uncovering; purification; petition to God; mourning; humbled; shame; judgement; natural baldness.
Acts 21:24, & 26 (See with Numbers 6:13-20, verse 18), Acts 18:18, Numbers 8:7, Job 1:20, Jeremiah 48:37-38, Isaiah 15:2, Ezra 9:3-6, Ezekiel 5:1, Ezekiel 29:18, Isaiah 22:12, Micah 1:16, Ezekiel 7:18, Jeremiah 47:5.

Balm - Healing; relief; anointing.
Jeremiah 8:22, Jeremiah 51:8, Ezekiel 27:17.

Band Aid - Insufficient Aid; patching up or covering something up instead of curing the real problem.
Jeremiah 8:22.
Wearing Band Aids = Being hurt or wounded.

Bank - Secure; dependable; safe; saved; certain; reward reserved in heaven; the Church.
Philippians 4:17, Luke 19:23, Matthew 6:20.

Banner or Flag - Identity; committed; God's protection; memorial; conquest; victory; warning; fearsome army; love.
See associated Colors in Part 2.
Numbers 1:52, Exodus 17:14-15, Psalm 20:5, Psalm 60:4, Isaiah 13:2, Isaiah 49:22, Song of Solomon 6:4b, & 10b, Song of Solomon 2:4.
White flag = Surrender; pure.

Banquet - God's provision; abundance; blessings; fellowship with God; feast; joy; celebration; to feed on; decadence, excessive indulgences (drunkenness); idolatry.
Song of Solomon 2:4, Isaiah 25:6 (See with Matthew 26:29,

& Revelation 19:9), Esther 5:4-6, Amos 6:7, Job 41:6, Daniel 5:1-4, 1 Peter 4:3.

Baptize - Change; repentance, dead to sin; raised up in new life; dead to self; alive to God.
Luke 3:3, Romans 6:1-11, Colossians 2:12-13.

Barber - Enemy; deceiver; seducer; groomer; cleaner.
2 Samuel 10:4, Isaiah 7:20, Judges 16:19, Leviticus 14:8-9.

Barbershop - Place of removal; the Church, removal of old covenant of sin; enemies' territory, causing loss. See Hair, Beard.
Judges 16:17, Romans 12:2, 2 Samuel 10:4, Ezekiel 5:1.

Barren - Unproductive; desolate; shame; in need of supernatural divine intervention.
Proverbs 30:16, 1 Peter 1:8-9, Isaiah 54:1-5, Galatians 4:27, Psalm 113:9.

Barn - Storehouse; church; relating to the work of the ministry; provision; large work; sound spiritual wealth. See Hay.
Matthew 13:30, Proverbs 14:4, Luke 12:18, Haggai 2:19.

Barricade - Closed; obstacle; hindered; path blocked.
Acts 16:7, 1 Thessalonians 2:18.

Baseball Cards - Hero Worship; esteem for another person (proper or improper); could reveal a soul tie.
1 Thessalonians 5:13a, 1 Samuel 17:4.

Baseball Game - Worship; idolatry; covetousness; true worship; spiritual warfare; striving; competition.

Basement - Soul; carnal nature; lust; discouragement; depression; refuge; retreat; hidden; beneath the surface; foundational issues; forgotten; secret sin; bloodline issue; demonic realm. See Foundation.
Jeremiah 38:6, Isaiah 24:22.
Valuables in the Basement = Inherited giftedness; great potential yet to be revealed or manifested.
Fault in the Basement = Broken foundation; bloodline issue needing repentance.

Basket - A measure; God's provision; judgement.
Deuteronomy 28:5, &17, Jeremiah 24:1-10, Amos 8:1-2, Zechariah 5:5-11.
Receive a Basket of Fruit = Impartation of the gift of the Holy Spirit.
Give a Basket of Fruit = Impart what you have to another; give to the Lord.
Deuteronomy 26:1-4.
Basket of Ripe Fruit = It's time; no more delay.
Basket of Bad Fruit = Not usable for the purpose of God; corrupt works.
Jeremiah 24:1-10, Matthew 12:33b.
Basket of Bread = Life-giving resources.
Basket of Flowers = Appreciation; honored; recognized; a show of love.
Covered Basket = Future reward or punishment.

Bat - Witchcraft; flighty, unstable, creature of the night, fear.
Leviticus 11:13-19, verse 19, Isaiah 2:20.

Bathing - Cleansing; sanctification; repentance; temptation, outward appearance of righteousness.
Psalm 51:2-3, Ephesians 5:25-26, 2 Samuel 11:2, Matthew 23:25-26.

Preparing a Bath = Contemplating how to rid oneself of surrounding evil practices.
Having a Bath = Resisting the influence of vileness.
Not Enough Water for the Bath = Need for more prayer; need to move more in the Holy Spirit; an indulgence hindering the desire for holiness.
Bathing in Public = Unashamed to disassociate from evil practices.
Bathing in Dirty Water = Desire for good, but unconcerned in not going about it in a corrupt or ungodly way; polluted environment.
Bathing in a Shrine = Worshiping an idol; putting faith in an idol. See Shrine.

Bathroom - Desire or Cleansing; prayer of repentance; confession of offenses or sins to another person; passion; strong lust. See Purging, Urinating, Feces, or Toilet; whichever was the focus in the dream.
Isaiah 1:16, Proverbs 17:14, 2 Samuel 11:2, & 4.
 Clean Bathroom = Conductive atmosphere to resist the influence of the evil one; right frame of mind to resist the devil.
 Unable to Access or Use Bathroom = Place or season that's not helpful in resisting evil practices; prideful attitude not allowing for true repentance.
 Attack in Bathroom = Need to be watchful of challenges in the area of vulnerability.

Bathroom Sink - Prayer; repentance; petition to God; self-justification.
Isaiah 1:16, James 4:8, Psalm 26:6, Job 9:30, Matthew 27:24.
 Soap = Cleansing; conviction; forgiveness; prayer; repentance.
Malachi 3:2, Jeremiah 2:22, Isaiah 1:16.

Washcloth = Truth; doctrine; understanding; enhances cleansing.
Psalm 51:7, John 15:3.
Dirty Washcloth = False doctrine; insincere apology; error.
Job 14:4.

Battery - Power; Holy Spirit; strength; life; prayer; motivation; weak; without spiritual power.
Acts 10:38, Luke 1:35, Acts 1:8, Romans 15:13, & 19, 2 Corinthians 13:4, Jude 1:20.

Battle - Spiritual warfare; attack; conflict.
Ephesians 6:10-12, Judges 3:10, 1 Timothy 1:18, Joshua 10:19, Psalm 27:2, Psalm 80:6.

Battleship - Support; Spiritual warfare; powerful evangelistic ministry; rescue.
Acts Chapter 27 (verses 22-25, & 31), 2 Corinthians 11:23-26, 1 Timothy 1:19.

Beam of Light - Illumination from God; exposure; spotlight.
Malachi 4:2 (AMPC), James 1:17.

Beam of Wood or Concrete - Pillar in the church; main support of a ministry; foundational truths.
Habakkuk 2:11, Matthew 7:3-5.

Bear - Destroyer; Destruction; an evil curse (through generational or personal sin, including financial loss or hardship); economic loss (bear market); danger; opposition; enemy; fierce anger; oppressive ruler; religious spirit; anti-Christ; Russia.

Amos 5:19, 2 Kings 2:23-24, 1 Samuel 17:34-37, Proverbs 17:12, Proverbs 28:15, Daniel 7:5 (See with Daniel 2:39, Daniel 8:20-21, & Daniel 10:20), Revelation 13:2, Ezekiel 38:16-18.

Beard - Covering; humanity; maturity; holy; relating to the heart.
Psalm 133:2, Leviticus 21:5-6.
Rough and Unshaven Face = Spiritual neglect or uncleanness; coarse or harsh personality.
Untrimmed Beard = Law, legalism; one who has made a vow.
2 Samuel 19:24.
Shaved Beard = Shame; mourning; humbled; judgement.
2 Samuel 10:4-5, Isaiah 15:2, Ezra 9:3-6, Jeremiah 41:5, Ezekiel 5:1.
Grabbed by the Beard = Warning of danger or death.
2 Samuel 20:9-10, 1 Samuel 17:35.
Beard Plucked Out = Gross indignity; disgrace; violence; ill treatment; highest insult; shame.
Isaiah 50:6 (See with Matthew 26:67), Nehemiah 13:25.
Spit in the Beard = Madness.
1 Samuel 21:13-14.

Beast - Inner spiritual nature; antichrist; kings; kingdoms; nations; principalities and powers.
Revelation 13:11-18; Daniel 7:17 &23, Daniel 10:13, & 20, Ephesians 6:12.

Beauty Shop - Church; preparation; holiness; a call for inward beauty; vanity; pride; gossip; slander. See Hair.
Revelation 21:2, Psalm 29:2, Corinthians 11:15, 1 Peter 3:3-4, 2 Samuel 14:25-26, Proverbs 31:30, Hosea 10:5.

Beaver - Industrious; diligent; clever; ingenious; busy; religious, stops flow of the Holy Spirit.
Proverbs 10:4, Proverbs 22:29, Luke 10:40-41, John 6:27.

Bed - Rest; salvation; meditation; intimacy; privacy; peace; covenant, spiritual or natural adultery; self-made, harmful conditions; illness.
Psalm 4:4, Isaiah 28:18-20, Hebrews 13:4, James 4:4, Proverbs 7:16-18, Psalm 139:8, Matthew 9:2.
Under the Bed = Inferior position; secret; hidden. Mark 4:21-22.
Mattress on the Floor = Humble position; poverty. 1 Peter 5:6, Psalm 113:7.

Bedroom - Rest; salvation; meditation; intimacy; privacy; peace; covenant in marriage; evil covenant, spiritual or natural adultery; self-made, harmful conditions.
Psalm 4:4, Psalm 139:8, Isaiah 28:18-20, Hebrews 13:4, James 4:4a.

Bees - Chastisement; judgement; offense; stinging words; affliction; busybody; gossip; busy. See Hornets, or Wasps.
Deuteronomy 1: 44, Psalm 118:12, Judges 14:8, 1 Timothy 5:13.

Bells - Change; times are changing; manifestations of the Spirit; bells as jewellery may mean pride; vanity. See Liberty Bells.
Exodus 28:34, 1 Corinthians 13:1, 1 Corinthians 14:22a, Isaiah 3:16.

Belly - Spirit; desire; heart; feelings; lust; selfishness; self-worship; sickness.
John 7:38, Proverbs 26:22, Philippians 3:19.

Bestiality - Inordinate Lust; unnatural deviant sex acts; obscene; abomination; cursed; darkened heart; willful denial of God; reprobate mind; hardened heart. See Sex.
Colossians 3:5, 1 Thessalonians 4:5, Leviticus 18:23, Leviticus 20:15-16, Exodus 22:19, Deuteronomy 27:21, Romans 1:21-31.

Bicycle - Works; flesh; legalism; self-righteousness; ministry depending on much human effort; one-man ministry; ministry with much exposure, making one vulnerable; limited capacity of influence.
Galatians 5:4, & 19-21, Ecclesiastes 9:15-16.
> **Riding Uphill or in Sand or Mud** = Working out life's difficulties.
> **Two-seater Bicycle** = Messenger as in bicycle courier.
> **Bicycle with a Child Seat** = Represents family, more than one person involved.

Bigfoot - Threatening authority; spirit of fear; intimidating threats; torment; demonic hoax; "wild man", based on a Roman mythical deity; deception; antichrist spirit, evolution versus creation and the Creator.
Daniel 3:13-15, Acts 9:1, 1 Samuel 17:4-11, 16, 23-24, 32, & 44, 1 Chronicles 20:6-7, Galatians 1:7-9, 1 John 4:2-3.

Bikini - Uncovered; carnal; seduction; temptation; insufficient covering.
Isaiah 47:3.

Bingo - Winner; sudden victory; correct; answer; idea; understanding; gambling.
1 Corinthians 9:24, Matthew 16:15-16.

Binoculars - Insight; looking ahead; understanding; prophetic vision; future event.
Revelation 4:1, John 16:13. See Telescope.
> **Unfocused or Blurred** = Difficulty in understanding or insight.
> John 16:12-13, 2 Corinthians 3:13.

Bird - Holy Spirit; angel; man; message; innocent; demon; gossip.

John 1:32, Ecclesiastes 10:20, Psalm 55:6-8, Psalm 124:7-8, Proverbs 1:17.

Dove = Holy Spirit; seal of approval; peace.

Matthew 3:16, Genesis 8:11.

Eagle = Leader; spiritual; prophet; to see from above; to see clearly; wisdom; insight; God's restorative power; swift; minister; rises above the storm; fierce predator; instrument of judgement; America.

Exodus 19:4, Isaiah 40:31, Isaiah 46:11, Proverbs 30:17, Ezekiel 17:3-20, Deuteronomy 28:49, Deuteronomy 32:11.

Hawk = Predator; sorcerer; evil spirit; a warmonger.

Acts 20:30.

Falcon = Hunter; minister.

Genesis 10:9.

Owl = Circumspect (looking around); wisdom; contemplator; demon; curse; spirit of craftiness.

Ephesians 5:15, Exodus 23:13a, Isaiah 34:13.

Woodpecker = One who seeks out areas of disturbance; nests where one's spirituality or life has been affected by the fires of trial; births new life out of chaos.

Isaiah 61:1-4, Luke 4:18, Acts 10:38.

Chicken = Fear; cowardliness.

Deuteronomy 1:29, Luke 13:34.

    Chick = Defenceless.

Hen = Gathering; protection; gossip.

Luke 13:34.

Rooster = Bragging; proud; boasting; arrogance; sexual pride.

John 18:27, Luke 22:33-34.

Turkey = Thanksgiving; provision, Christmas; contemptuously rich; forgetting God; foolish, dumb; clumsy, in word or deed.

Psalm 107:22, Psalm 116:17, Esther 5:4, Proverbs 30:8-9, Luke 12:19-20, Ecclesiastes 9:12, Proverbs 7:22-23.

Peacock - Pride; pious; beauty.

Job 39:13, 1 Kings 10:22, 2 Chronicles 9:21.

Ostrich = Denial; fear; careless; cruel, hardened heart, lacks wisdom and understanding.

Lamentations 4:3, Job 39:13-17.

Raven or Crow = Unclean spirit; confusion; outspoken person; person operating under or out of a spirit of envy or strife (which causes confusion and disorder); hateful; depression; grief; death; suicide; straight path or direct route; God's minister(s) of justice or provision.

Revelation 18:2, Isaiah 13:20-22, Isaiah 34:11-15, James 3:16, Psalm 35:26, Proverbs 30:17, 1 Kings 17:4-6.

Vulture or Buzzard = Evil spirit; preys on human weakness; opportunistic; scavenger; unclean; impure; an evil person; all seeing and waiting.

Deuteronomy 14:12-13, Proverbs 30:17.

Parrot = Mimics; copies; mocks; repeats; divination. See Echo.

2 Kings 2:23, Luke 23:21.

Crane = Chatter; knows one's time and season; punctual; repentant; loyal.

Isaiah 38:14, Jeremiah 8:7.

Penguin = Specialized; graceful in water; awkward on land; vigilantly watches out for its natural predator, sharks.

1 Corinthians 7:20, 1 Peter 5:8.

   Out of Water = Out of its natural element.

Stork = Expectant; new birth; pregnancy; new baby; new experiences; forthcoming.

Jeremiah 8:7.

Sparrow = Divine provision; desire of God to provide.

Matthew 10:31, Luke 12:6-7, Matthew 6:26, Luke 12:22-24, & 30-32.

Birds Flying in V-formation = Working together in unity; keeping the unity of the Spirit; follows one in charge; when one leader tires, another switches place, keeping

the strength of the formation; followers dependant on the strength of the leader; every part doing its share; communicating effectively; skilled; naturally flowing in the things of God; operating in the gifts; operating in its divine design; alert to the purpose and will of God; dependant on one another; faithful.
Psalm 133:1-3, Ephesians 4:1-16, 1 Corinthians 12:4-28, Romans 12:1-10.
Various Kinds of Birds = All the parts working together; no partiality; multi-generational; humble; in covenant.
1 Corinthians 3:6-10, 1 Corinthians 12:4-28, Romans 15:20, Romans 12:1-16, 2 Corinthians 10:13-16.
All the Same Type of Birds = Associating only with ones' own kind ("Clique"); excluding others different than ones' group; partiality; fear; pride; selfishness; not willing to move out of comfort zone; familiar spirit; could be a smaller unified and specialised ministry.
James 2:1-9, Romans 12:9-16.
Birds Flying out of Formation = Disunity; low or no communication; careless; going astray; concerned only with worldly cares; unorganized; self-reliant; could be in collision course.
2 Timothy 4:3-4, 1 John 2:19, Matthew 22:1-10, 1 John 2:15-16.
Various Kinds of Birds = Compromise for the sake of unity; false unity; fear of man; sold out to the world system.
Romans 12:2a, James 4:4, Romans 1:21-32.
All the Same Kind of Birds = Disloyal; covenant breakers; betrayers; out of the will of God; never were a part of the ministry; have developed their own little group ("Clique"); rejecting ones who are "different"; partiality; fear; pride; selfishness; not willing to move out of comfort zone; familiar spirit; offense; could be weaker members (newer believers) not properly equipped.

1 John 2:19, Acts 15:24, Acts 20:30, , Matthew 26:21-25, 1 Timothy 1:19-20 Jude 1:19, Matthew 18:6.
A Flock of Black Birds = Gossip; slander; bitter words. 1 Samuel 17:44, Jeremiah 12:9, Ezekiel 39:4.

Black Box (Airplane) - Record of conversations; to investigate; search out the answers; find evidence. Genesis 18:21, Exodus 2:11-14, Mark 14:72, John 21:24-25, 1 Corinthians 2:9-10.

Black Clouds - The presence of evil spirits; a swarm of demonic forces; death; sorrow; blocked prayers; judgement. Isaiah 44:22, Lamentations 3:44, 2 Samuel 22:12, Psalm 18:11-12, Psalm 97:2.

Black Horse - Famine; bad times; evil; could have apocalyptic meaning. See Horse, and Black in Part 2. Revelation 6:5, Amos 8:11.

Black Widow Spider - Great danger; deadly; life-threatening; evil; slander. James 3:8.
> **Fangs** = Evil intent or motive: danger. Psalm 57:4, Psalm 58:6, Proverbs 30:14, Daniel 7:5-7, Revelation 9:8.

Bladder - An urge to release something; strife; temptation; lust. Proverbs 17:14, 1 Samuel 25:22, 1 Kings 21:21, Genesis 49:4.
> **Full Bladder** = Pressure; compelling urge.
> **Bladder infection or cancer** = Offense; enmity.

Blanket - Covering; warmth; covenant; protection; hidden. Exodus 25:20-22, Ezekiel 16:8-10, Psalm 91:4-5, Proverbs 31:22, Proverbs 7:16, Job 31:20.

Patchwork Quilt = Memories or influence of one's foremothers.
Comforter = Holy Spirit; the Spirit of truth.
John 14:16, & 26, John 16:7, John 15:26.

Bleeding - Wounded heart; natural or emotional hurting; spiritually dying; offence; strife; gossip; unclean.
Psalm 147:3, Proverbs 18:8, Leviticus 17:11.

Blimp - Weak; moved by every wind; wimp; controlled; powerless; slothful; aimless; puffed up.
Ephesians 4:14.

Blind - Ignorance; unseeing; without understanding; foolish; self-justification; self-righteousness; hatred; sealed; unlearned.
Matthew 15:14, Matthew 23:16-28, John 9:39-41, 2 Corinthians 4:4, Mark 8:23-24, Revelation 3:17, 2 Peter 1:9, 1 John 2:11.
Near-sighted = Sees only one's own church or denomination; eyes only on the present rather than on the future; vision too small; limited spiritual insight; lack of foresight; vulnerable to the attacks of the enemy.
2 Peter 1:9, Judges 9:36.
Squinting = Straining to see further ahead; hindrance to spiritual insight.
Mark 8:24, 1 Corinthians 13:9-12.

Blood - Life of the Flesh; covenant; murder; defiled; unclean; pollution; purging; testimony; witness; guilt.
Leviticus 17:11a, Leviticus 15:19, Deuteronomy 27:25, Psalm 106:38, Ezekiel 33:8.

Blood Transfusion - Change; regeneration; salvation; deliverance.
1 Peter 1:18-19, Hebrews 9:12-14, 1 John 1:7, Colossians 1:13-14.

Blushing - Spiritual shedding of innocent blood; being shamed; causing embarrassment; guilt.
Psalm 10:7-8, Proverbs 6:17, 2 Samuel 19:5, Ezra 9:6, Ezekiel 16:61-63, Romans 6:21.
Embarrassment = Shame; disgraced; perceived or actual failure.
Genesis 9:22-24, 1 Samuel 20:34, 2 Samuel 19:5-6, Psalm 142:4, Psalm 31:11.

Blueprints - Plans; word of God; personal prophecies; specific instructions.
Jeremiah 29:11, Hebrews 8:5, 1 Chronicles 28:19.

Boa Constrictor - Divination; familiar spirits; ancestral spirits; a regional spirit; a coiling spirit that squeezes out the breath of life (the Holy Spirit) and cut off a believer's lifeline to God (prayer); puts believers in bondage; thwarts a believer's purpose; high level of spiritual warfare needed. See Snake.
Acts 16:16-18, Ephesians 6:12, Psalm 91:13, Daniel 10:13 & 20.

Boar - Persecutor; hostile to virtue; vicious; vengeful; danger.
Psalm 80:13, 2 Timothy 3:2-3.

Board Games (Fun Games) - Passing of time; leisure; entertainment; strategizing for eternal or temporary things; competition; playing with one's Christian life; not enough concern for souls.
1 Peter 1:17, Mark 9:33-34, Matthew 11:16-19.
   Chess = Strategy; consultation; plan the next move; deliberate; purposeful course of action.
   Genesis 3:15, Proverbs 20:18, Proverbs 24:6, Luke 14:31-32, Joshua 6:2-20, 1 Samuel 17:1-57.
      Stalemate = Standstill.
      1 Samuel 17:16, Ephesians 6:13.

Checkmate = Defeating the enemy or defeated by the enemy.
1 Samuel 17:45-51, Joshua 7:2-5.

Boat - Support; life; person; recreation; spare time.
Genesis 6:16, Luke 8:22-23, 1 Timothy 1:19.
Large Boat = The Church.
Small Boat= Small or personal ministry.
Sailboat = Moved by the Spirit.
Row Boat = Exercise (prayer) in the Spirit.
Rescue Boat = Intercessory ministry.
Submarine = The Underground Church; persecuted; hidden ones; spies out new or enemy territory; flows with the Spirit of God; the Holy Spirit searching out the spirit of believers. See Water, Telescope, Torpedo.
John 8:59, John 12:36, Acts 8:1-4, John 14:22, John 17:6, Romans 16:25-26, Numbers 13:17-21, Numbers 14:6-8, Proverbs 20:27, Romans 8:27, Psalm 139:1-4, & 23-24.
Powerboat = Powerful ministry.
Speed Boat = Acceleration into the new season and ministry.
On Dry Ground = Without the move of the Spirit; the work of the flesh; a miracle if moving on dry ground.

Body - Physical human body (vessel); the temple of God; the Church; any mass of people following a founder or are members of an institution; followers of the beast of Revelation.
Acts 9:15, 2 Timothy 2:20-21, 1 Thessalonians 4:4-5, 1 Corinthians 3:16-17, 1 Corinthians 6:18-20, Ephesians 4:16, 1 Corinthians 12:12-27, Romans 12:1, & 4-5, 1 Kings 18:17-19, Revelation 13:3-4, & 8.

Body Odour - Uncleanness; bad attitude; filthiness of the flesh; rejected.
2 Corinthians 7:1, James 1:21a, James 4:8, Ecclesiastes 10:1.

Body Wash - Cleansing; conviction; forgiveness; prayer; repentance.
Malachi 3:2, Jeremiah 2:22, Isaiah 1:16.

Boiling or Hot Water - Spiritual condition; anger; war; judgment. See Water.
Isaiah 64:2, Jeremiah 1:13-16, Ezekiel 24:3-14.

Bolts - Essential; the bottom line; indispensible; wisdom; to fasten. See Lock Washer.
Proverbs 4:7.

Bomb - Power; miracle power; sudden destruction, explosive words; can have apocalyptic meaning. See Stealth Bomber.
Acts 1:8, 1 Thessalonians 5:3, Luke 17:27-29.

Bomber Jet - Individual ministry, person, or minister; powerful, fast, effective, attacking; a call to intercessory ministry; spiritual warfare. See Airplane.
Genesis 41:43, 2 Kings 10:16, Zechariah 6:1-8, Isaiah 5:26-28.

Bones - Spirit; condition of the heart; death; that which is eternal.
Matthew 23:27, Ezekiel 37:11, Proverbs 17:22.

Book - Record; word of God; heart of man; witness; remembrance (good or evil); conscience; education; preparation; knowledge. See Library.
Malachi 3:16, Revelation 20:12, Jeremiah 36:8-10, 2 Corinthians 3:2-3, Hebrews 10:7,
Revelation 22:10, Daniel 12:4.
   Open Book = Access to knowledge and a call to release its revelation.
   Daniel 7:10, Revelation 20:12, Jeremiah 36:8-10.

Reading a Book = Gaining knowledge and revelation; gaining information.

Inability of Difficulty in Reading a Book = Life issues or circumstances hindering knowledge or revelation; circumstances hindering information.

Book Title or Topic = The main message.

Closed Book to the Right = Knowledge to be studied, learned, and explored.

Revelation 5:1.

Closed Book to the Left = The end of a study season, preparation, or learning process.

Book on a Shelf = Untapped truth and revelation.

Daniel 12:4, Isaiah 29:11.

Diary, Journal or Book of Remembrance = A record of life; records of encounters with God; a record of God's righteous dealings on one's behalf; recorded thoughts of God's power, omniscience, justice, goodness, mercy, peace and truth.

Malachi 3:16, Job 19:23-25, Psalm 56:8.

Boots - Words; gospel; covenant; preparation. See Feet.

Ephesians 6:15, Ruth 4:7, Galatians 5:16.

> **New Boots** = New ministry or way of life.
>
> **Combat or Heavy Boots** = Spiritual warfare.
>
> **Steel-toed Boots** = Protection.

Border - Boundary; security; spiritual landmark; ministry progress; peace; refuge; safety.

Psalm 16:5-11, 2 Corinthians 10:13, & 15-16, Job 26:10 (ASV), Micah 7:11 (NAS), Leviticus 26:6, Psalm 147:14, Numbers 35:25-28.

Bow - Source of attacks; power of a nation or person; heart from where issues of life come. See Arrows.

Genesis 49:24, Jeremiah 9:3, Jeremiah 49:35.

Bowels - Wickedness; remorse; disease; wounded, spirit of man, heart, gut instinct, mercy.
Job 20:12-15, Acts 1:18, 2 Chronicles 21:15, &18-19, 2 Samuel 20:10, Proverbs 20:27, Psalm 22:14, Jude 1:10, Colossians 3:12, 1 John 3:17.

Bowl - Vessel; doctrine; tradition; a determination or resolve; form of the truth; a person.
Romans 2:20, Exodus 25:29, Isaiah 28:9-10, Jeremiah 1:13, 2 Kings 21:13, 1 Thessalonians 4:3-5.
God's bowls of wrath, judgement and plagues.
Revelation 15:7, Revelation 16:2-21, Revelation 17:1, Revelation 21:9.

Bowling - Striving; preaching; deliverance; trial; tribulation.
2 Timothy 4:7, 1 Corinthians 9:25-26.

Box - Container; emotions of the heart; religious traditions; legalistic doctrine.
Mark 14:3, Matthew 26:7, & 10-13, Romans 10:10, Isaiah 29:13, Matthew 15:7-9, Ephesians 4:18, Romans 1:21.
Collection of Boxes = Memories.
Philippians 3:13.
Plastic Box = Insincere heart.
Isaiah 29:13, Matthew 15:7-9.
Black Box = Hard heart; no understanding.
Ephesians 4:18, Romans 1:21.
Disposing Old Boxes = Renouncing and forsaking the past.
Philippians 3:13.
Gift Wrapped Box = Special gift; spiritual gift.
Mark 14:3, Matthew 26:7, & 10-13, 2 Kings 9:1-3.
White Box = Innocence; righteousness.

Boxing - Striving; trial.
1 Corinthians 9:25-26, 2 Timothy 4:7.

Breakdown, Vehicle, Ship, Train, Airplane etc - Problem; sickness; spirit of poverty; demonic attack; hindrance to one's life, ministry, career, livelihood. See Driver, Captain, Conductor, or Pilot, and associated means of transportation.
1 Thessalonians 2:18, Acts 16:6-7.

Brake Failure - Overcome; inability to stop a bad habit or change a tradition; no resistance to temptation.
2 Peter 2:14.

Brakes - Slowing down; compelled to stop; stopping; hindrance; resist; wait.
1 Thessalonians 2:18, Acts 16:6-7.

Brass - Word of God; word of man; judgment; hypocrisy; self-justification; fake; man's tradition.
Revelation 1:15, 1 Corinthians 13:1, 2 Corinthians 12:10, Ephesians 6:16, Isaiah 48:4.

Bread - Life; word; doctrine; covenant; the Church; substances; provision.
Matthew 4:4, Judges 7:13-14, John 13:18, 2 Thessalonians 3:8.

> **Mouldy Bread** =Unfit; tradition; old revelation; stale; defiled.
> Joshua 9:5b, Malachi 1:7, 1 Corinthians 5:8, Matthew 15:2-3, & 6, Exodus 16:20.

Bricks - Man-made stone; man's effort; work of the flesh; bondage; incorruptible building material.
Exodus 20:25, Isaiah 65:3, Exodus 1:14, Psalm 68:13, Psalm 81:6, Nahum 3:14.

Bride - Church; covenant (good or bad); natural marriage. See Marriage.
Isaiah 62:5, Ephesians 5:31-32, John 3:29, Revelation 21:9, 2 Corinthians 6:14.
Groom = Christ; headship; natural groom.
Isaiah 62:5, Ephesians 5:31-32, 2 Corinthians 6:14.
Wedding = Beginning of fruitful union; new level of intimacy with Jesus; beginning of spiritual responsibility; new covenant.
Wedding Dress = State of preparation.
Stained or Wrinkled Wedding Dress = Still issues that need to be dealt with.
Holes in Wedding Dress = Faulty preparation; correction needed.
Wedding Cake = Means of joyful celebration; fruitful relationship with Jesus; God's provision.
Running out of Ingredients when Baking a Wedding Cake = Inadequate preparation.
Wedding Wine = Holy Spirit empowerment; God's miraculous provision; caution to avoid over indulgence.
Key People Missing from Wedding = Have not completely put key things in place.

Bridge - Support; way; faith; trial (of faith); transition; season change; joined.
Genesis 32:22, Isaiah 43:2a, 1 Corinthians 10:13.

Briers (Thickets) - Snare; obstacles; hindrances; trial; wicked person; rejected; cursed. See Thorns.
Ezekiel 2:6, Isaiah 32:13a, Micah 7:4a, Hebrews 6:8.

Bronze - Demotion; primitive; unrefined; displacement of gold and silver with bronze is a consequence of sin; lewdness; harlotry.
1 Kings 14:25-27.

Broom - Cleaning; witchcraft; clean house, put away sin. See Sweeping.
John 2:15, Galatians 5:19-20a.

Broom or Juniper Tree - One who provides just enough shade, or rest from the desert experience. See Trees.
1 Kings 19:4-5.

Brother - Self; spiritual or natural brother; someone he reminds you of; may represent someone you can trust. See Friend.
Romans 2:1, Romans 14:10a, Hebrews 13:3.

Brother-in-law - Partiality; adversary; fellow minister; someone he reminds you of; problem relationship; partner; oneself; he may represent himself. See Friend.
1Timothy 5:21, Esther 7:6a.

Brother's Wife - The brother himself. See Brother.

Bubble Gum - Childish; foolishness; immaturity.
Proverbs 15:14, Proverbs 22:15.

Buck (Male Deer) - Regal; rule; authority; strength; power.
Psalm 42:1-2, Song of Solomon 2:9, & 17, Song of Solomon 8:14, Isaiah 35:6.
    Deer = Graceful; divine enabling, swift; sure-footed; agile; spiritual longing; provision; timid; skittish.
    2 Samuel 22:34, Psalm 18:33, Habakkuk 3:19, Psalm 42:1-2.

Bugs - Plague (plagues of Egypt); pest; small; problem; trouble; annoyance; religious spirit (bad-mouthing those led by the Spirit); broken (there's a bug in this); spying device.
Exodus 5:3, Exodus 8:16-18, & 21-24, Psalm 78: 45-46, Psalm

105: 31, & 34, Isaiah 7:18, Matthew 23:24, Luke 18:5, John 7:12, John 9:16, Isaiah 1:14, Luke 18:5, John 9:16.

Ant = Industrious; wise; diligent; prepared for the future; nuisance, stinging or angry.

Proverbs 6:6-8, Proverbs 30:25.

Invasion of Large Numbers of Ants = Challenging or dangerous situation; overwhelming situation; onslaught of the enemy.

Fire Ant = Fiery, angry words; attack of the enemy; volatile, dangerous situation.

James 3:6, Proverbs 16:27.

Stung or Bitten by Ants = Attacking words; stinging words; dangerous situation; attack of the enemy; strife.

Proverbs 26:20-21.

Bees = Chastisement; judgement; offense; stinging words; affliction; busybody; gossip; busy.

Deuteronomy 1: 44, Psalm 118:12, Judges 14:8, 1 Timothy 5:13.

Hornets or Wasps = Affliction; stinging; biting words; slander; strife; curse (because of sin); persecution; trouble; offense; demon spirits.

Deuteronomy 7:20, Exodus 23:28, Joshua 24:12.

Spider = Evil; sin; false doctrine; temptation; deceiver; difficult escape from entanglement; conflict; stronghold; threatening issue with danger of entanglement or possibly death; false trust; tenacious; clever; evil spirit; religious spirit; predatory person.

Proverbs 30:24, & 28, Proverbs 7:22-23, Isaiah 59:5-6, Genesis 31:27, 2 Corinthians 10:4-5, Acts 4:17, 21, & 29, 1 Peter 2:23, Job 8:13-15, 1 Timothy 6:9, 2 Timothy 2:26, Matthew 23:27-28; Psalm 91:3, Psalm 124:7, Hosea 9:8.

Black Widow = Great danger; deadly; life-threatening; evil; slander.

James 3:8.

Fangs = Evil intent or motive: poisonous; great danger. Psalm 57:4, Psalm 58:6, Proverbs 30:14, Daniel 7:5-7, Revelation 9:8.

Spider Web = Snare; lies and deception; scheme; trap; ruin; internet.
Ecclesiastes 7:26, Isaiah 59:5-7; Psalm 91:3, Psalm 124:7, Ecclesiastes 9:12; Psalm 140:5, Psalm 119:110, Psalm 141:9.

Flea = Insignificant; nuisance; irritant; hunted; elusive. 1 Samuel 24:14, 1 Samuel 26:20.

Lice = Condemnation; accusation; shame; guilt; affliction. Exodus 8:16-17, John 8:6, & 9.

Tic = Hidden unclean spirit; oblivious to one's true self, self-justification and self-righteousness; parasite; life-stealing; draining; pest.
Leviticus 5:2, Jeremiah 17:9.

Flies = Beelzebub "Lord of the flies" is a reference to the devil. Evil spirits; Satan; doctrines of demons (fly in the cup); unclean; corruption; curse; nuisance; foolishness destroying one's reputation.
Exodus 8:21-31, Matthew 12:24, &26-27, 1 Corinthians 10:21, 2 Corinthians 6:15-17, Ecclesiastes 10:1, Isaiah 7:18.

Covered by Flies = Corruption that breeds unclean spirits.

Fly Screen = Covering; protection from demonic attacks.
Ecclesiastes 10:1(See with Ecclesiastes 9:18).

Cockroaches = Unclean; infestation; crept in; defiled; hidden sin; in darkness; lies.
Leviticus 5:2, Leviticus 11: 31, & 43, 2 Corinthians 7:1; 2 Timothy 3:6, Jude 1:4,
1 Corinthians 4:5, 1 John 1:6.

Mosquito = Parasite; evil spirit; unseen attack sapping the life out of another; stealing of finances; irritation.

John 12:6, John 10:10, Deuteronomy 25:18, Micah 7:2-3, Matthew 27:6 (See with Exodus 21:30, Leviticus 17:11).

Grasshoppers = Small; very little; insignificant; many together can destroy crops; instrument of judgement.
Numbers 13:33, Isaiah 40:22, Amos 7:1-2.

Locusts = Judgement; famine; death; devourer; pestilence; plague; demonic spirits; oppressive multitude; invades their enemy in military order (like a swarm of locusts); weak when alone; flighty; restoration possible.
Exodus 10:4-6, 14-15, &17-19, Deuteronomy 28:38, & 42, 2 Chronicles 7:13, 1 Kings 8:37, Psalm 78:46, Psalm 105:34-35; Joel 1:4, Revelation 9:3-10, Psalm 109:22-24, Joel 2:7-9, Nahum 3:15-17, Joel 2:25.

Slug or Snail = Slowly eats away the truth of the word of God; corruption of injustices; unclean issues; lawlessness.
2 Timothy 2:17, Nahum 3:15, James 5:3, Leviticus 11:29-30, & 41-45, Leviticus 22:5-6, Habakkuk 1:14.

Worm = Corruption; weak; insignificant; filthiness of the flesh; evil; eats from the inside; pride; transgressor; death; rotten motives; bitter; temptation leading to sin; fearful; reproached; despised.
Job 17:14, Job 25:6, Job 7:5, Isaiah 14:11, Isaiah 66:24, Proverbs 5:4, Mark 9:43-50, Isaiah 41:14, Psalm 22:6.

Maggot = Corruption; filthiness of the flesh; despised; decay; evil; death; judgement; rotten motives.
Job 17:14, Psalm 22:6, Exodus 16:20, Acts 12:23, Deuteronomy 28:39, Job 24:20.

Leech = Sucks the life out of another; a sponge; soaks up others' resources and strength; insatiable appetite to steal the life of others.
Proverbs 30:15 (See with Habakkuk 2:5, Proverbs 27:20).

Termites = Corruption; hidden destruction; secret sin; deception; demons; unclean spirits.
Psalm 11:3, Haggai 1:6.

Moth = An insect of darkness; loss through deceit; secret or undetected trouble; rotten; corruption; riches eaten up; destruction; chastisement.
Hosea 5:12, Job 13:28, Isaiah 50:9, Isaiah 51:8, Matthew 6:19-20, James 5:2,
Job 4:19, Psalm 39:11.
Butterfly = Freedom; new believer; new creation; beauty; fragile flighty or flitting about; temporary glory.
2 Corinthians 5:17, John 3:3, 1 Peter 1:23-25, Isaiah 41:14, & 16 (See with Genesis 32:28).

Building - Spiritual or emotional condition of a person, or church; life of the person or church.
Matthew 16:18, Luke 6:48, Matthew 7:24-25.
Building under Construction = Not ready; not complete; still being built up in Jesus.
Shaky or Collapsed Building = Unstable; ill health; uncontrollable circumstances.
Matthew 7:26-27, Luke 6:49, Luke 14:28-30.
Flooding Building = Imminent challenge; imminent disaster.
Basement = Soul; carnal nature; lust; discouragement; depression; refuge; retreat; hidden; beneath the surface; foundational issues; forgotten; secret sin; bloodline issue; demonic realm.
Jeremiah 38:6, Isaiah 24:22.
Valuables in the Basement = Inherited giftedness; great potential yet to be revealed or manifested.
Fault in the Basement = Broken foundation; bloodline issue needing repentance.

Building Foundation - Established; stable; sound; level; solidified.
Psalm 11:3, Luke 14:29, 1 Corinthians 3:10-11, Ephesians 2:20.

Under Construction = Not ready; not complete; still being built up in Jesus.

Not Cured = Unstable; ill health; uncontrollable circumstances.

Deluge of Rain = Imminent challenge.

Matthew 7:24-27, Luke 6:48-49.

Building Frame - The gospel; sound doctrine; church government; building program.

Psalm 11:3, Luke 14:29, 1 Corinthians 3:10-11, Ephesians 2:20-22.

Under Construction = Not ready; not complete; still being built up in Jesus.

Shaky or Collapsed = Unstable; ill health; uncontrollable circumstances.

Deluge of Rain = Imminent challenge; imminent disaster.

Matthew 7:24-27, Luke 6:48-49.

Bull - Persecution; spiritual warfare; opposition; accusation; slander; threat; economic gain 'bull market.' See Calf.

Psalm 22:12.

Bulldog - Unyielding; stubborn; dangerous; tenacious. See Dog.

Judges 2:19.

Bulldozer - Very powerful ministry, good or evil; evangelist; apostle; prophet; preparation ministry; powerful pioneering ministry; heavy-handed leader.

Acts 8:5-10, Isaiah 40:3-4, Matthew 3:1-3, 1 Samuel 22:11-18.

Bullets - Words; accusations; slander; gossip; power.

2 Samuel 11:24, Psalm 64:4, Luke 11:21-22.

Being Shot with Bullets = Powerful words coming against a person; curses; attacks.

In Possession of Bullets = Equipped with authority or ability; power; unhindered.

Broken or Inoperative = Without authority or ability; without power; hindered.

Smaller Calibre = Weak or ineffective weapon; without power; lack of prayer and fasting.

Revelation 3:8.

Larger Calibre = Powerful; spiritual power through acceptable service; covenant; effective; the power of evil working through agreement (acquiescence) or conquest (our defeat).

2 Corinthians 10:4.

Burrs - Irritant; Irritated; minor afflictions. See Thorns.

Hebrews 6:8, Exodus 22:6, Matthew 13:22.

Bus - Church; large ministry; working together; group mission. See Vehicle.

2 Kings 4:38, 2 Timothy 2:2, Hebrews 11:9a.

Tour or Passenger Bus = sojourners, Christians, sight-seers.

School Bus = Teaching ministry; youth ministry; learning and working together.

To Miss the Bus = Possible missed divine appointment; a call to prayer.

To Board the Wrong Bus = Misdirected; misplaced priorities.

To Leave the Bus at the Wrong Stop = Wrong timing; destination misinterpreted; wrong decision; preoccupation.

Stalled Bus = Ministry on hold; operation in one's own strength; need to take authority; hindrance by Satan; opposition.

Isaiah 49:2, Exodus 14:13-16, Galatians 5:7-12, Nehemiah 4:1-18, 1 Thessalonians 2:18.

Bus Breakdown - Problem; sickness; spirit of poverty; demonic attack; hindrance to one's life, ministry, career, livelihood. 1 Thessalonians 2:18, Acts 16:6-7.

Bus Crash - Strife; contention; conflict; confrontation; calamity; offense; mistake or sin in ministry; failure; church split; personal disaster (failed marriage, business venture, ministry, project etc.); end of one phase (for whatever reason unbeknownst to the dreamer). Nahum 2:3-4, 2 Corinthians 11:25-27, 1 Timothy 1:19-20.

Bus Driver - Self; if the bus driver is a teacher in the dream, then the passengers represent the driver's students. See Friend. 2 Kings 9:20.

Bus Station -Wait; prepare; be made ready (for ministry, travel, change, etc.); the Church. 1 Peter 3:20, Jeremiah 23:22.

Business - Market-place; Commerce; industrious; employment; kingdom business; occupation for provision; work of a missionary, work for the advancement of the gospel. See Employer, Balances. Deuteronomy 8:18, Proverbs 31:14-22, Acts 16:14, Luke 19:12-15, Matthew 25:14-15, Colossians 4:1, Psalm 112:5, & 9, Acts 18:3, 1 Thessalonians 2:9, 2 Thessalonians 3:7-10, Acts 20:34-35, Ephesians 6:5-9.

Butter – Works; doing, or not doing the word or will of God; deceptive motives; words; works; smooth talker; deceiver. See Cheese. Psalm 55:21, Proverbs 30:33, Isaiah 7:15.

Butterfly - Freedom; beauty; fragile flighty or flitting about; temporary glory.
2 Corinthians 5:17, John 3:3, 1 Peter 1:23-25, Isaiah 41:14, & 16 See with Genesis 32:28.

Buzzard - Scavenger; unclean; impure; an evil person; all seeing and waiting; evil spirit; preys on human weakness; opportunistic.
Deuteronomy 14:12-13, Proverbs 30:17.

C

Cafeteria - Service or Ministry; people or work; teaching; helps ministry; deacon ministry.
Matthew 16:18, 1 Corinthians 12:28, Numbers 11:16-17, Acts 27:17.

Cage - Restriction; limited mobility; captivity; guard against evil. See Prison.
Jeremiah 5:27.
> **Prisoners** - Lost Souls; stubborn; sinners; persecuted saints.
> Luke 4:18, Hebrews 2:15, 2 Peter 2:14, 2 Timothy 2:25-26, Jeremiah 38:6, Zechariah 9:12a.
> **Put Someone in a Cage** = Put in bondage; limit freedom.
> 1 Samuel 30:1-3.
> **Help Someone to Get out of a Cage** = Break bondages; release freedom; remove limitations.
> 1 Samuel 30:3-8, & 18-19.
> **Broken Iron Bars** = Deliverance; broken limitations.
> Isaiah 45:2, Psalm 107:16.

Cake - Provision from heaven; nourishment from God.
Numbers 11:8.
> **Bake a Cake** = Help to bring celebration of joy.

Running out of Ingredients when Baking a Cake = Inadequate preparation.

Birthday Cake = Major celebration; important day.

Wedding Cake = Means of joyful celebration; fruitful relationship with Jesus; God's provision.

Caldron or Pot of Boiling Water - Spiritual condition; anger; war; judgment. See Water, and Hot Water subheading.
Isaiah 64:2, Jeremiah 1:13-16, Ezekiel 24:3-14, Psalm 58:9.

Calendar - Time; date; event; appointment. See Clock.
Hosea 6:11, Jeremiah 51:33.

Calf - Increase; prosperity; children of the Kingdom; youthfulness; idolatry; false worship; stubbornness.
Malachi 4:2, Hosea 4:16, Hosea 10:5, Exodus 32:4, & 35.
Fatted Calf = Hospitality; celebration.
Luke 15:23.
Cow or Heifer = Rebellious woman.
Amos 4:3, Judges 14:15-18, Hosea 4:16, Hosea 10:11, Jeremiah 50:11.

Camcorder - Focusing; recording; memories; publishing; fame; reliving memories; seeing the promises of God. See Movie.
Hebrews 12:1-2, Mark 5:20, Mark 7:36, Matthew 26:13, John 21:25, 1 Corinthians 2:9-10.
Camcorder Operator = Seer; prophet; one with clear focus.
Numbers 24:4, & 16, 2 Samuel 18:24, Acts 10:10-20.

Camel - Endurance; long journey; able to bear other's burdens; intercessory spirit; ungainly and non-graceful.
Hebrews 6:15, Genesis 24:61-64, 1 Samuel 30:17, Matthew 3:4, 2 Kings 1:8, Matthew 11:8-9.
A Loaded Camel = Abundance; plentiful supply.

Camera - Focus; record; memories; publish; fame; relive memories; sees the promises of God.
Hebrews 12:1-2, Mark 5:20, Mark 7:36, Matthew 26:13, John 21:25, 1 Corinthians 2:9-10.

Camera Operator - Seer; prophet; one with clear focus.
Numbers 24:4, & 16, 2 Samuel 18:24, Acts 10:10-20.

Camp - Temporary; transient; traveling.
Numbers 33:11-37, Exodus 19:2.
> **Camp of Angels** = Divine encounter; divine help.
> Genesis 32:1-2, 2 Kings 6:17, Psalm 34:7.
> **Camp of Friends** = Divine appointment of help; alignment; gathering; leisure.
> **Camp of Enemies** = Opposition.
> Psalm 3:6, Psalm 27:3, 2 Kings 6:15.
> **Camping Out** = Recreation; vacation; rest; youth ministry.
> **Camp Fire** = Fellowship.

Cancer - Sin within the church; offence; sinfulness; heresy; consuming destructive words; bitterness; unforgiveness; stress; literal cancer disease.
Genesis 13:7, 2 Timothy 2:16-17, Hosea 9:9, Job 21:25, Job 2:4-5.
> **Tumor** = Judgement; corruption; literal tumor.
> 1 Samuel 5:6, 2 Corinthians 10:5, 2 Timothy 2:16-17.
> > **Brain Tumor** = Self-destructive thoughts and words.
> > 2 Corinthians 10:5, 2 Timothy 2:16-17.

Candle - Word of God; Jesus; spirit of man.
Zephaniah 1:12, Psalm 132 :17, 2 Samuel 22:29, Psalm 18:28, Job 29:3, Proverbs 20:27, Matthew 25:1-12, Proverbs 13:9.
> **Unlit Candle** = Lack of God's presence; the wicked; unbeliever.

Matthew 25:8, Proverbs 20:20, Proverbs 24:20, Job 18:5-6, Job 21:17.

Candlestick - The lamp stand; Spirit of God; the Church; believers.
Exodus 25:31-37, Exodus 27:20-21, 1 Chronicles 28:14-15, Zechariah 4:2-6, Revelation 4:5, Revelation 5:6, Revelation 1:12, Matthew 5:14-16.
Candlestick = Menorah, means Light Bearer
Hammered or Beaten Work, the Forming of the Candlestick = The beaten, bruised body of Jesus.
Exodus 25:31, Isaiah 52:14, Isaiah 53:4-5.
Seven Branches = Three Branches out of one (left) side of the Middle Shaft, and three Branches out of the other (right) side of the Middle Shaft.
Exodus 25:32, Exodus 37:18.
Three Divine Pairs (Branches) = Representative of Elohim, the plural name of God as Creator.
Genesis 1:1-2, Genesis 2:4, Romans 1:20, Colossians 2:9.
Revelation 4:5 Divine Pair = Flashes of lightnings, and thunderings... *which are the seven Spirits of God.*
> **Lightnings** = Enlightening. (Glare: Lightning, bright shining. Strong's Number. G796).
> **Thunderings** = Power. (To roar; thunder. Strong's Number G1027).
Revelation 6:5 Divine Pair = Seven horns and seven eyes... *which are the seven Spirits of God.*
> **Seven Horns** = Fullness of power.
> **Seven Eyes** = Fullness of insight.
The Bible, a Divine Pair = Old Testament and New Testament:
The first (left) side of the Candlestick, consists of 3 Branches of 9 objects = 27 objects, attached to 12 objects of the Main Shaft = 39 objects.
39 objects = The 39 Books of the Old Testament.

The other (right) side of the Candlestick, consists of the remaining 27 objects.

27 objects = The 27 Books of the New Testament.

39 objects + 27 objects = The 66 Books of the Bible.

The Seven Spirits of God = Represented by the seven Branches (Middle Staff included). Jesus is the BRANCH. Revelation 4:5, Zechariah 4:2, & 8-10, Revelation 5:6, Zechariah 3:8-9.

> **The Seven Eyes** = Fullness of insight.
> **The Seven Horns** = Fullness of power.
> Isaiah 11:2.

The Spirit of the LORD, the Spirit of Wisdom and Understanding, the Spirit of Counsel and Might, the Spirit of Knowledge and the Fear of the LORD.

Functions of the Seven Spirits of the LORD = Imparted to believers.

> **The Spirit of the LORD** = Boldness; courage; strength of God; conquest.
> Luke 4:18-21, Isaiah 61:1-4, Judges 3:7-11, Judges 15:14-16, 1 Samuel 16:13.
> **The Spirit of Wisdom** = Creative insight; strategies.
> Ephesians 1:17, Exodus 31:3-6, Exodus 35:35, Exodus 36:1-2.
> **The Spirit of Understanding** = Discernment.
> Ephesians 1:18, Proverbs 2:10-11, 1 Chronicles 12:32.
> **The Spirit of Counsel** = Repairer of breaches; adviser; gives aid.
> John 14:16-17, &26, John 16: 7-15.
> **The Spirit of Might** = Warfare; do exploits.
> Zechariah 4:6, Isaiah 40:27-31, Romans 15:19.
> **The Spirit of Knowledge** = Truth; intelligence.
> John 8:32.
> **The Spirit of the Fear of the LORD** = Reverence and awe of God.

Proverbs 8:13, Proverbs 14:27, Proverbs 16:6, Job 28:28, Ecclesiastes 12:13-14.
Associated Colors of the Seven Burning Lamps = Represented by the seven colors of the rainbow. See Colors in Part 2.
Emerald Green = The Spirit of the LORD, the Main Staff in the middle of the Candlestick. Revelation 4:3b.
Red = The Spirit of Wisdom, the farthest Branch on the first (left) side.
Purple = The Spirit of Understanding, the farthest Branch on the other (right) side.
Amber / Fire-Orange = The Spirit of Counsel, the second farthest Branch on the first (left) side. Deuteronomy 4:36 See with Ezekiel 1:26-28.
Indigo Blue = The Spirit of Might, the second farthest Branch on the other (right) side. Ezekiel 23:6.
Golden Yellow = The Spirit of Knowledge, the inside Branch on the first (left) side. Psalm 68:13, Habakkuk 2:14, 2 Corinthians 2:6.
Medium Light Blue = The Spirit of the Fear of the LORD, the inside Branch on the other (right) side.

The colors travel from the outside branches inward to the inside branches, which form the same order of the colors of the rainbow.

Colors from the outside of the First (Left) Side to the Middle Staff and from the outside of the Other (Right) Side = Red, Orange, Yellow, Green, Blue, Indigo, Violet (Purple). The same order as seen in the rainbow.

This whole section is included, particularly the above Associated Colors of the Seven Burning Lamps, to help show how some of the color symbolisms, in Part 2, have originated, and to help put all the different symbolisms together accurately.

Cane - Support; strength; discipline; abuse; judgement. See Staff.
Zechariah 8:4, 1 Samuel 17:40, & 43, Mark 6:8, Hebrews 11:21, Psalm 23:4, Exodus 21:19-20, Numbers 22:27, Isaiah 10:5.

Captain - In charge; Christ; overseer; elder.
Joshua 5:14-15, Hebrews 2:10.

Car - Life; person; ministry; if new, then new ministry or new way of life; if fast may mean a reckless, self-righteous, or unsaved person (living life in the fast lane).
Genesis 41:43, 2 Kings 10:16, 1 Chronicles 13:7, Acts 16:6-7, Genesis 45:27, Nahum 2:3-4, Isaiah 37:24.

Air Conditioning = If in good condition, adequate comfort; if not working, faulty provision for comfort.

Brakes = Slowing down; compelled to stop; stopping; hindrance.
1 Thessalonians 2:18, Acts 16:6-7, 2 Peter 2:14.

Driver's Seat = Indicates leadership; taking control.

Engine = Holy Spirit power; supernatural empowerment.

Catalytic Converter - New anointing of fire; transformative power; yoke-destroying power; gains territory; destroys strongholds; bringer of change; pioneer of new beginnings.
Acts 3:19, James 5:19-20, Ezekiel 18:30-32, Lamentations 5:21, Jeremiah 31:18-20, Isaiah 1:16-20, Psalm 51:13, Acts 15:3, Acts 26:16-18.

Rear-view Mirror = Looking back; focus on the past; warning to watch your back; warning to look ahead.
Genesis 19:7, & 26, Luke 17:31-32.

Seatbelts = Security; safety; preparedness when fastened; assurance; careless when unfastened.

Steering Wheel = The controlling or leading part; the means by which leadership is affected.

Tires = Spirit; life; relates to the spiritual condition. Exodus 14:25, Ezekiel 1:16-21.

> **Fully Inflated Tires** = Encouraged in the Lord; enabled in ministry; prayerful; going in the power of the Lord.
>
> **Deflated Tires** = Discouragement; dismay; hindrance; lack of prayer; lack of covering; lack of power.
>
> **Tires with no Tread** = Worn out; unsafe ministry; careless ministry.
>
> Exodus 18:18, 1 Timothy 1:19-20, Psalm 73:2.

Keys = Authority; power to bind or loose; lock or unlock; wisdom; knowledge; important.
Matthew 16:19, Isaiah 22:22, Revelation 3:7, Luke 11:52, Proverbs 4:7.

> **To be Given Keys** = Given power and authority.
> Isaiah 22:22.
>
> **To Lose One's Keys** = Lose the power and authority one was given.

Trunk = Heart; baggage.
Proverbs 14:14, Hebrews 13:9 (KJV), Luke 11:46, Matthew 23:4, Acts 15:28.

Being Given a Replacement Car for One's Current Car = New assignment or ministry is being given to one, possible change of ministry.

Difficulty or Inability to Find One's Car = Hindrance; subversion or distraction; interference; opposition; being hidden from the car owner; losing one's way.

Vandalized Car = Ministry being destroyed, could be from all sorts of wrong motives.
John 10:10, Matthew 23:14.

Stolen Car = Ministry being taken away through opposition; attack of the enemy to destroy one's purpose; trip one up from an assignment; over-reaching of boundaries; restraint from living out one's heritage.

John 10:10, Genesis 27:35-36, Matthew 16:22-23, Jeremiah 9:4, 2 Corinthians 10:13-16, Micah 2:2.

Junkyard = Abandoned ministries; ministries need repair.

Convertible = Capable of open heaven administration; indicative of revelatory ministry.

With the Top Up = Covered; protected; closed heaven; closed to revelation.

With the Top Down = Uncovered; exposed; vulnerable; open heaven; open to receive revelation.

Indy Race Car = Acceleration into the new season and ministry.

All-wheel Drive = Powerful ministry; ground breaking; capable of global influence; personal ministry or work in the natural; dependable; hard work; rescue; solid Biblical and gospel foundation.

Nahum 2:4, Isaiah 37:24.

Station Wagon = Natural or spiritual family; family ministry; fellowship.

Ephesians 3:14-15, 1 John 1:7.

Van = Natural or spiritual family; family ministry; fellowship.

Ephesians 3:14-15, 1 John 1:7.

Stalled Car = Ministry on hold; operation in one's own strength; need to take authority; hindrance by Satan; opposition.

Isaiah 49:2, Exodus 14:13-16, Galatians 5:7-12, Nehemiah 4:1-18, 1 Thessalonians 2:18.

Car Breakdown - Problem; sickness; spirit of poverty; demonic attack; hindrance to one's life, ministry, career, livelihood.
1 Thessalonians 2:18, Acts 16:6-7.

Car Crash - Strife; contention; conflict; confrontation; calamity; offense; mistake or sin in ministry; failure; church split; personal disaster (failed marriage, business venture,

ministry, project etc.); end of one phase (for whatever reason unbeknownst to the dreamer).
Nahum 2:3-4, 2 Corinthians 11:25-27, 1 Timothy 1:19-20.

Car Trunk - Heart; baggage.
Proverbs 14:14, Hebrews 13:9 (KJV), Luke 11:46, Matthew 23:4, Acts 15:28.

Car-carrier Transport Truck - Riding on another's ministry; large ministry about to release new ministries. See Truck.
2 Kings 5:20, Matthew 28:19-20, Luke 9:1-2.

Cards - Facts; blunt honesty; wisdom, hold or fold; truth; past time entertainment; to expose; reveals; dishonest dealing; gambling; bluffing; cheating.
Romans 12:17, 1 Chronicles 24:5, Acts 1:24-26, Joshua 18:10, Jonah 1:7, 1 Samuel 14:41-42, Acts 5:3-4, & 8-9, Matthew 22:17-21.

Gambler/Gambling = Risk taker; taking chances on eternal destiny; living by chance instead of on purpose for and trusting in God; covetous; addiction; greed; cheat; underhanded.
1 Samuel 14: 9-10, Matthew 16:25-26, Luke 12:19-21, 1 Timothy 6:9-10, Proverbs 1:19, Proverbs 15:27, Acts 5:3-4, & 8-9.

Tarot Cards = Consulting the demonic realm instead of God; necromancy; familiar spirits; deception; error.
1 Samuel 28:7-10, Mark 12:27, 1 Chronicles 10:13-14, Deuteronomy 18:10-12, Micah 5:12.

Cargo Airplane - Large ministry; bearer of large loads; apostolic ministry; releases international ministries. See Airplane.
Acts 13:1-5, 13-14, & 46-51, Romans 15:19, 2 Corinthians 10:13, Colossians 1:6, & 23-29.

Carnival or Fair - Flesh; worldly: festivity; party spirit; exhibitionism; divination; competition. See Roller Coaster.
Luke 21:34, Acts 16:16.

Carpenter - Builder; preacher; evangelist; labourer (good or evil); Christ.
2 Kings 22:6, Isaiah 41:7, Mark 6:3.

Carpet - Covering; covenant; Holy Spirit; deception or covering things up.
Mark 4:22.

Cartoon Character - Person; superficial; animated; relates to the nature of the cartoon character; fable; myth. See Super Hero.
Judges 9:14, 1 Timothy 4:7.
Some examples below:
Mickey Mouse = Sensitive hearing (big ears); insignificant ("Mickey mouse thing").
Ecclesiastes 9:15-16, Judges 6:15.
Goofy = Silly; can be prone to foolish actions.
2 Samuel 24:10, Matthew 25:2-3, Proverbs 14:24.
Scooby Doo = Fearful but comes through when pressed; cheerful and friendly.
Judges 6:23, John 20:19, Isaiah 41:10.
Scrappy Doo = Courageous; feisty.
2 Chronicles 15:8, Judges 4:4-9, 14, & 17-22.
Superman = Super strength; humble (Clark Kent); strong sense of morality and compassion. Reflects the ability and characteristics of God.
Jeremiah 32:27, Psalm 136:1-26.
Superman can be an antichrist.
2 Thessalonians 2:9.

Cat - Self-willed; untrainable; unteachable; predator, arrogant; unclean spirit, demon, bewitching charm; witchcraft; stealthy; sneaky; crafty; deception; self-pity; lustful.
Proverbs 7:10-12, & 21, Psalm 73:7 (NLT).
Alley cat or Tom-cat = Unfaithful.
Personal Pet = Something precious; a precious habit that could be dangerous.
Kitten = Precious gift; helpless; must be attended to.
1 Corinthians 12:4, 1 Timothy 4:14.

Catalytic Converter - New anointing of fire; transformative power; yoke-destroying power; gains territory; destroys strongholds; bringer of change; pioneer of new beginnings.
Acts 3:19, James 5:19-20, Ezekiel 18:30-32, Lamentations 5:21, Jeremiah 31:18-20, Isaiah 1:16-20, Psalm 51:13, Acts 15:3, Acts 26:16-18.

Caterpillar - Devourer; potential.
Joel 1:4.

Cave - Safety; hidden from danger; secret place; burial place.
1 Samuel 22:1, 1 Kings 18:4, & 13, Psalm 57:1, Psalm 142:1, Hebrews 11:38, Genesis 49:30, John 11:38.
Hide in a Cave = Fear; lack of faith.
Joshua 10:16-17.
Put Valuables in a Cave = Hidden from the enemy.
1 Kings 18:4, & 13.

CD - Recorded music; record of memories; praise and worship; celebration; reliving past memories.
Mark 14:72, Luke 15:25.
Listening to Music on a CD = Reliving memories of praise and worship; reliving time when music was played.

Cedar Tree - Rooted and grounded in the things of God; firm in the faith; persistent; determined. See Trees.
1 Kings 5:8, & 10, Ezekiel 17:22-23, Psalm 92:12, Isaiah 41:19.

Ceiling - Covering; authority, good or bad; limitation; hindered prayer (prayers that hit the ceiling).
Acts 10:1-9, 22-24, & 27, 1 Kings 6:12-15, Genesis 19:8, Job 42:8, 1 Peter 3:7, James 4:3, Romans 8:26-27.

> **Glass Ceiling** = Fragile covering due to weakened relationship and opposition with godly authority; transparency with authority.
> 2 Timothy 3:8-9.

Roof = Covering; protection; mind; thought; vantage point, for good or bad; authority, good or bad; prayers; visions; proclamation; preaching; evil practices revealed.
Isaiah 30:1, Deuteronomy 22:8, Mark 2:4, Luke 5:18-19, 2 Samuel 11:2, Matthew 8:8-9, Genesis 19:8, Acts 10:9, Matthew 10:27, Zephaniah 1:5, Jeremiah 19:13, Luke 12:2-3.

> **Roof with a Leak** = A gap in authority structure or covering; lack of maintenance.
> Mark 2:4, Luke 5:18-19, Ezekiel 13:5, Ezekiel 22:30.

Chair - Place of authority; position of power; throne of God; seat of Satan; rest; quietness.
Matthew 23:2-6, Matthew 20:21, Acts 2:32-33, 1 Peter 3:22, Ephesians 1:20, Hebrews 10:12, Isaiah 30:15.

> **Someone Else Sitting on a Chair** = In place of authority; in position of power; throne of God; seat of Satan.
> 1 Peter 3:22, Ephesians 1:20, Hebrews 10:12, Hebrews 12:2, Matthew 23:1-2, Revelation 2:13.

> **Sitting on One's Chair** = One's place of authority; one's position of power; rest.
> 1 Peter 3:22, Ephesians 1:20, Hebrews 10:12.

Difficulty Finding One's Chair = Hindrances to obtaining one's place of authority.
1 Samuel 18:8-29.
Stolen Chair = Warfare needed to maintain or recover one's authority, or designated place or position.
2 Samuel 15:1-36.

Channel - Passage; time; a way out.
Isaiah 8:7, Isaiah 43:2, Exodus 14:29, Hebrews 11:29.
Passing through a Channel = Going through something.
Psalm 66:12, Isaiah 8:7.
Dark Channel = Difficult time.
Psalm 23:4.

Chase - Pursuit; flee away. See Run.
Leviticus 26:7-8, & 36, Deuteronomy 32:30, Joshua 23:10, Psalm 35:5.
Chased by an Insane Person = Mental instability; irrational decision.
Chased by a Dangerous Animal = Spiritual attack; weakness in spiritual issue represented by the specific animal.

Check - Faith; provision; trust; if it is a bad check, fraud, deception, hypocrisy, lack of faith or prayer.
Hebrews 11:1, Mark 4:40, Luke 17:5.

Cheese - Works; doing, or not doing the Word or will of God. See Butter.
John 4:34, Job 10:10.

Chess - Strategy; consultation; plan the next move; deliberate; purposeful course of action.
Genesis 3:15, Proverbs 20:18, Proverbs 24:6, Luke 14:31-32, Joshua 6:2-20, 1 Samuel 17:1-57.

Stalemate = Standstill.
1 Samuel 17:16, Ephesians 6:13.
Checkmate = Defeating the enemy or defeated by the enemy.
1 Samuel 17:45-51, Joshua 7:2-5.

Chewing - Meditate; receiving wisdom and understanding. See eating, food, milk, teeth.
1 Timothy 4:15, Psalm 49:3, Proverbs 24:9.
Chewing Bubble Gum = Childishness; foolishness.
Chewing on Tough Meat = A hard saying or difficult work. John 6:60.

Chicken - Fear; cowardliness.
Deuteronomy 1:29, Luke 13:34.
Hen = Gathering; protection; gossip.
Luke 13:34.
Rooster = Bragging; proud; boasting; arrogance; sexual pride.
John 18:27, Luke 22:33-34.
Chick = Defenceless.

Child/Children - Similar characteristics or behavior of oneself; someone they remind the dreamer of; innocence; purity; humble; trusting; new believer; immaturity; undisciplined; disobedient.
Ezekiel 16:44, Isaiah 3:4, & 12a, Matthew 18:3-6, 1 John 2:12-14, 1 Corinthians 13:11, Hebrews 12:8, Ephesians 5:6, Colossians 3:6.
Many Children = Future children of God; the church.
Jeremiah 31:17, John 1:12.

Chiropractor - One who brings alignment into the body of Christ; makes adjustments by manipulation.
Ephesians 4:12, & 16, Colossians 2:19.

Choking - Hindrance; stumbling; too much; too fast; hatred; anger; unfruitful; spiritually draining.
Mark 4:19.

Christmas - Gift; new life in Christ; celebrating Christ; season of rejoicing; spiritual gifts; a surprise; good will; benevolence; tradition; commercialism.
Luke 11:13, Ephesians 4:7-8, 1 Corinthians 12:1, 4, 7-11, & 28-31, 1 Corinthians 14:1, Luke 2:1-20, Matthew 10:8, Matthew 15:3-6.
   Christmas Tree = Celebration; spiritual gifts.
   Luke 2:10-11, 1 Corinthians 2:12, Ephesians 4:7-8, 1 Corinthians 12:1, 4, & 7-11.

Church Building - One's own congregation; a church in general; house of worship; individual member.
1 Timothy 3:15, Revelation 2:1, 8, 12, & 18, Matthew 16:18, Romans 16:15, 1 Corinthians 3:16, 1 Corinthians 6:19-20.
   Synagogue = Jewish place of worship; Jewish people gathering together; a Jewish place of teaching the Torah.
   Luke 4:16-20, John 12:42, John 18:20, Acts 14:1, Acts 17:1-2, & 10-11.

Church Service - Worship; praise; fellowship; message; tradition; false worship.
2 Chronicles 29:28, Hebrews 2:12, Acts 2:36-42, John 4:24, Mark 7:7.

Cigar Boat - Support; powerful; fast progress; life; person; smuggling; prideful; wasteful; recreation; spare time. See Shipwreck.
Genesis 6:16, Luke 8:22-23, 1 Timothy 1:19.
   A Large Boat or Ship = Big business.
   A Small Boat or Ship = Small or personal business.

Cigar Smoking - Intellectual pride; haughty; arrogant; offence. Isaiah 65:5, Proverbs 21:24, 1 Corinthians 8:1, Deuteronomy 29:19-20, Job 19:17.

Cigarette Smoking - Pride; bitterness; bitter memories; offense; unforgiving; envy; jealousy; self-righteousness. Isaiah 65:5, Proverbs 21:24, 1 Corinthians 8:1, Deuteronomy 29:19-20, Job 19:17.

Circle - Eternal; God; everlasting covenant; goes on forever; wandering endlessly; judgement comes around full circle; continue in the same mistakes (keep going around about the mountain). See Round.
Isaiah 40:22, Deuteronomy 33:27, Psalm 102:25-28, Numbers 14:29-33, Psalm 78:40-41, & 56-57, Deuteronomy 2:3.

Circumcision - Covenant with God; blood relationship; born again; believer; cutting away fleshly desires; changed heart. Genesis 17:11, Jeremiah 4:4, Acts 7:8, Romans 2:25-29, Romans 4:9-13, Philippians 3:3, Colossians 2:11-13.

Circus - Show; entertainment; worldly church service. Matthew 6:5, Mark 12:38-39, 3 John 1:9-10.

City - Characteristics; that for which a city is known; the Church; a person's character.
Jude 1:7, Acts 20:23, Proverbs 25:28.

Civil Trial - Judgment; trial; persecution; justice; legal matters; conviction. See Courthouse, Miscarriage.
Deuteronomy 16:18, Deuteronomy 17:6-13, Isaiah 43:12, Psalm 94:20, 1 Corinthians 6:1, Matthew 18:15-19.

Classroom - Spiritual preparation; taught in the things of God; training in ministry.

1 John 2:13-14, Matthew 20:23, 2 Timothy 3:16-17, Mark 12:35-37.
Childhood Classroom = New foundational teaching; knowledge imminent.
Difficulty Finding Classroom = Hindrances to get proper training.

Clay - Frailty of man; delicate; not secure; molded by God.
Job 4:19, Daniel 2:33-34, & 41-43, 2 Corinthians 4:7-11, Isaiah 64:8, Romans 9:20-21, Jeremiah 18:2-6, 2 Corinthians 4:7-11.
Mold a Vessel with Clay = Creation; God's restorative power; trials.
Job 10:9, Isaiah 64:8, Jeremiah 18:2-6.

Clean - Redeemed; pure; holy; undefiled; sanctification; righteous; only have outward appearance instead of true change.
Titus 2:14, Psalm 51:7, &10, Matthew 8:2-3, John 15:3, Revelation 19:8, 1 John 1:7, Matthew 23:25-28.

Cleanse - Confession; repentance; to make right a wrong.
See Bathroom.
1 John 1:9, Psalm 51:2-4, Ephesians 5:26, Luke 19:8-9.

Clock - Timing; late; early; delay. See Calendar.
John 11:9-10, Ephesians 5:16, Colossians 4:5.
Clock Hands Moving Faster than Normal = There is an acceleration coming in one's life.
John 4:35.
Clock Hands Nearing Midnight = The end of something is near; opportunity nearing an end.
John 9:4-5, John 11:9-10, John 12:35, Colossians 4:5, Ephesians 5:15-17.
Clock Hands Slow or Stopped = Hindrance to one's assignment.

1 Thessalonians 2:18, Romans 15:22, Luke 11:52, Ezra 4:21-24, Ezra 6:7-8.
Grandfather Clock - Past.

Close - To shut up; keep silent; walled up.
Isaiah 29:10-12, Matthew 13:15.

Closet - Private; personal; prayer; secret sin; something hidden; stored away.
Matthew 6:6, Luke 8:17, Luke 12:2.

Clothing - Covering; righteousness; spiritual attitude; fleshly attitude. See Coat, Pants, Skirt; whichever applies to the dream.
Romans 13:14, Psalm 132:9, James 2:2, Isaiah 64:6, Zechariah 3:3-7, Psalm 109:18.
Clean Clothing = Honor; mantle; glory of God; righteousness.
Zechariah 3:5-7.
Wrinkled Clothing = Still issues that need to be dealt with.
Filthy Clothes = Unrighteousness; sin; iniquity; self-righteousness; uncleanness.
Psalm 109:18, Isaiah 64:6, Zechariah 3:3-4.
Worn out Clothing = Useless; poor; humble; unrighteous; self righteous.
Isaiah 64:6, Proverbs 23:21.
Put on a Garment of Praise (Bright and Colorful Clothing) = Joy; thanksgiving.
Isaiah 61:3.
Tearing Clothing = Mourning.
2 Samuel 1:11-12, Joel 2:12-13.

Clouds - Change; covering; trouble; distress; threatening; thoughts (of trouble); confusion; hidden; covered. See Fog.
Zechariah 10:1, 1 Corinthians 10:1-2, Zephaniah 1:15.

White Clouds = Good change; glory; rest; manifest presence of God; covering; government and protection of God; revival.
Exodus 13:21, Leviticus 16:2, Zechariah 10:1.
Dark Clouds = Time of difficulty; the Lord's appearance.
2 Samuel 22:12, Psalm 18:11-12, Matthew 24:30, Zephaniah 1:15.

Clown - Foolish works of the flesh; the 'old man'-flesh; childish; mischief. See Joker.
Ecclesiastes 7:4, Proverbs 10:23a.

Clutter - Obstacles; oppositions; distractions.
Nahum 3:3, Jeremiah 18:15.

Coat - Covering: Anointing; authority; protection; grief; shame; confusion. See Clothing.
2 Kings 2:14-15a, Psalm 109:17-19, & 29.

Cobra - Power to rule; authority; under the grip of Satan; spiritual warfare. See Snake.
Exodus 7:9-12, Psalm 91:13.
King Cobra = Satan.
Revelation 12:9, Genesis 3:1, 2 Corinthians 11:3, & 14, Ephesians 6:12, & 16.

Cocklebur (Xanthium) or Sticker Thorns - Irritant; irritated; minor afflictions. See Thorns.
Hebrews 6:8, Exodus 22:6, Matthew 13:22.

Cockroaches - Unclean; infestation; crept in; defiled; hidden sin; in darkness; lies. See Bugs.
Leviticus 5:2, Leviticus 11: 31, & 43, 2 Corinthians 7:1; 2 Timothy 3:6, Jude 1:4, 1 Corinthians 4:5, 1 John 1:6.

Cocoon - Metamorphosis; transformation; change.
Romans 12:2.

Coffee - Stimulant; desire for revenge; bitter envy; bitter memories; wake-up call; become sober.
James 3:14, Ephesians 5:14, Titus 2:6.

Coins (Money) - Wealth; spiritual riches; provision; natural talents and skills; power; strength of man; greed; covetousness.
Deuteronomy 8:18, Ecclesiastes 7:12, Matthew 17:27, Luke 16:11, Genesis 31:15, Ezekiel 22:12, 1 Timothy 6:10, James 5:1-4.

> **Finding Silver Coins** = Receiving Biblical revelation, knowledge and understanding; receiving the Lord's instruction.
> Proverbs 2:1-5, Proverbs 8:10.
> **Getting Coins** = Literal financial increase; increase in favor.
> Matthew 17:27.
> **Bundle of Coins** = Season of abundance of money or favor.
> **International Currency** = Privilege or favor from that country.
> **Short of Money** = Season of a lack of money or favor.
> **Changing Paper Money into Coins or needing to make Change** = Impending change of location or church etc.

Cold Feet - Retreat; renege on deal; does not keep promises; fearful.
1 Samuel 17:24. See Feet.

Combat, Military Self-defence - Severe spiritual warfare; powerful deliverance ministry; spiritual combat; self-defence.
Ephesians 6:12, 1 Timothy 6:12, 2 Corinthians 10:3-6.

Comforter - Holy Spirit; the Spirit of truth.
John 14:16, & 26, John 16:7, John 15:26.

Blanket = Covering; warmth; covenant; protection; hidden. Exodus 25:20-22, Ezekiel 16:8-10 Psalm 91:4-5, Proverbs 31:22, Proverbs 7:16, Job 31:20.
Quilt = Covering; warmth; covenant; protection; hidden. Exodus 25:20-22, Ezekiel 16:8-10, Psalm 91:4-5, Proverbs 31:22, Proverbs 7:16, Job 31:20.
Patchwork Quilt = Memories or influence of one's foremothers.

Compass - Directions; word of God; correction; advice. Proverbs 6:23.

Communication - Inform; avenue of information and knowledge and revelation being conveyed, the distribution of important facts or details.
Luke 24:17, 1 Corinthians 15:33.

Computer - Channel of communication; artificial communication; programmed; heart (CPU); man-made or worldly spirit; spirit of arrogance.
2 Timothy 2:2, Proverbs 22:6, Romans 12:2, Proverbs 4:23, James 3:15, Isaiah 14:11-14.
Web = Snare; lies and deception; scheme; trap; ruin; internet; search tool; research.
Ecclesiastes 7:26, Isaiah 59:5-7; Psalm 91:3, Psalm 124:7, Ecclesiastes 9:12; Psalm 140:5, Psalm 119:110, Psalm 141:9, Ecclesiastes 7:25, John 1:38, Luke 19:10.

Concorde - Soaring; fast; powerful; high-functioning church; fully empowered by the Spirit; deep in the Spirit; moving in the deep things of God; extreme acceleration into the new season and ministry. See Airplane, Flying.
2 Kings 2:9-11, Psalm 104:3-4.

Concrete Slab - Foundation; established; stable; sound; level; solidified.
Psalm 11:3, Luke 14:29, 1 Corinthians 3:10-11, Ephesians 2:20.
Pouring Concrete = Not ready; not complete; still being solidified in Jesus.
Not Cured = Unstable; ill health; uncontrollable circumstances.
Deluge of Rain = Imminent challenge.
Matthew 7:24-27, Luke 6:48-49.

Conductor (Railway Operator) - Control; self; Christ; pastor; teacher; Satan; the emphasis is on the nature of the driver (Confident, kind, careful, frantic, careless, selfish, rude ...).
2 Kings 9:20.

Convertible Car - Life; person; ministry; capable of open heaven administration; indicative of revelatory ministry. See Car, Driver.
Genesis 41:43, 2 Kings 10:16, Isaiah 30:1, Genesis 9:21, 1 Corinthians 11:5.
With the Top Up = Covered; protected; closed heaven; closed to revelation.
With the Top Down = Uncovered; exposed; vulnerable; open heaven; open to receive revelation.

Cord - Bondage; sin; covenant; vow; hindrances; rescue; salvation.
Proverbs 5:22, Psalm 118:27, Jeremiah 38:11.

Corn Field - Harvest field; economy.
Genesis 41:26-27, Hosea 6:11, John 4:35.
Ears Large and Full = Prosperity.
Genesis 41:26-27.
Ears Shrunk and Dried = Famine.
Genesis 41:26-27.

Cornet - Voice; announcement; preaching; prophesying; warning; call to assemble; worship; tongues; the rapture; if sounding reveille, beginning, wake-up, call to assemble; finished.
Isaiah 58:1, 1 Corinthians 14:8, 1 Corinthians 15:52, Joel 2:15, Ephesians 5:14.

Cornucopia - Abundance without measure or limitation; goodness without end; blessed.
Deuteronomy 28:2, & 4-5, Galatians 5:22-23, Ephesians 3:20.

Corridor - Passage way; transition; restricted journey; focused journey.
Jeremiah 6:16.
 Long Corridor = Passage of time.
 Enclosed Corridor = Limits but compels one's transition.
 Dark Corridor = Ominous time; trouble; sickness.
 Lighted Corridor = Enlightened journey.
 Psalm 119:105.
 Clear Corridor = Obstacle free.
 Cluttered Corridor = Obstacles; opposition.
 Nahum 3:3, Jeremiah 18:15.

Costume - Change of one's appearance; wanting to be someone else; hiding true identity; to feel the need to be someone else; false Christian.
1 Samuel 21:13, Romans 7:18-19, Genesis 27:15-16, Proverbs 6:19, Galatians 2:4.

Couch - Rest; at ease; unconcerned; lazy.
Psalm 25:13, Amos 6:4.

Country - Offspring; a move to another country; characteristics of the specific country representative to the dreamer; entering our heavenly country.

Genesis 10:20, & 31, Genesis 12:7a, Genesis 11:1-9, Joshua 1:11, John 3:5, Hebrews 11:14-16. Some examples below:
Israel = Inventions; innovation; prudent entrepreneurship; humanitarian; chosen; prince of God; warfare. See Krav Maga.
Psalm 46:6-11, Genesis 32:24-28, Luke 21:9-10.
Germany = Industrious; hardworking; world war.
China = Industrious; global economic dominance; power; influence; world dominance; communist; antichrist, the Dragon is China's national symbol; underground church; persecution.
Revelation 16:12-16, Isaiah 49:12, Acts 19:22-31.
France = Romance; tourism; arrogant, surrender.
Nation or Nationality = That for which the people are generally known; may represent the actual nation in the natural.
1 Kings 9:7.

Countryside- Isolated; quiet; peaceful; restful; leisurely; pleasant; removed from the city; fresh; creation.
Mark 6:31, Psalm 23:2, Isaiah 55:12, Genesis 49:15, Deuteronomy 3:20, Joshua 1:13, Song of Solomon 7:11-13, Genesis 1:12, Genesis 2:9.
Country Road = Country ministry; wilderness training; alone; off track.
Acts 8:26, Matthew 3:1-3, 1 Kings 19:4, Deuteronomy 8:2-3, Luke 15:4.

Courthouse - Judgment; trial; persecution; justice; legal matters; conviction.
Deuteronomy 16:18, Deuteronomy 17:6-13, Isaiah 43:12, Psalm 94:20, 1 Corinthians 6:1,
Matthew 18:15-19.

Kangaroo Court = Prejudiced; verdict already decided before hearing the defence.
Proverbs 18:13, John 7:51.
Before a Kangaroo Court = Unfair judgement at hand or imminent.
Judge = Authority; God; conscience.
Psalm 75:7, James 5:9, 1 Corinthians 11:31.
Fair and Just Judge = Rule of God.
Unjust Judge = Prejudiced; verdict already decided before hearing the defence.
Proverbs 18:13, John 7:51, Luke 18:2-6.
Evil Judge = Satan; evil authority.
Psalm 94:20, Matthew 5:25-26, Luke 12:58-59.
Before an Unfair or Evil Judge = Evil power's influence over one's situation.
Lawyer = Advocate; Christ; a legalistic minister.
1 John 2:1, Luke 11:46, Revelation 12:10.
Evil Lawyer = Devil's advocate; the accuser of the brethren.
Revelation 12:10.

Cousin - Spiritual brother or sister in the faith.
Luke 1:36, & 58, Romans 16:1, Ruth 4:14.

Cow - Rebellious woman. See Calf.
Amos 4:3, Judges 14:15-18, Hosea 4:16, Hosea 10:11, Jeremiah 50:11.

Crab - Moving sideways; disgruntled; ill-tempered; easily angered; potential to hurt; self centered; complaining; critical.
Philippians 2:14.

Crane (Bird) - Chatter; knows one's time and season; punctual; repentant; loyal. See Bird.
Isaiah 38:14, Jeremiah 8:7.

Crane Truck - Burden lifter; load made easy; powerful salvation ministry; burden. See Truck.
Matthew 11:30, Matthew 27:32, Isaiah 49:22, Isaiah 59:19b, Psalm 3:3, James 4:10, Psalm 113:7, Psalm 27:6a, Matthew 23:4, Luke 11:46.

Crash, Vehicle, Ship, Train, Airplane etc. - Strife; contention; conflict; confrontation; calamity; offense; mistake or sin in ministry; failure; church split; apostasy; personal disaster (failed marriage, business venture, ministry, project etc.); end of one phase (for whatever reason unbeknownst to the dreamer). See Driver, Captain, Conductor, or Pilot, and associated means of transportation.
Nahum 2:3-4, 2 Corinthians 11:25-28, 1 Timothy 1:19-20.

Crawling - Humility; humbled; judgement.
1 Samuel 14:11, Ezekiel 8:10, Genesis 3:14.

Crooked - Distorted; wicked; perverse.
Isaiah 40:4, Psalm 125:5, 2 Peter 2:15, Acts 2:40.

Crawfish - Retreat; coward; renege on a promise; if it has raised claws, defensive or cautious.
1 Samuel 17:24.

Crocodile - Ancient; evil out of the past from generational or personal sin; danger, destruction, evil spirit; large mouthed enemy; verbal attack. See Snake.
Job 41:1, & 10, Psalm 74:14, Isaiah 27:1.

Cross - Redemption; gospel of Salvation; forgiveness of sin; victory; deliverance; healing; dead to self. See Crucify.
Colossians 1:20, 1 Corinthians 1:17-18, Colossians 2:14-15, Colossians 1:12-22, 1 Peter 2:24, Matthew 16:24, Mark 8:34-35.

Crossroads - Decision; confusion; choice; job or career change; geographical move.
Luke 18:18, & 22-23.
    Left Turn = Spiritual change.
    Right Turn = Natural change.

Crouch - Hide; ready to attack.
Joshua 8:4, Deuteronomy 19:11, Genesis 4:7.

Crow - Confusion; outspoken person; person operating under or out of a spirit of envy or strife (which causes confusion and disorder); hateful; depression; grief; death; suicide; straight path or direct route; God's minister(s) of justice or provision. See Bird.
James 3:16, Isaiah 13:20-22, Isaiah 34:11-15, Psalm 35:26, Proverbs 30:17, 1 Kings 17:4-6.
    Flock of Crows = Gossip; slander; bitter words.
    1 Samuel 17:44, Jeremiah 12:9, Ezekiel 39:4.

Crown – Authority; glory; honor; victory; righteousness; life; reward; rejoicing; incorruptible; pride.
Hebrews 2:7-10, Proverbs 4:9, 1 Peter 5:4, 2 Timothy 2:5, 2 Timothy 4:8, James 1:12, Revelation 2:10, 1 Thessalonians 2:19, 1 Corinthians 9:25, Isaiah 28:1, & 3.
    To be Crowned = Rewarded; honored; given authority.
    To be Given a Crown = To be given power.
    Crown of Thorns = Humiliation; Ridicule.
    Matthew 27:29.

Crying - Sorrow; grief; disagreement; complaining; anger; repentance.
1 Samuel 30:4, Numbers 11:13, Hosea 13:8, Acts 21:13, Joel 2:17, Job 30:23-27, Joel 2:12-13, Nehemiah 8:9, 2 Chronicles 34:27.

Crying Out or Speaking Out - Communication in prayer; message from God; conversation with God; counsel; gossip; the enemy's voice.

Psalm 4:1, Psalm 20:9, 2 Samuel 22:7, Psalm 18:6, Jeremiah 33:3, Psalm 32:1-11, 1 Timothy 5:13, Genesis 3:3-4, Jeremiah 29:8-9, 1 John 4:1.

Crucify - Death to self; weakness of man, the power and wisdom of God; die to the flesh (old nature) live through the Spirit (new nature); torturous death. See Cross.

Galatians 2:20, 1 Corinthians 2:1-5, Galatians 5:24-25, Mark 8:31, Isaiah 52:14, Isaiah 53:3.

Crystal Ball - Future vision; divination; fortune telling; prediction.

Jeremiah 14:14, Ezekiel 13:6-7, & 23, Micah 3:11, Acts 16:16.

Cup - Symbol of life and health; or death and evil.

1 Corinthians 10:21.

God's cup of wrath, judgement and plagues.

Revelation 15:7, Revelation 16:2-21, Revelation 17:1, Revelation 21:9.

Cursing or Cussing - Curse; uncontrolled anger; hatred.

Psalm 109:17-18, Matthew 5:22, Colossians 3:8, Ephesians 4:29-31, Ephesians 5:4.

Curtain - Concealment; hidden; covering; deception; without understanding; law versus liberty; flesh versus the Spirit.

2 Corinthians 3:13-18; Isaiah 25:7-8, Hebrews 9:3, & 8.

> **Separated by a Curtain** = Unrevealed; not exposed.
> 2 Corinthians 3:13-16.
> **Torn Curtain** = Revealed; exposed; barrier removed.
> Mark 15:37-38, Luke 24:45, Isaiah 25:7-8.

Cyclone - Great disturbance; intense spiritual warfare; witchcraft; sudden calamity or destruction; judgement; trial; persecution; opposition; outpouring of revival; powerful move of the Spirit. See Tornado, Whirlwind.
Isaiah 25:4, Acts 27:14-15, & 18-25, 1 Thessalonians 5:3, Nahum 1:3, 2 Samuel 22:10-15, Psalm 18:9-14, Psalm 104:3, Psalm 58:9, Hosea 13:3, Zechariah 7:14.

Cymbals - Instrument of praise; without love; noise.
Psalm 150:5, 1 Corinthians 13:1.

Cypress Tree - One who is a provider of shade, or rest from the desert experience; grateful for the one who provides relief; godly; durable (the White Cedar). See Trees.
1 Kings 5:8, & 10, Isaiah 55:12-13, Isaiah 60:13, Isaiah 41:19.

Dam - Being held back; restricted; hindrance; obstacle; blocked; reserve; power.
Joshua 3:16.

Dancing - Worship of God; joy; celebration; idol worship; romance; seduction; lewdness.
Psalm 149:3, Lamentations 5:15, Matthew 14:6, Exodus 32:19.

Darkness or Night - Ignorance; hidden; lost; spiritual blindness; sin; power of darkness; stealth (under cover of darkness).
John 11:10, Jonah 4:10, 1 Thessalonians 5:7, Luke 22:53, Matthew 13:25, Jude 1:4, Galatians 2:4, 2 Timothy 3:6.

Daughter - Themselves: or someone whom they remind you of; having the characteristics of that child; innocence; purity.

Ezekiel 16:44, Isaiah 3: 12, Genesis 20:12, Genesis Chapter 34, Leviticus 18:9-11.

Day - Light; knowledge; truth; good; manifest; evil revealed.
2 Corinthians 4:6, Genesis 1:4-5, 2 Peter 1:19, 1 Corinthians 3:13, Ephesians 5:13.

Death - Termination; repentance; loss; sorrow; failure; separation; end of relationship; physical death; spiritual death, from sin.
John 12:24, 1 Corinthians 15:31, Hebrews 2:14, Isaiah 26:14, John 11:14, Jeremiah 9:21, Romans 6:23.

Death Row - Death sentence; cursed; judgement; certain death of something if unrepentant; in need of the Lord's intervention.
Genesis 20:3, Ezekiel 33:14, Luke 13:3-5.

Deer - Graceful; divine enabling, swift; sure-footed; agile; spiritual longing; provision; timid; skittish.
2 Samuel 22:34, Psalm 18:33, Habakkuk 3:19, Psalm 42:1-2.
   Buck (Male Deer) = Regal; rule; authority; strength; power.
   Psalm 42:1-2, Song of Solomon 2:9, & 17, Song of Solomon 8:14, Isaiah 35:6.

Defecation - Unclean; offensive; impure; need for repentance.
See Toilet, Bathroom.
2 Corinthians 7:1, Ephesians 5:3-5.

Deflated Tires - Discouragement; dismay, hindrance, lack of prayer, lack of covering, lack of power. See Tires.
Exodus 14:25.

Den - Revealed; everyday or current affairs; that which is hidden be manifest; truth exposed; without hypocrisy; can be a place of hidden predators.
Mark 2:4-5, Amos 3:4, Daniel 6:16, & 23, Psalm 10:9, Jeremiah 7:11, Matthew 21:13.

Dentist - Physician; dreaded; fearful encounter; trial; Christ; minister of the Gospel.
See James 3:10 with Psalm 50:16-20, Jeremiah 7:4-10, and Micah 3:11.

Desert - Barren; test; humbled; heart revealed; infertile; spiritual wasteland; result of turning away from God; tempted.
Deuteronomy 8:2-3, Psalm 107:4-5, Proverbs 30:16, Isaiah 5:17, Isaiah 49:19, Jeremiah 17:5-6; Matthew 4:1.

Desk - Work; position; ministry; office.
1 Timothy 3:1.
   Cluttered Desk = Disorganized; too much responsibility; behind schedule.

Detective - Investigate; search out the answers; spy.
Genesis 18:21.

Diamond - Eternal; gift of the Spirit; pure; valuable; precious; engraves something; unchangeable; hard-headed; heard-hearted.
Proverbs 17:8, Ezekiel 28:13, Exodus 28:18, Jeremiah 17:1, Ezekiel 3:7-9, Zechariah 7:12.

Diary or Book of Remembrance - A record of life; records of encounters with God; a record of God's righteous dealings on one's behalf; recorded thoughts of God's power, omniscience, justice, goodness, mercy, peace and truth.
Malachi 3:16, Job 19:23-25, Psalm 56:8.

Digging - Uncovering truth; fertilizing; digging a well.
Matthew 13:44, Luke 13:8, Genesis 26:18-19.

Dim Light - Without full knowledge or understanding.
2 Samuel 22:29, Psalm 18:28, John 3:19-20, Ephesians 5:11-14.

Dining Room - Spiritual growth; spiritual food.
Psalm 34:8, Psalm 23:5, Hebrews 5:12-14.

Diploma - Graduated to the next level; completed; recognition of achievement, promotion.
2 Timothy 2:15, Proverbs 22:6, 2 Timothy 3:15-17.

Dirt - Soiled; defiled by sin.
Isaiah 57:20, Job 18:10, Psalm 18:42.
Digging = Uncovering truth; fertilizing; digging a well.
Matthew 13:44, Luke 13:8, Genesis 26:18-19.
Digging up Dirt = Looking for shameful or criminal activity in another's life.
Good Soil = Disciple.
Matthew 13:23.

Dirty Laundry - Sin; shameful; hidden; need for repentance.
Isaiah 1:16, Ephesians 5:26-27, Revelation 7:14.

Dirty or Muddy Water - Corrupted spiritually; causing strife; bitter words; unstable hypocrite; sin; false doctrine; unattractive or too common to the proud.
Ezekiel 32:2, Ezekiel 34:18-19, Isaiah 57:20, Exodus 15:23-24, Job 8:11, 2 Kings 5:12, Ezekiel 47:11.

Ditch - Snare; habit; religious tradition; addiction; lust; passion; sin.
Psalm 7:15, Proverbs 23:27, Matthew 15:14.

Divorce - Broken covenant; permanent separation; end of relationship.
Malachi 2:14-16, Mark 10:9.

Doctor - Healer; authority; Christ; preacher; medical doctor; illness.
Mark 2:17, Mark 5:26, 2 Chronicles 16:12, 1 Corinthians 11:30-32.

Dog - Strife; contention; offense; unclean spirit; obsession; guilt, shame, cowardly.
Galatians 5:15, Proverbs 26:17, Proverbs 26:11, Luke 16:21, 2 Peter 2:22, Matthew 7:6, 2 Timothy 3:2-4, Isaiah 56:10-11, Revelation 22:15.
Attacks You = Unthankful.
Matthew 7:6, Galatians 5:15, Philippians 3:2.
Biting the Hand That Feeds It = Incessant nuisance and annoyance.
Galatians 5:15.
Barking Repeatedly = Single-minded pursuit of evil; demonized; deliberately evil; contagious evil; persecution.
Philippians 3:2, 2 Timothy 3:2-4, Psalm 59:6, & 14.
Rabid Dog = Great danger.
Psalm 59:6, & 14.
Fangs = Evil intent or motive: poisonous; great danger.
Psalm 57:4, Psalm 58:6, Proverbs 30:14, Daniel 7:5-7, Revelation 9:8.
Animal Teeth = Danger.
Psalm 57:4, Psalm 58:6. Job 4:10, Proverbs 30:14, Daniel 7:5-7, Revelation 9:8.
Bulldog = Unyielding; stubborn; dangerous; tenacious.
Judges 2:19.
Wolf = Predator; devourer; false prophet; evil minister or governor; person seeking their own gain; opportunistic; womanizer; loner; God's minister of justice.

Matthew 7:15, Acts 20:29-30.

Fox = Subtlety; deceptive; cunning; secretly; a con man; false prophet; wicked leader; hidden sin; counter-productive.

Song of Solomon 2:15, Nehemiah 4:3, Luke 13:32, Ezekiel 13:4, & 6.

Hyena = Warning of attack against the spiritually asleep; a call to stay awake and alert.

Isaiah 52:1, Luke 22:45-46.

Watchdog = Watchman elder; minister; alert; beware; warning; wake up.

Isaiah 56:10-11, Psalm 68:23, Ezekiel 33:1-9.

Sheepdog = Brings together; one used by God for a good means of control.

John 10:3.

Hunting Dog = Persistence; determination; pursuit; chase after; serving the Master; obsessed.

Greyhound Dog = Runs well in the race of faith; unencumbered for action; swift; very fast; graceful and efficient; intelligent; gentle.

1 Corinthians 9:24-27, Proverbs 30:29, & 31, 1 Kings 18:46, 1 Kings 19:7-8, Ephesians 6:14, Luke 12:35.

Puppy = Precious gift; helpless; must be attended to.

1 Corinthians 12:4, 1 Timothy 4:14.

Trailing Game = Persistence.

A Positive Bark = Warning.

Tail = End of something; last time; the least; subservient; disobedient; beneath; cursed; trouble maker; powerful sting; support; powerful weapon; false prophet; influence; allegiance.

Exodus 4:4, Deuteronomy 28:13, & 44, Isaiah 7:4, Revelation 9:10, & 19, Job 40:17, Judges 15:4, Isaiah 9:14-15, Revelation 12:3-4.

Wagging Tail = Friend or acceptance.

Large Tail = Powerful support or weapon.
Job 40:17.
Tail Tucked In = Betrayal; guilt; shame; cowardly.

Dolphin - Wise; intelligent; teacher; physically weak but spiritually strong in the Lord; prophesier; easily flows in the Holy Spirit.
Job 12:7-8, Job 35:11.

Dominos - Continuous; chain reaction.
Leviticus 26:37.

Donkey - Obnoxious; self-willed; bragging, if braying; stubborn; unyielding; tenacious.
Proverbs 26:3, Numbers 22:25, 2 Peter 2:16.
Mule = Stubborn; self-willed; rebellious; tenacious; strong; unbelief.
Psalm 32:9, Zechariah 7:11.

Door - Entrance; Christ; way; avenue; mouth.
John 10:7-9, Revelation 4:1, Colossians 4:3, Psalm 141:3, Isaiah 22:22, Revelation 3:7-8.
Open Door = New opportunity; grace for progress.
Revelation 3:8.
Closed Door = Obstacle; hidden activities.
Ezekiel 8:3-18.
Keys to the Closed Door = Authority over the obstacle; authority to create opportunity; power to bind or loose; lock or unlock; wisdom; knowledge; important.
Matthew 16:19, Isaiah 22:22, Revelation 3:7, Luke 11:52, Proverbs 4:7.
To be Given Keys = Given power and authority.
Isaiah 22:22.
To Lose One's Keys = Lose the power and authority one was given.

Dove - Spirit; Holy Spirit; peace; innocent; message. See Bird. Matthew 3:11, Genesis 8:8-12, Luke 3:22, Luke 10:5-6, Matthew 10:16, Psalm 68:13.

Down - Beneath: Humbled; demotion; worldly. Psalm 75:7, Psalm 113:5-6, 2 Samuel 22:28, Psalm 18:27, James 1:9-10, James 2:3.

Dragon - Satan; high level demonic spirit; global level of wickedness; the nation of China (the Dragon being China's national symbol); antichrist, extreme level of spiritual warfare needed. Revelation 12:3-17, Ephesians 6:12, & 16, Isaiah 27:1, Isaiah 51:9, Revelation 13:2-4, Psalm 74:13, Ezekiel 29:3, Revelation 20:2.

Drawer - Stored thoughts; memories; life; organized. Proverbs 6:20-23, 1 Corinthians 11:2, 1 Corinthians 15:1-2.
> **Messy Drawer** = Cluttered thoughts; disorganized life. 1 Corinthians 14:33, James 1:6-8.

Drawing - Conceptualization; method of illustration; fluent in expression; truth; doctrine; deception. Proverbs 20:5, Ezekiel 32:20, Isaiah 5:18.

Dream - Prophesy; warning; message; direction; instruction. Matthew 2:13, & 19-20, Daniel 2:9.

Dreaming a Dream - Message within a message; deep spiritual message; futuristic message. Genesis 40:8, Judges 7:13.
> **Interpreting a Dream within the Dream** = Unlocking the mystery; expounding of the message. Judges 14:12, Ezekiel 17:2, Genesis 41:25-32, Daniel 2:28-45.

Drinking - Receiving from the spirit realm (good or bad); receiving one's portion in life.
Jeremiah 2:13, John 4:10-15, John 7:37-39.

Drinking Fountain - Spirit; source; words of life; spirit of man; Holy Spirit; salvation.
Revelation 21:6, James 3:11-12, Jeremiah 2:13.

Driver - Control; self; Christ; pastor; teacher; Satan; the emphasis is on the nature of the driver (Confident, kind, careful, frantic, careless, selfish, rude ...).
2 Kings 9:20.
> **Keys** = Authority; power to bind or loose; lock or unlock; wisdom; knowledge; important.
> Matthew 16:19, Isaiah 22:22, Revelation 3:7, Luke 11:52, Proverbs 4:7.
> > **To be Given Keys** = Given power and authority.
> > Isaiah 22:22.
> > **To Lose One's Keys** = Lose the power and authority one was given.

Driving Backwards - Operating by the letter of the law or word; usually while looking in the rear-view mirror; legalism; not by the spirit of the law or God's Spirit; looking back; not looking forward; backsliding; wanting to return to Egypt or a dog to its vomit.
2 Corinthians 3:6, Philippians 3:16.
> **Rear-view Mirror** = Looking back; focus on the past; warning to watch your back; warning to look ahead.
> Genesis 19:7, & 26, Luke 17:31-32.

Drought - Trial; testing; judgement; financial trouble; lacking the love of God; famine, physically or spiritually.
Deuteronomy 8:15, Isaiah 58:11, Jeremiah 17:8, Hosea 13:5,

Psalm 32:4, Jeremiah 50:38, Haggai 1:11, Ezekiel 37:2-6, Amos 8:11.

Drowning - Overcome; overwhelmed; depression; grief; sorrow; temptation; excessive debt.
Isaiah 43:2, Isaiah 61:3, 2 Peter 2:19, 1 Timothy 6:9.

Drugs - Influence; spell; sorcery; witchcraft; control; medicine, regulate body systems; relief of symptoms; healing.
Galatians 5:20-21, Acts 8:9-11, Acts 13:6-8, Deuteronomy 18:10-11, Galatians 3:1, Revelation 22:2, Ezekiel 47:12.

Drunk - Influenced; under a spell; controlled; addicted; fool; unchangeable; stubborn; rebellious; selfish; self-indulging; proud; violent; conceited; arrogant; boastful.
Ephesians 5:18, Acts 2:13-18, Luke 21:34, Deuteronomy 21:20, Proverbs 12:15, Proverbs 14:16.

Drunkard - Influenced; under a spell; controlled; addicted; fool; unchangeable; stubborn; rebellious; selfish; self-indulging; proud; violent; conceited; arrogant; boastful.
Ephesians 5:18, Acts 2:13-18, Luke 21:34, Deuteronomy 21:20, Proverbs 12:15, Proverbs 14:16.

Dune Buggy - Powerful itinerate ministry. See Vehicle.
Luke 1:80, 1 Samuel 3:19-20, Judges 13:24-25, Luke 1:15.

Dust - Temporary nature of humanity; frailty of man; curse; humiliation; large numbers.
Genesis 2:7, Isaiah 52:2, Psalm 103:14, Genesis 3:14, Genesis 28:14.
Dust on the Head = Grief.
Lamentations 2:10, Joshua 7:6, Job 2:12, Ezekiel 27:30.
Sitting in Dust = Repentance.
Job 42:6, Lamentations 2:10.

Lying in Dust = Humiliation.
Isaiah 29:4-5, Micah 1:10.
Throwing Dust in the Air = Expression of shock.
Acts 22:23.
Lying Down in Dust = Death.
Psalm 30:9, Psalm 44:25, Psalm 104:29.
Enemies Licking the Dust = Defeat of the enemy.
Psalm 72:9, Micah 7:17.
Shaking Dust off of Feet = Rejection of a place.
Mark 6:11, Acts 13:51.

Dusty Relics from the Past - Memories, good or bad. See Attic.
Philippians 3:13.

Dwarf - Small; made small by comparison.
Psalm 119:141, Isaiah 40:22, Numbers 13:33, 1 Samuel 17:42.

Dynamite - Power; miracle; potential; danger; destruction.
Acts 10:38, Matthew 9:8, Mark 9:1, Luke 10:19, Luke 22:53.
Having Dynamite in a vehicle = Powerful ministry.

Dinosaur - Extinct; ancient generational issues; hidden generational sins (buried fossils); strongholds; evil; guilt of past sins (buried fossils). See Dragon.
Job 40:15-24.

Eagle - Leader; spiritual; prophet; to see from above; to see clearly; wisdom; insight; God's restorative power; minister; rises above the storm; fierce predator; instrument of judgement; America.

Exodus 19:4, Isaiah 40:31, Isaiah 46:11Proverbs 30:17, Ezekiel 17:3-20, Deuteronomy 28:49, Deuteronomy 32:11.

Eagle's Nest - Prophetic School; heavenly dwelling and rest. Deuteronomy 32:11-12, Exodus 19:4b, Revelation 12:14, 2 Kings 4:38, Job 39:27, Proverbs 23:5b, Obadiah 1:4, Jeremiah 49:16.

School of the Prophets = Organization of true prophets who supervise the training of up-and-coming prophets. 1 Samuel 10:10, 1 Samuel 19:20, 1 Kings 18:4.

Ear - Symbol of a prophet; hears spiritual things that build up or tear down; pay attention. Deuteronomy 32:1-4, Jeremiah 22:29-30, 1 Samuel 9:15-16, Isaiah 50:5, Matthew 10:27, Revelation 2:7.

Ear that is Listening = Receiving instructions from God; eavesdropping; gossiper. Acts 8:6, Isaiah 30:21.

Ear Eager to Listen = Understands the things of the Spirit. Proverbs 8:6-9, Luke 2:46-47.

Ear Hard of Hearing or Deaf = Not paying attention to what is being said by God or man. Isaiah 6:9-10, Matthew 13:14-15, Acts 28:25-27, Hebrews 5:11.

Closed Ear = Deliberate refusal to listen when capable of hearing; hindered by extraneous influence. Zechariah 7:11, Proverbs 28:9, Acts 7:57, 2 Timothy 4:4, Amos 8:11-12.

Ear Itching to Hear = Mind not yielded to Jesus; prone to deception. 2 Timothy 4:3.

Earrings - Hearing; desire to hear. Acts 17:19-21, 2 Timothy 4:3.

Gold Earrings = Desire for man's honor; desire for financial prosperity; idolatry; vanity. Exodus 32:1-4, Hosea 2:13, Judges 8:24-27.

Earthmover - Leadership working in the flesh; the dead raised up. See Truck. 1 Corinthians 15:47-49.

Excavate = Prepares foundation; opens one's heart; searching one's heart; uncovering secrets of the heart; clearing one's heart; enlarging one's heart. Matthew 7:25, Song of Solomon 5:2, Acts 16:14, Psalm 139:1, & 23, 1 Chronicles 28:9, Jeremiah 17:10, Romans 8:27, Psalm 44:21, Genesis 26:18 See with 2 Corinthians 4:7. **Digging** = Uncovering truth; fertilizing; digging a well. Matthew 13:44, Luke 13:8, Genesis 26:18-19.

Earthquake - Upheaval; trial; judgement; sudden release of power; ground-shaking changes; disaster; trauma; shock. Acts 16:26, Isaiah 29:6, Isaiah 64:2-4, Hebrews 12:26-27.

East - Beginning; God's glory; Law of Moses (therefore, blessed or cursed); birth; first; anticipate; false religion; judgement (east wind). Genesis 11:2, Job 38:24, Genesis 41:23, & 27, Exodus 10:13, Psalm 103:12, Hosea 12:1, Job 15:2.

Eating - Partake; participate; meditating on God's word; experience; doing God's work; covenant; agreement; friendship; fellowship; devour; consume. See Chewing, Food. John 4:34, Proverbs 30:20, Joshua 9:14-15, John 13:18.

Echo - Repetition; gossip; accusation; voice of many; mocking; mimic. See Parrot. 2 Kings 2:23, Luke 23:21.

Egg - New idea; revelation; plan; potential; promise; gift; sustenance, fragile.
Luke 11:12, 1 Timothy 4:15.

Egg Yolk = Heart; life; keeps promise.
Jeremiah 17:10-11, Job 6:6.

Egg White without Yolk = Heartless; dead; empty promise.
Jeremiah 17:10-11, Job 6:6.

Rotten Egg = Bad company; bad idea; bad plan; schemes; no potential; unsure; without promise; promise breaker.
Isaiah 59:5.

Abandoned Egg = Unprotected; exposed to the elements; left to die.
Job 39:13-16.

Electricity - Holy Spirit; potential for God's flow; spiritual power; sorcery.
1 Corinthians 4:20, Luke 24:49, Acts 1:8, Romans 15:19; 2 Thessalonians 2:9.

Power Lines = Spiritual power; dangerous obstacle if flying near. See Flying (Sub heading: Flying near Electrical Power Lines).

Fallen Power Line = Dangerous obstacle; potential of fatal encounter with the enemy.
2 Thessalonians 2:9.

Electrical Outlet = Power source; Holy Spirit.

Burned Outlet = Offense; anger.

Unplugged Cord = No power; lack of prayer; lack of authority.

Damaged Cord = Limited or blocked flow of the Spirit; wounded by the enemy; carelessness in maintaining connection with God.

Elementary School - Infant stage; not yet mature.
Hebrews 5:12, Hebrews 6:1-3.

Elephant - Invincible; hard to offend; powerful; immovable; strong; strong prophetic voice; the largest among others; retains the things of God; has great memory.
Philippians 4:13, 1 Corinthians 15:10, Acts 19:11, Amos 3:6-7, Luke 7:28, Hebrews 7:4.
> **Elephant Trunk** = Voice; channel to the Spirit; brings cleansing; strength.
> Isaiah 40:3, Matthew 3:1-3, Revelation 4:1; John 4:14, John 7:38-39, Isaiah 51:9, Isaiah 62:8-11.
> **Baby Elephant** = Potential for greatness; the beginning of something large or great.
> 1 Samuel 2:21, & 26, Luke 1:15, &80.
> **White Elephant** - Unusable item; unwanted.

Elephant Ears - Extra sensitive hearing.

Elevator - Change of position; moving up or down in levels of godly authority; moving up or down in the spiritual realm.
Revelation 4:1, Proverbs 3:35.
> **Going Up** = Promotion; victory; rising up in the things of God.
> **Going Down** = Demotion; trial; backsliding.

Embarrassment - Shame; disgraced; perceived or actual failure.
Genesis 9:22-24, 1 Samuel 20:34, 2 Samuel 19:5-6, Psalm 142:4, Psalm 31:11.
> **Blushing** = Spiritual shedding of innocent blood; being shamed; causing embarrassment; guilt.
> Psalm 10:7-8, Proverbs 6:17, 2 Samuel 19:5, Ezra 9:6, Ezekiel 16:61-63, Romans 6:21.

Employee - Servant; slave; submitted to authority; the actual person in the natural.

Colossians 3:22, 1 Peter 2:18-19, Titus 2:9-10, 1 Timothy 6:1-2, Ephesians 6:5-7.

Fellow Employee = Servant; co-worker in Christ, the Kingdom; actual person in the natural, or oneself.
Colossians 3:22, 1 Timothy 6:1, Titus 2:9-10, Ephesians 6:5-7, 1 Peter 2:18-19, Philemon 16-17.

Employer - Authority; pastor; Christ; Satan; evil leadership; someone he or she resembles, in position action or character; actual employer in the natural.
Colossians 4:1, 1 Timothy 6:2.

Engine - Holy Spirit power; supernatural empowerment. See Vehicle.

Envelope - Important message from God; prophecy; personal instructions.
Job 33:14-16, Deuteronomy 29:29.
   Sealed = Prophecy un-interpreted; message or instruction not revealed.
   Daniel 8:26, Daniel 9:24, Daniel 12:4, & 9.
   Opened = Prophecy interpreted; message or instruction revealed.
   Revelation 22:10.
   Postage Stamp = Seal; authority; authorisation; empowerment; small but powerful.
   Esther 8:8, 2 Timothy 2:19.
   Letter = Important message from God; prophecy; personal instructions.
   Job 33:14-16, Deuteronomy 29:29.

Eunuch - Set apart for God's service; spiritual purity; God given gift of celibacy; undistracted service to the Lord; un-regenerated nature incapable of bearing service to the Lord;

nature of man mutilated by the enemy; officials in the courts of ancient kings; could be natural in nature. Isaiah 56:3-5, 1 Corinthians 7:32-38, 1 Corinthians 7:7, Matthew 19:11-12, Isaiah 39:7, Acts 8:27.

Evergreen Tree (Pine, Spruce, & Fir Trees etc.) - Long-lasting life; everlasting life. Isaiah 55:13, Isaiah 60:13. See Trees.

Excavate - Prepares foundation; opens one's heart; searching one's heart; uncovering secrets of the heart; clearing one's heart; enlarging one's heart. Matthew 7:25, Song of Solomon 5:2, Acts 16:14, Psalm 139:1, & 23, 1 Chronicles 28:9, Jeremiah 17:10, Romans 8:27, Psalm 44:21, Genesis 26:18 See with 2 Corinthians 4:7.

Earthmover = Leadership working in the flesh; the dead raised up. 1 Corinthians 15:47-49.

Digging = Uncovering truth; fertilizing; digging a well. Matthew 13:44, Luke 13:8, Genesis 26:18-19.

Explosion - Sudden expansion or increase; quick work; sudden outburst; swift change; devastating change. Isaiah 48:3, Acts 2:2, Malachi 3:1, Acts 9:3, Luke 9:39, Luke 2:13, Jeremiah 4:20.

Explosives - Power; miracle; potential; danger; destruction. Acts 10:38, Matthew 9:8, Mark 9:1, Luke 10:19, Luke 22:53.

Having Explosives in a vehicle = Powerful ministry.

Exportation or Shipping - Means of moving from the spiritual realm to the physical realm; releasing generational inheritances; distributing and speaking into existence what has been prayed for.

Genesis 28:12-17, Genesis 32:1-2, John 3:8, Ezekiel 37:9, Revelation 8:3-5.

Freight Ship = Business, spiritual or natural. See port, and its subheading exportation or shipping. See Port.

1 Kings 10:15, Psalm 107:23, Acts 21:3.

Freight Truck = Business. See Truck.

1 Kings 10:15, 2 Chronicles 9:14.

Eyes - Seer's anointing; revelation; understanding; window of the soul; to watch; being watched; desire; covetousness; lust; passion.

Ephesians 1:17-18, Luke 11:34-36, Luke 6:41-42, Psalm 101:3, Proverbs 23:5, Proverbs 27:20, Isaiah 44:18.

Eye of God = God's omniscience; God's ability to watch over us,

Zechariah 4:10, 2 Chronicles 16:9, Psalm 32:8, Psalm 33:18, Psalm 34:15, Job 36:7, Proverbs 15:3, 1 Peter 3:12.

Eyes Opened = Enlightened; understanding; knowledge.

Ephesians 1:17-18, Acts 26:18, Psalm 119:18.

Eyes Focused = Thinking; thoughtful; no distraction.

2 Peter 3:14.

Bright Eyes = Intelligent; highly knowledgeable.

Ephesians 1:17-18, John 6:45.

Steering Eyes = Being watched by another, good or evil; being watched over by God.

Exodus 2:11, 2 Kings 9:17, Judges 1:24-25, Joshua 6:22-25.

Dim Eyes = Grief; lack of knowledge.

Lamentations 5:17, Job 17:7, 1 Corinthians 13:12.

Winking Eyes = Deceitfulness; perversity; cunning; concealed intention; overlooking a matter.

Proverbs 6:13, Acts 17:30.

Dissatisfied Eyes = Greed; lack of agreement; sign of disapproval.

Proverbs 27:20, Acts 28:25, & 29.

Eyes Closed = Unbelief; willful ignorance; spiritually blind. Isaiah 44:18.

F

Face - Heart; identity; character; countenance.
Proverbs 27:19, Leviticus 21:5, James 1:22-24.
Shining Face = Emanating God's glory; goodness of God; image of Jesus.
Matthew 17:2, Exodus 34:29-30, 2 Corinthians 3:7-8, & 18, 2 Corinthians 4:6.
Smiling Face = Agreement; friendship.
Job 33:26.
Happy Face = Cheerful heart.
Proverbs 15:13.
Hard Looking Face = Resolute; strong; determined; bold; stubborn; hardened.
Isaiah 50:7, Ezekiel 3:8-9, Isaiah 48:4, Galatians 2:11.
The Face of Something = Public image given to something.
Rough and Unshaved Face = Spiritual neglect; uncleanness; coarse or harsh personality. See Beard.
Leviticus 21:5, 2 Kings 1:8, Matthew 3:4, Genesis 25:25, Genesis 27:11.
Sad Face = Sorrow; repentance.
Nehemiah 2:2-3, Ecclesiastes 7:3, 2 Corinthians 7:10.
Angry Face = Disagreement; hatred.
Genesis 4:5-6.
Seductive Face = Temptation.
Person with a Face of an Animal = Hidden characteristics of the animal.
Animal with a Human Face = A spirit working through humans.

Factory - Production; getting things done; the Kingdom of God; the Church; the world; the motions of sin. Luke 2:49, Romans 12:11.
Working in a Factory = Being useful in the corporate plan.
Factory Not Working Well = Set-up not in order.
Flooding or Flooded Factory = Overwhelming situation; challenge.
Factory on Fire = End of one phase; significant change. See Fire.
Abandoned Factory = Non- Productive: Is not reaching full potential, lazy, sloth, or actual workplace.
Basement = Soul; carnal nature; lust; discouragement; depression; refuge; retreat; hidden; beneath the surface; foundational issues; forgotten; secret sin; bloodline issue; demonic realm. See Foundation. Jeremiah 38:6, Isaiah 24:22.
> **Supplies in the Basement** = Inherited giftedness; great potential yet to be revealed or manifested.
> **Fault in the Basement** = Broken foundation; spiritual forefathers' issues needing repentance.

Fair or Carnival - Worldly; festivity; party spirit; exhibitionism; divination; competition. See Roller Coaster. Luke 21:34, Acts 16:16.

Falcon - Hunter; minister. See Bird. Genesis 10:9.

Fall Season - End; completion; change; transition; close of harvesting; entering difficult times; sin; repentance. Isaiah 64:6, Jeremiah 5:24, Jeremiah 8:20.

Falling - Loss of support; financial loss, moral failure, trial; succumb; a falling out; attacked; robbed; without counsel; backsliding; one who gloats over another's failure.

Psalm 20:8, Hebrews 12:1-2, Proverbs 11:28, James 1:2, Proverbs 16:18, Proverbs 22:14, Genesis 45:24, Exodus 1:10, Luke 10:30, Proverbs 11:14, Proverbs 24:17.

Family - Spiritual family; the Church; natural family.
1 Chronicles 13:14, Ephesians 3:15.
Family Reunion = Reconciliation; love.
Family Home = Past; love; security. See Home.
Family Feud = Unresolved past issues of personal or spiritual family.

Family Room - Community; fellowship; family oriented.

Famous Person - Jesus Christ; an acquaintance that relates as a parallel to the famous person; the role or character of the famous person; the actual person; the world's glory.
Mark 1:28, Luke 4:14, & 37, Matthew 17:12-13, Luke 1:17, Malachi 4:5-6, Matthew 4:8-10.
A Famous Person, Passed Away and was Righteous = The spirit of the famous person.
Matthew 17:3, Luke 9:30-31, Matthew 22:32.

Fangs - Evil intent or motive: danger.
Psalm 57:4, Psalm 58:6, Proverbs 30:14, Daniel 7:5-7, Revelation 9:8.

Farm - Labour; field of labour; area of ministry; the Kingdom of God; the Church. See Barn, Garden.
Mark 4:14, 2 Corinthians 9:10.

Farm Tractor - Powerful work; slow but powerful ministry; if ploughing, represents preaching and teaching. See Truck.
Acts 1:8, Acts 4:33.

Farmer - Labourer; preacher, pastor; sows; reaps; Christ; minister; plants; nurtures.
Mark 4:14, 2 Corinthians 9:10.

Fat - Abundance; excess; laziness.
Genesis 49:20, Genesis 45:18, Leviticus 3:15-16, Leviticus 17:6b, Jeremiah 50:11.

Father - Authority; God; author; originator; source; inheritance; tradition; custom; Satan; religious leader; natural father.
Malachi 2:10a, Ephesians 6:1-4, Colossians 3:19-21, 2 Corinthians 12:14b, Genesis 4:20-21, John 8:44.

Caring, Loving Father = A caring leader; like a loving father; nurturing; God's provision; godly discipline; self-sacrificing.
1 Corinthians 4:15, Ephesians 6:4b, Hebrews 12:5-11, Romans 9:3-5, Exodus 32:32, Acts 7:22-26.

Absent Father = Negligent, emotionally, spiritually, or physically; wrong priorities; rejection; spirit of rejection; spirit of abandonment.
1 Timothy 5:8.

Children Absent = Thankless; wrong priorities; unresolved past issues; resentment; spirit of rejection; spirit of abandonment.
1 Timothy 5:4, Ephesians 6:2-3, Colossians 3:20, Job 18:19.

Abusive Father = Abusive authority figure; abuse of the past; wounded; spirit of past abuse in the present authority figure; can have image of Father God; trouble relating to Father God.
1 Timothy 5:8, Ephesians 6:4a, Colossians 3:21, 1 Samuel 20:30-34.

Father-in-law - Law; authoritative relationship based upon law; legalism; not from the dreamer's church; problem (authoritative) relationship; spirit of delegation; father figure of organization; advisor; he may represent himself. Exodus 18:17.

Feathers - Covering; Spirit; presence of God; protection; weightless.
Psalm 91:4, Psalm 68:13, Ezekiel 17:3-7.
Wet Feathers = Offense (madder than a wet Hen).

Feces - Unclean; offensive; impure; need for repentance. See Toilet, Bathroom.
2 Corinthians 7:1, Ephesians 5:3-5.

Feeding - Partaking of spiritual provision.
Luke 4:4, Deuteronomy 8:3, Matthew 6:11, Exodus 16:16-35, Matthew 26:26, John 6:33-35, & 47-58, 1 Corinthians 11:23-24.
Good Food = The Word of God; good spiritual doctrine; spiritual nourishment.
Matthew 26:26, John 6:33-35, & 47-58, 1 Corinthians 11:23-24, Luke 4:4.
Food going mouldy = Unfit; tradition; old revelation; stale; defiled.
Joshua 9:5b, Malachi 1:7, 1 Corinthians 5:8, Matthew 15:2-3, & 6, Exodus 16:20.
Bread with Spider Web within = Looks good but has a trap in the end; deception; betrayal.
Proverbs 14:12, Proverbs 16:25, Proverbs 12:26, Joshua 9:3-16.

Feet - Walk; heart; thoughts (meditation); way; stubborn (unmovable); sin. See Toes.
Ephesians 6:15, John 13:5-16, Acts 9:5, Ezekiel 6:11, Ezekiel 32:2, Ezekiel 34:17-21, 2 Chronicles 16:12, 2 Samuel 22:37-43, Proverbs 25:19, Hebrews 12:13.

Barefoot = Unprepared; unsaved; unprotected; reverence before God.
Exodus 3:5, Joshua 5:15.
Cold Feet = Retreat; renege on deal; does not keep promises; fearful.
1 Samuel 17:24.
Diseased = Offense.
Ezekiel 32:2, Ezekiel 34:17-21, 2 Chronicles 16:12.
Kicking = Rebellion.
Acts 9:5, Acts 26:14.
Stomping = Defiant; temper tantrum; aggressive.
Ezekiel 6:11.
Tread Down = Oppression; injustice; disregard; take advantage of.
Ezekiel 32:2, Ezekiel 34:17-21.
Under Feet = Enemy subdued.
2 Samuel 22:37-43.
Lame = Unbelief; error; unfaithful.
Proverbs 25:19, Hebrews 12:13.
Washing Feet = Cleansing; humble service.
John 13:5-16.
Shaking Dust off Feet = Rejection.
Luke 9:5, Acts 13:51.

Fellow Employee - Servant; co-worker in Christ, the Kingdom; actual person in the natural, or oneself.
Colossians 3:22, 1 Timothy 6:1, Titus 2:9-10, Ephesians 6:5-7, 1 Peter 2:18-19, Philemon 16-17.
Employee = Servant; slave; submitted to authority; the actual person in the natural.
Colossians 3:22, 1 Peter 2:18-19, Titus 2:9-10, 1 Timothy 6:1-2, Ephesians 6:5-7.

Fence - Boundary; protection; security; limitation; obstacle; barrier; stronghold.
Psalm 62:3, Daniel 11:15, Jeremiah 15:20.

Ferret - Unclean spirit; false friend; false innocence; out for blood.
Leviticus 11:29-31 (KJV), Psalm 55:12-14, John 13:18, Job 33:4 See with Leviticus 17:11.

Field - World; God's work; the kingdom of heaven; harvest; opportunity; mixed multitude; life situations; personal purpose in life.
Matthew 13:24-32, 38, & 44, John 4:35, Job 5:10, Psalm 23:1-6, Malachi 3:11, Luke 2:8.

Fig - Israelites; first-fruit; healing.
2 Kings 20:7, Isaiah 38:21.
Green Fig = Not yet fruitful; not ready.
Song of Solomon 2:13.
Ripe Fig = Fruitful; ready for the work of God; believer.
Jeremiah 24:1-3, & 5-7.
Bad Fig = Not usable for the purpose of God; unbeliever.
Jeremiah 24:1- 3, & 8-10.

Fig Leaves - Self-atonement; self-made covering; profession of religion but bearing no fruit; broken promise of fruit (figs come before the leaves); barren.
Genesis 3:7, Matthew 21:19.

Fig Tree - Israel; prosperity.
Hosea 9:10, Luke 13:6-9, 1 Kings 4:25, Micah 4:4, Zechariah 3:10.

Fight - Wrestle; struggle; warfare; resist.
Ephesians 6:10-18, Hebrews 10:32, 1 Timothy 6:12, 1 Timothy 1:18, Hebrews 11:32-34, 1 Peter 5:8-9, James 4:1-2, & 7.
Fight with an Angry Person = Warfare against issues that trouble the mind; struggle with difficult situations.
Hebrews 10:32, Psalm 35:1, 1Timothy 6:12, 2 Corinthians 10:3-5, Ephesians 6:10-18, 1 Peter 5:8-9, James 4:1-2, & 7, Proverbs 6:5, Psalm 91:3-6.
Fight with an Animal = Internal struggle with characteristics of that animal.
Proverbs 6:5.
Fight with an Evil Spirit = Spiritual conflict; torment; generational issue with characteristics of the evil spirit.
Ephesians 6:10-18, 2 Corinthians 10:3-5, 1 Peter 5:8-9, Psalm 91:3-6.

Fighter Jet - Individual Ministry, person, or minister; powerful, fast, effective, attacking; a call to intercessory ministry; spiritual warfare. See Airplane, Pilot.
Genesis 41:43, 2 Kings 10:16, Zechariah 6:1-8, Isaiah 5:26-28.

Filthy Clothes - Unrighteousness; uncleanness; sin. See Clothes.
Zechariah 3:3-5.

Fingers - Holy Spirit (finger of God); kingdom of God; ownership; spiritual sensitivity; discernment; recognition; rule of God; imminent judgement recorded; warfare; sin; uses sign language; mischievous; sows discord; repentance; fragrant; anointing; brings relief. See Hand.
Luke 11:20, John 8:6, Leviticus 4:6, 17, 25, 30, & 34, Isaiah 2:8, Exodus 8:19, Exodus 31:18, Deuteronomy 9:10, Daniel 5:5, Psalm 144:1, Isaiah 59:3, Proverbs 6:13, Song of Solomon 5:5; Luke 16:24.

Pointing Finger = Accusing; blaming; showing direction.
Proverbs 6:13-14, Isaiah 58:9.
Finger of God = Work of God.
Exodus 8:19, Exodus 31:18, Deuteronomy 9:10, Daniel 5:5, Luke 11:20.
Clenched Finger = Pride.
Six Fingers = Ultimate means of dominion; excess.
2 Samuel 21:20.
Fingernails = Beautified woman; preparation; flirting; unkempt; insanity.
Deuteronomy 21:12, Daniel 4:33.
Thumb = Apostle; power; control; leverage; service.
Ephesians 4:11, Judges 1:6-7, Exodus 29:20, Leviticus 8:23-24, Leviticus 14:14, 17, 25, & 28.
Index Finger = Prophet; points the way; knowledge; revelation; shows direction; accuser; blame shifter.
Ephesians 4:11, John 8:6, Proverbs 6:13-14, Isaiah 58:9.
Middle Finger = Evangelist; derogatory; crude.
Ephesians 4:11.
Ring Finger = Pastor.
Ephesians 4:11.
Little Finger = Teacher; oppressor.
Ephesians 4:11, 1 Kings 12:10-11.

Fingerprints - Identity; ownership; recognition; mischievous acts exposed (from fingerprints left at the crime scene).
Exodus 8:19, Proverbs 7:3, John 20:25, John 8:6, Proverbs 6:13.

Fir Tree - One who is a provider of shade, or rest from the desert experience; grateful for the one who provides relief; godly; durable (the White Cedar). See Trees.
1 Kings 5:8, & 10, Isaiah 55:12-13, Isaiah 60:13, Isaiah 41:19.

Fire - Passion; God's word or Spirit; God's presence; power; revival; fervency; zeal; anger; envy; jealousy; strife; desire; lust; trial; persecution; punishment; judgement; affliction; gossip. Jeremiah 23:29, Jeremiah 5:14, 1 Corinthians 7:9, Matthew 3:11, James 3:5-6, Psalm 79:5, Psalm 89:46, Proverbs 26:20, Exodus 22:6, Genesis 19:24.
Fireplace = Heart.

Firearms - Words; accusations; slander; gossip; power.
2 Samuel 11:24, Psalm 64:4, Luke 11:21-22.
Being Shot by a Firearm = Powerful words coming against a person; curses; attacks.
Holding a Firearm = Equipped with authority or ability; power; unhindered.
Broken or Inoperative Firearm = Without authority or ability; without power; hindered.
Smaller Calibre = Weak or ineffective weapon; without power; lack of prayer and fasting.
Revelation 3:8.
Larger Calibre = Powerful; spiritual power through acceptable service; covenant; effective; the power of evil working through agreement (acquiescence) or conquest (our defeat).
2 Corinthians 10:4.

Fireman - Helper; Christ; Holy Spirit; pastor; minister; counselor; public servant.
Psalm 46:1, John 14:16, & 26, John 15:26, Jeremiah 33:3.

Fire Truck - Emergency assistance; quick response to an urgent need; help on its way. See Truck.

Fish - New believers; redeemed; miraculous provision; person; character or motive; Holy Spirit; outreach; sport; spirit of man; unclean spirit. See Fishing.

Mark 1:17, Luke 11:11, John 21:6-12, Luke 5:4-11, Ezekiel 47:10, Matthew 13:47-50, Isaiah 50:2.

Fish Hook - Evangelistic ministries; take the bait; support of the minister; messages from the Word of God; overtaken; drag into or out of something against one's will.
Acts 8:5-7, & 12, Genesis 3:6, Matthew 17:27, 1 Corinthians 9:14, Ezekiel 29:4-5, Ezekiel 38:4, Isaiah 37:29.

Fish Pond - Humanity; one's own fishing hole; a church.
Matthew 4:18-19, Acts 8:5, 25-29, & 39-40, Acts 21:8, Romans 16:5.

Fish Tank - The church.
Romans 16:16, & 21-27.

Fishing - Witnessing; evangelizing; preaching; hope; asking questions (fishing for answers).
Matthew 4:18-19, John 21:3-12, Ezekiel 47:10, Matthew 13:47-50, Mark 9:10-16, Acts 17:18-21.

Fishing Line - Means of catching the lost; the Gospel.
Matthew 4:19, Romans 1:16.

Fishing Rod - Tool of evangelism; inward motives of the heart manifesting.
Matthew 4:19, John 21:6, Jeremiah 9:8, Matthew 12:34.
    Black Rod = A heart caught up in the things of the world.
    1 John 2:16, James 3:14-16.

Flag or Banner - Identity; Committed; God's protection; memorial; conquest; victory; warning; fearsome army; love.
See associated Colors in Part 2.
Numbers 1:52, Exodus 17:14-15, Psalm 20:5, Psalm 60:4,

Isaiah 13:2, Isaiah 49:22, Song of Solomon 6:4b, & 10b, Song of Solomon 2:4.

White Flag = Surrender; pure.

Flashlight - Personal knowledge or understanding; guidance. Psalm 119:105, Ephesians 5:13, John 3:21.

Flea - Insignificant; nuisance; irritant; hunted; elusive. See Bugs. 1 Samuel 24:14, 1 Samuel 26:20.

Flies - Beelzebub "Lord of the flies" is a reference to the devil. Evil spirits; Satan; doctrines of demons (fly in the cup); unclean; corruption; curse; nuisance; foolishness destroying ones' reputation. See Bugs.
Exodus 8:21-31, Matthew 12:24, &26-27, 1 Corinthians 10:21, 2 Corinthians 6:15-17, Ecclesiastes 10:1, Isaiah 7:18.

Covered by Flies = Corruption that breeds unclean spirits.
Fly Screen = Covering; protection from demonic attacks. Ecclesiastes 10:1(See with Ecclesiastes 9:18).

Flood - Abundance, overflowing, outpouring; a global deluge of Holy Spirit; a submersion of spiritual teachings and revival; a great harvest; increase; extending borders; cleansing of old ways; warning of disaster; judgment; overwhelmed; overcome; depression.
Isaiah 59:19, Isaiah 8:7-8, Isaiah 54:2-3, Isaiah 43:2, Isaiah 28:15, &17, 2 Samuel 22:5-6, Psalm 69:15, Psalm 93:3-4, Jeremiah 47:2, Amos 8:8, Genesis 6:17, Daniel 9:26, Revelation 12:15.

Flowers - Glory; temporary; gift; offering; romance; man's glory.
Psalm 103:15-16, 1 Peter 1:24, Isaiah 28:4, James 1:10.
Flower Bud = Potential.

Job 14:9, Psalm 132:17, Isaiah 27:6, Isaiah 61:11, Ezekiel 29:21.

Flower Bud Unfolding = Good growth; fulfillment at hand; glory revealed.
Numbers 17:8, John 15:1-6.

Flowers that are Dead or Dried Up = Withdrawn affections; without passion; needs watering (prayer); untended.

Lily = Jesus Lily of the valley; death; funeral; mourning.
Song of Solomon 2:1.

Rose = Romance; Christ; love; courtship.
Song of Solomon 2:1.

> **Red Rose** = Passion.

> **Yellow Rose Garden** = Marriage counseling.

Fly or **Flies** - Beelzebub "Lord of the flies" is a reference to the devil. Evil spirits; Satan; doctrines of demons (fly in the cup); unclean; corruption; curse; nuisance; foolishness destroying ones' reputation. See Bugs.
Exodus 8:21-31, Matthew 12:24, &26-27, 1 Corinthians 10:21, 2 Corinthians 6:15-17, Ecclesiastes 10:1, Isaiah 7:18.

> **Covered by Flies** = Corruption that breeds unclean spirits.

Fly Screen - Covering; protection from demonic attacks.
Ecclesiastes 10:1(See with Ecclesiastes 9:18).

Flying - Moved by the Spirit; ministering in the gifts of the Spirit. See Airplane, Pilot.
Habakkuk 1:8, Judges 13:25.

> **Flying Near Electrical Power Lines** = Caution; danger; need for prayer.

> **Flying Too Low** = Insufficient power, prayer, preparation, or training; only partially operating in the spirit; not following, being led by the Spirit.

> **Flying High** = Fully empowered by the Spirit.
> Habakkuk 1:8, Judges 13:25.

Soaring = Deep in the Spirit; moving in the deep things of God.
2 Kings 2:9-11, Psalm 104:3-4.

Supersonic Flight = Fast; powerful; soaring in the Spirit; fully empowered by the Spirit; deep in the Spirit; moving in the deep things of God; extreme acceleration into the new season and ministry.
2 Kings 2:9-11, Psalm 104:3-4.

Fog - Confusion; clouded thoughts; uncertain circumstances; obscurity; temporary.
Psalm 71:1, Job 10:15, Daniel 9:7-8, Hosea 6:4, James 4:14.

Food - Work of God, spiritual provision. See Feeding.
Genesis 41:35, John 4:34, Hebrews 5:12-13.

Foreigner - Alien; unbeliever; demonic; not of God; of the flesh; outcast; foreigner; believer (pilgrim on the earth), not of this world. See Nation.
Lamentations 5:2, Proverbs 25:25, Ephesians 2:12, Job 19:15, Genesis 47:9, 1 Chronicles 29:15, Psalm 119:19, Hebrews 11:13-16, & 34, 1 Peter 2:11.

Forehead - Thought process; reasoning; retaining and recalling ability; revelation; commitment to God; resolute; strong; determined; bold; stubborn; hardened. See Head.
Exodus 28:38, Ezekiel 3:8-9, Isaiah 48:4, Jeremiah 3:3.

Forest - Foreboding; frightful surroundings. See Trees.
Psalm 104:20, Psalm 107:4-5, & 40, Genesis 21:14-16, Deuteronomy 8:15, Job 12:24.

Forklift Truck - Organizer; burden lifter; lying spirit, falsely raising hopes. See Truck.
Nehemiah 12:44, Matthew 11:28, 1 Kings 22:22, Micah 2:11.

Found - Revelation or gift received from God. See Lost. Jeremiah 15:16.

Found what was Lost = Understanding; revelation; knowledge; sound direction; proper application and timing of a prophetic word; decisive; gift of God. Jeremiah 15:16, Ezekiel 3:1-3, Luke 15:4-10.

Foundation - Established; stable; sound; level; solidified. Psalm 11:3, Luke 14:29, 1 Corinthians 3:10-11, Ephesians 2:20.

Under Construction = Not ready; not complete; still being built up in Jesus.

Not Cured = Unstable; ill health; uncontrollable circumstances.

Deluge of Rain = Imminent challenge. Matthew 7:24-27, Luke 6:48-49.

Four Wheel Drive Vehicle - Powerful ministry; ground breaking; capable of global influence; personal ministry or work in the natural; dependable; hard work; rescue; solid biblical and gospel foundation. See Vehicle. 1 Chronicles 13:7, Genesis 45:27, Galatians 6:5.

Fox - Subtlety; deceptive; cunning; secretly; a con man; false prophet; wicked leader; hidden sin; counter-productive. Song of Solomon 2:15, Nehemiah 4:3, Luke 13:32, Ezekiel 13:4, & 6.

Tail = End of something; last time; the least; subservient; disobedient; beneath; cursed; trouble maker; powerful sting; support; powerful weapon; false prophet; influence; allegiance. Exodus 4:4, Deuteronomy 28:13, & 44, Isaiah 7:4, Revelation 9:10, & 19, Job 40:17, Judges 15:4, Isaiah 9:14-15, Revelation 12:3-4.

Larger than Normal Tail = Support or weapon. Job 40:17.

Tail Tucked In = Betrayal; guilt; shame; cowardly.

Freezer - Stores spiritual food for the future; preservation of life.
Psalm 12:6-7, Genesis 45:5-7, Psalm 31:23, Psalm 37:28, Psalm 121:8, Psalm 145:20, Psalm 116:6, John 10:28-30, 2 Timothy 4:18, 1 Thessalonians 5:23.

Discover Food in the Freezer = Recovery of the reward of one's labor.

Spoiled Food in the Freezer = Must leave past hurts and losses behind.

Freight Ship - Business, spiritual or natural. See Port, Ship.
1 Kings 10:15, Psalm 107:23, Acts 21:3.

Exportation or Shipping = Means of moving from the spiritual realm to the physical realm; releasing generational inheritances; distributing and speaking into existence what has been prayed for.
Genesis 28:12-17, Genesis 32:1-2, John 3:8, Ezekiel 37:9, Revelation 8:3-5.

Freight Truck - Business. See Truck.
1 Kings 10:15, 2 Chronicles 9:14.

Friend - Self; the character or circumstances of one's friend reveals something about oneself. Sometimes one friend represents another (look for another with the same name, initials, hair color, job, or trade, or one with similar traits, character, talents, personality, features, circumstances, etc.); the actual friend in the natural.
1 Samuel 15:8a, Proverbs 18:24, Proverbs 27:6.

Frog - Unclean spirit; demon; demonic powers; deception; lying spirit; witchcraft; curse; evil words; puffed up.
Exodus 8:2-13 (the plagues reflecting the gods of Egypt, therefore empowered by demons. See with 1 Corinthians 10:19-20), Psalm 78:45, Psalm 105:30, Revelation 16:13, 1 Kings 22:22.

Front - Future or Now (as in Front Yard); in the presence of prophecy; immediate; current.
Genesis 6:11-13, Revelation 1:19.

Front Half of Horse - First part of time or work; beginning; ready. See Horse.

Front Porch - Public; open to everyone; community; recreation; leisure; exposed; revealed.
Mark 14:68, Acts 5:12, Joel 2:17.

Fruit - Nourishment; increase; reward of labor; the work of the Lord; harvest; gifts of the Spirit; fruit of the Holy Spirit, consisting of all the Christian virtues.
Psalm 1:3, Psalm 92:14, John 15:8, Galatians 5:22-23.
    Receive a Basket of Fruit = Impartation of the gift of the Holy Spirit.
    Give a Basket of Fruit = Impart what you have to another; give to the Lord.
    Deuteronomy 26:1-4.
    Ripe Fruit = It's time; no more delay.
    Bad Fruit = Not usable for the purpose of God; corrupt works.
    Jeremiah 24:1-10, Matthew 12:33b.

Fuel - Source of energy; prayer; capable of reviving; source of food for the Spirit; inflammatory gossip; contention; strife; danger.
Jude 1:20, Proverbs 26:20-21.

Fumes = Deception; deceiving spirit; evil motive; envy; false accusations; slander; poisonous doctrine; danger. Proverbs 24:28, Matthew 24:4, James 3:14-15.

Funeral - Loss; grieve; closure; brought to an end. 2 Samuel 12:22-23, Job 7:8-10, Genesis 37:35, Luke 23:43.

Furnace - Affliction; heat; wrath; judgement; zeal; the Lord's presence; trial; pruning; the heart; holy activities.
Isaiah 48:10, Daniel 3: 19-26, Deuteronomy 4:20, Isaiah 31:9, Malachi 4:1, Genesis 19:28, Exodus 19:18, Psalm 17:3, Psalm 39:3, Psalm 12:6, Revelation 1:15.

Gallows - Death; nemesis; severe punishment.
Deuteronomy 21:22-23, Esther 7:9-10, Esther 9:13-14, & 25.

Gambler/Gambling - Risk taker; taking chances on eternal destiny; living by chance instead of on purpose for, and trusting in God; covetous; addiction; greed; cheat; underhanded.
1 Samuel 14: 9-10, Matthew 16:25-26, Luke 12:19-21, 1 Timothy 6:9-10, Proverbs 1:19, Proverbs 15:27, Acts 5:3-4, & 8-9.

Game of Cards or Poker - Facts; blunt honesty; wisdom, hold or fold; truth; past time entertainment; to expose; reveals; dishonest dealing; gambling; bluffing; cheating.
Romans 12:17, 1 Chronicles 24:5, Acts 1:24-26, Joshua 18:10, Jonah 1:7, 1 Samuel 14:41-42, Acts 5:3-4, & 8-9, Matthew 22:17-21.
  Playing with Tarot Cards = Consulting the demonic realm instead of God; necromancy; familiar spirits; deception; error.

1 Samuel 28:7-10, Mark 12:27, 1 Chronicles 10:13-14, Deuteronomy 18:10-12, Micah 5:12.

Games or Sports Competitions - Teamwork; contest; competition; recreation; sportsmanship; unsportsmanlike conduct.
2 Timothy 2:5, 1 Corinthians 9:24-27.
Stepping out of Bounds = Disqualified; conduct out of order.
Galatians 5:7.

Gap - Breach; weak spot; loophole; opening.
Ezekiel 13:5, Ezekiel 22:30.

Garage - Rest from job or ministry, not using talents, storage; protection; restoration.
1 Samuel 4:13-18, Isaiah 49:2, Genesis 42:16-19, Galatians 6:1, Revelation 3:2.

Garbage - Sin; transgression; unclean; flesh; abandoned; works of the flesh; reprobate.
Isaiah 66:24, Mark 9:43-48, Philippians 3:8, Galatians 5:19-21.
Getting Something from the Garbage = Lack; poverty; resorting to the things of the past.
Proverbs 26:11, 2 Peter 2:22.
Eating from the Garbage = Severe famine; insanity.

Garbage Dump - Rejected; filth; hell; evil; vile; corruption.
Mark 9:47-48, 1 Corinthians 9:27.

Garbage Truck - Large deliverance ministry; removes sin; unclean ministry; unclean church; corrupt business. See Truck.
Matthew 8:16, Job 8:4, Isaiah 31:7, John 2:14-16, Revelation 19:2-3, Isaiah 1:4.

Garden - Church; field of labor; purpose; cultivated; life situation; increase; fruitfulness; productivity.
Genesis 2:8, Genesis 4:2-3, Isaiah 58:11, Jeremiah 2:21.
The Crop = Fruit of one's labor.
Genesis 4:2-3.

Garden Pests - Weights and sins that devour one's fruit.
Isaiah 5:5-10.

Gardener - Labourer; preacher, pastor; Christ; minister.
Genesis 4:2-3, Mark 4:14, 2 Corinthians 9:10; 1 Timothy 4:14-15.

Gardening - Working; church; ministry; area of labor; putting things in order; harvest; pleasant past time. See weeds and flowers.
Isaiah 58:11, 1 Timothy 4:14-15.

Garments - Covering; righteousness; spiritual attitude; fleshly attitude.
Romans 13:14, Psalm 132:9, James 2:2, Isaiah 64:6, Zechariah 3:3-7, Psalm 109:18.
Clean Garments = Honor; mantle; glory of God; righteousness.
Zechariah 3:5-7.
Wrinkled Garments = Still issues that need to be dealt with.
Filthy Garments = Unrighteousness; sin; iniquity; self-righteousness; uncleanness.
Psalm 109:18, Isaiah 64:6, Zechariah 3:3-4.
Put on a Garment of Praise (Bright and Colorful Clothing) = Joy; thanksgiving.
Isaiah 61:3.
Tearing Garments = Mourning.
2 Samuel 1:11-12, Joel 2:12-13.

Gasoline - Source of energy; faith-filled prayer; capable of reviving; source of food for the Spirit; inflammatory gossip; contention; strife; danger.
Jude 1:20, Proverbs 26:20-21.
Gasoline Fumes = Deception; deceiving spirit; evil motive; envy; false accusations; slander; poisonous doctrine; danger.
Proverbs 24:28, Matthew 24:4, James 3:14-15.

Gate - Doors; opening; entrance; salvation; passage; business bargaining.
Psalm 87:2, Revelation 21:21, Psalm 107:16, Isaiah 45:2, Deuteronomy 3:5.

Gazelle - Sure-footed; graceful.
2 Samuel 2:18-19, Psalm 18:33, Habakkuk 3:19, 2 Samuel 2:18.

General - Highest Authority; Christ; apostle; or evil principality.
1 Corinthians 12:28, Ephesians 4:11, Ephesians 6:12.

Giant - Strongman; powerful demonic spirit; champion; stronghold; challenge; obstacle; trouble; spiritual warfare; one's own fleshly nature to be overcome; imagination that magnifies a problem bigger than it is; powerful angel.
Numbers 13:28-33, Deuteronomy 1:28, Job 16:14, Revelation 7:1.
Being a Giant = Great in faith; powerful spiritual warrior; a great threat to the enemy.
Matthew 8:8-10, Joshua 15:14.

Girdle - Prepare for use; righteousness; might; potency; made ready; support.
Isaiah 11:5, 2 Kings 4:29, Jeremiah 1:17-19, Job 38:3, 1 Kings 18:46; Ephesians 6:14, 1 Peter 1:13, Luke 12:35.

Ghost - Demonic spirit; haunt; torment; issue from past; unjustified fear.
Matthew 14:26.

Gloves - Covering; divine fitting to do God's work specific to one's purpose; protection; safe; careful. See Hands.
Ezekiel 1:8, Psalm 44:3.
White Gloves = Clean; inspection. See White in Part 2.
Black Gloves = Evil works; hidden works; formality. See Black in Part 2.
Soiled Gloves = Contaminated from the work; corrupted work. See Dirt.
Work Gloves = laborious work; spiritual warfare.
Jude 1:23.
New Gloves = New work; fresh mandate from God.
Wrong Size Gloves = Not suited to one's specific purpose; work one's not called to; someone else's work.
Romans 15:20, 1 Corinthians 3:6-10, 2 Corinthians 10:13-16.

Glue - Adherence; unity; cleaves; tenacious.
Acts 11:23.

Goat - Sinner; unbelief; stubborn; unyielding; strife; devourer; argumentative; negative person; foolish; scapegoat (miscarriage of judgement).
Matthew 25:33, Leviticus 16:10.

Gold - Pure; tried; God's glory; seal of divinity; enduring holiness; faithful; high value; honor.
Revelation 1:12, Exodus 25:11, & 31, 2 Timothy 2:20.

Gorilla - Stronghold; defiant; strong man; strength; valiant; affluence; mammon.
1 Samuel 17:4, & 23-25, Matthew 12:29, Luke 11:21-22, 1 Samuel 14:52, Psalm 19:5, 2 Chronicles 9:21, 1 Kings 10:22.

Governor - Rule; Christ; evil principality; person in charge, good or bad.
Malachi 1:8, Ephesians 6:12.
Governor's Statement or Order = A call from a person of high spiritual authority, good or evil.

Graduation - Graduated to the next level; completed; recognition of achievement, promotion.
2 Timothy 2:15, Proverbs 22:6, 2 Timothy 3:15-17.

Grain - Seed; word of God; harvest.
Luke 8:11, Genesis 41:22-23, & 27.
Condition of Grain = Indicative of future economy.
Genesis 41:22-23, & 27.

Grandchild - Heir; oneself; inherited blessing or iniquity; one's spiritual legacy; actual grandchild in the natural.
2 Timothy 1:5, Exodus 34:7, 2 Kings 17:41.

Grandfather - Past; generational authority; past wisdom; past gifting; spiritual inheritance, good or bad; a call for self-examination for inherited traits, faults, or sins.
2 Timothy 1:5, Proverbs 13:22a, Leviticus 26:39-40, & 42.

Grandfather Clock - Past. See Clock.

Grandmother - Past; generational authority; past wisdom; past gifting; spiritual inheritance, good or bad; a call for self-examination for inherited traits, faults, or sins.
2 Timothy 1:5, Proverbs 13:22a, Leviticus 26:39-40, & 42.

Grandparents - Past; generational authority; past wisdom; past gifting; spiritual inheritance, good or bad; a call for self-examination for inherited traits, faults, or sins.
2 Timothy 1:5, Proverbs 13:22a, Leviticus 26:39-40, & 42.

Grapes - Fruit of the Promised Land; success; evidence of fruitfulness.
Amos 9:13, Numbers 13:23, Hosea 9:10, Revelation 14:18.
Carry Grapes = Rich inheritance; future prosperity.
Numbers 13:23.
Spoiled Grapes = Corrupted promises; corrupted wisdom.
Deuteronomy 32:32-33.

Grass - Divinely provided; maintenance required; fragility of life; word of God; sustenance for animals.
Matthew 6:30, Psalm 72:16, 2 Samuel 23:3-4, 2 Kings 19:26, Psalm 103:15-16, 1 Peter 1:24, Isaiah 40:7-8, James 1:10-11, Job 5:25, Zechariah 10:1, Deuteronomy 32:2, Deuteronomy 11:15.
Dried Grass = Death of the flesh; repentance; spiritual drought.
Psalm 102:4, & 11, Isaiah 40:7-8.
Mowed Grass = Disciplined; obedience; chastisement; sickness; financial distress; depression; anguish.
Amos 7:1-2, Psalm 37:2, Psalm 72:6, 1 Corinthians 11:27-32.

Grasshoppers - Small; very little; insignificant; many together can destroy crops; instrument of judgement. See Locusts.
Numbers 13:33, Isaiah 40:22, Amos 7:1-2.

Grave - Death; old tradition; generational demonic influence; buried potentials; darkness; hell.
Job 21:13, Proverbs 1:12, Psalm 88:5, Isaiah 14:11, Psalm 30:3, 1 Corinthians 15:54-55, Psalm 6:5, John 12:17, Matthew 27:53, Psalm 31:17, Job 17:3, Proverbs 30:16, Hosea 13:14, Job 33:22, Revelation 20:13-14.
Digging the Grave = Discovering what was hidden from the ancient past'
Burying something in the Grave = End of a phase; putting an end to something.

Grave clothes = Bound.
John 11:44.
Graveyard = Hidden; curse from the past; evil inheritance; hypocrisy; death; demon.
Matthew 23:27, Luke 11:44.

Gravel - Deceit; mockery; shame; offspring.
Proverbs 20:17, Matthew 7:9, Lamentations 3:16, Isaiah 48:19-20 (KJV).

Gravel Pit - Source; the Word of God; abundant supply.
Deuteronomy 8:9, 2 Timothy 2:15.

Gravel Road - Difficult way, narrow way.
Psalm 17:5, Matthew 7:13-14.

Grey Hair - Worldly wisdom, wisdom gained from living a long life; old age; on a younger person, exceptional wisdom.
Proverbs 16:31, Proverbs 20:29.

Greyhound Dog - Runs well in the race of faith; unencumbered for action; swift; very fast; graceful and efficient; intelligent; gentle. See Dog.
1 Corinthians 9:24-27, Proverbs 30:29, & 31, 1 Kings 18:46, 1 Kings 19:7-8, Ephesians 6:14, Luke 12:35.

Groom - Christ; headship; natural marriage. See Marriage.
Isaiah 62:5, Ephesians 5:31-32, 2 Corinthians 6:14.
    Bride = Church; covenant (good or bad); natural groom.
    Isaiah 62:5, Ephesians 5:31-32, John 3:29, Revelation 21:9, 2 Corinthians 6:14.
    Waiting for a Groom = Waiting for the manifestation of the words of Jesus in one's life; growing in intimacy with Jesus.
    Matthew 25:4-7.

Delayed arrival of a Groom = Hindrances to the work of Jesus in one's life; hindrances or issues to intimacy with Jesus.
Matthew 25:5, Hebrews 10:36-37, 2 Peter 3:4-9, Matthew 24:42-51.
Appearance or Arrival of a Groom = Manifestation of the work of Christ; ready for the marriage.
Matthew 25:10.

Ground Floor - Revealed: Everyday or current affairs; that which is manifest; truth exposed; without hypocrisy. See Porch.
Mark 2:4-5.

Guard - Ability to keep on right path; vigilant; protector.
Ezekiel 38:7, Nehemiah 4:22-23, 2 Kings 11:4-13.
Faceless and Protective Guard = Holy Spirit.
Forceful and Frustrating Guard = Situation that has power to limit a person.

Guest - Spiritual messengers; angel; evil presence.
Hebrews 13:2, Genesis 18:2-10, Genesis 19:1-3, Judges 13:15-25, Luke 1:11-13, Galatians 1:8-9, 2 Corinthians 11:13-15.

Gum - Sticky situation; offence; grudge.
1 Kings 11:2, Mark 11:25-26.
Chewing Gum = Contemplating; meditating; idling away one's time; annoyance.
Genesis 24:63, Psalm 19:14, Psalm 119:145-152, Psalm 63:6, 1 Timothy 4:15, Psalm 103:3-5.
Bubble Gum = Childish; foolishness; immaturity.
Proverbs 15:14, Proverbs 22:15.

Gun - Words; accusations; slander; gossip; power.
2 Samuel 11:24, Psalm 64:4, Luke 11:21-22.

Being Shot by a Gun = Powerful words coming against a person; curses; attacks.

Holding a Gun = Equipped with authority or ability; power; unhindered.

Broken or Inoperative Gun = Without authority or ability; without power; hindered.

Smaller Calibre = Weak or ineffective weapon; without power; lack of prayer and fasting.
Revelation 3:8.

Larger Calibre = Powerful; spiritual power through acceptable service; covenant; effective; the power of evil working through agreement (acquiescence) or conquest (our defeat).
2 Corinthians 10:4.

Hail - Judgement; punishment; destruction; bombardment.
Exodus 9:18, & 23-24, Ezekiel 38:22, Isaiah 28:17, Haggai 2:17.

Hair - Covering; covenant; glory; beauty; humanity; man-made religious doctrine or ritual; tradition; worldliness; vanity.
Numbers 6: 5, Song of Solomon 5:11, Daniel 7:9, Revelation 1:14, Song of Solomon 7:5, 2 Samuel 14:25-26; Song of Solomon 4:1, Song of Solomon 6:5, 1 Corinthians 11:3-7, 11, &14-16, 1 Peter 3:3, 1 Timothy 2:9.

Hair Standing on Edge = Fright; shock.
Job 4:15.

Hair Shaved Off = Uncovering; purification; separation to God; petition to God; mourning; humbled; shame; judgement.
Acts 21:24, & 26 (See with Numbers 6:13-20, verse 18), Acts 18:18, Numbers 8:7, Job 1:20, Jeremiah 48:37-38,

Isaiah 15:2, Ezra 9:3-6, Ezekiel 5:1, Ezekiel 29:18, Isaiah 22:12, Micah 1:16, Ezekiel 7:18, Jeremiah 47:5.
Hair Growing Back = Restoration of the covenant. Judges 16:22, & 28-30.
Long Hair = Covenant; consecrated or separated (Nazarite) to God.
Judges 13:5, Judges 16:17, Numbers 6:2, 5, &13, Luke 1:15-17, 2 Kings 1:8.
Note: The two illustrations below have been judged according to man-made religious doctrine or ritual. I have made note of some more grace-centered entries, along with supporting Scriptures. Spiritually, in Christ there is no distinction between the genders (Jew or Greek, male or female), Galatians 3:28. Outside of marriage, a woman's role, or calling and liberty in Christ are only limited by a male-dominated culture. Her spiritual covering is Jesus. In Genesis 3:16, the husband's "rule" over the wife, is a result of the curse. Jesus redeemed us from the curse of the law, Galatians 3:13. The order of the household remains with the husband being the head of the wife and children, but length of hair is strictly a man-made religious doctrine. See 1 Corinthians 11 verse 11 and especially verse 16.
Woman with Long Hair = Glory; beautiful. (1 Corinthians 11:15. See with Numbers 6:2, 5, & 18). Long or styled hair is just natural and shows beauty. Song of Solomon 4:1; Song of Solomon 6:5, Song of Solomon 7:5.
> **Woman with Short Hair** = Can still show glory and be beautifully styled; possible special covenant with God.
> Numbers 6:2, 5, & 18.

Man with Long Hair = Mourning; covenant with God; shame. (1 Corinthians 11:14). In Jewish tradition, a man would pray and preach with his head covered. Men also covered their heads while mourning, 2 Samuel 15:30,

Esther 6:12. Also, a Nazarite did not cut his hair so a more accurate interpretation could be mourning rather than shame, or one who has made a special covenant with God, or one keeps himself well groomed (whose hair grows out quickly, if that fits in the dream.
2 Kings 1:8, Song of Solomon 5:11, 2 Samuel 14:25-26.
> **Man with Short Hair** = Headship of his household; Christ as his Head; natural grooming; business demeanour.
> 1 Corinthians 11:3.

This all should be taken into context for an accurate interpretation.

Hair Color - Each color listed below. See Colors in Part 2.
Blonde Hair = Faddish; worldly glory; God's glory; fair; natural beauty.
Revelation 12:1 (stars = glory, the color of blonde hair. See with Daniel 12:3).
Red Hair = Fiery; healthy (ruddy); natural beauty; hot-headed; impulsive.
Song of Solomon 5:10; 1 Samuel 16:12, 1 Samuel 17:42.
Dark Hair = Cool temperament; thoughtful; typical.
Song of Solomon 5:11; Song of Solomon 7:5 (purple = glossy splendor of black hair).
White Hair = Wisdom; glory; elevation in status; victory; grace.
Revelation 1:14, Daniel 7:9.
Grey Hair = Worldly wisdom, wisdom gained from living a long life; old age; on a younger person, exceptional wisdom.
Proverbs 16:31, Proverbs 20:29.

Haircut - Putting away tradition or bad habits; repenting of bad attitudes. See Beauty Shop or Barber Shop.
Judges 16:17.

Hairdresser - Vanity; self glory; grooming; separation to God. 2 Samuel 14:25-26, 1 Timothy 2:9, 1 Peter 3:3, Numbers 6:18-19, Acts 18:18.

Halloween - A satanic holiday; a high offering day for witches, sorcerers, occultists and Satanists, to demonic spirits; a celebration of death.
Deuteronomy 18:10-12, 2 Kings 21:6-7, 2 Chronicles 33:6-7, Micah 5:12, Acts 8:9-11, Isaiah 8:19-20, Mark 12:26-27.
Jack-O-Lantern = Witchcraft; deception; snare; appeasement; trickery.
2 Kings 21: 7, 2 Chronicles 33: 7, Isaiah 8:19-20, Judges 18:17-20, Acts 8:9-11.

Hallway - Passage way; transition; restricted journey; focused journey.
Jeremiah 6:16.
Long Hallway = Passage of time.
Enclosed Hallway = Limits but compels one's transition.
Dark Hallway = Ominous time; trouble; sickness.
Lighted Hallway = Enlightened journey.
Psalm 119:105.
Clear Hallway = Obstacle free.
Cluttered Hallway = Obstacles; opposition.
Nahum 3:3, Jeremiah 18:15.

Hammer - Word of God; force; preaching; evil words; destruction; a tool of creative or destructive power by the one in authority.
Jeremiah 23:29, Proverbs 25:18.

Hand - Symbol of strength; power; action; possession. See Fingers.
Psalm 128:2, Psalm 28:4, Proverbs 14:1, Psalm 115:4, Proverbs 6:1-5, Proverbs 22:26, Acts 8:17-18.

The Hand of God = Power of God to deliver and to set free; powerful word of God; power to heal; performs signs and wonders.

Acts 11:21, Deuteronomy 4:34, Acts 4:29-31.

Working Hands = Deeds, good or evil; labor; service; idolatry; spiritual warfare.

Psalm 128:2, Psalm 28:4, Psalm 115:4.

Holding Hands = In agreement.

Right Hand = Oath of allegiance; power; honor; natural strength; takes bribes.

Isaiah 62:8, Isaiah 41:10-13, Isaiah 48:13, Exodus 15:6, Deuteronomy 33:2, Psalm 20:6, 2 Samuel 20:9, Psalm 26:10, Psalm 144:11.

Left Hand = Something spiritual.

Judges 3:21 (divine justice).

Clapping Hands = Joy; worship; mockery.

Psalm 47:1, Psalm 98:8, Isaiah 55:12, Job 27:23, Lamentations 2:15, Nahum 3:19.

Outstretched Hands with Palms Up = Helplessness.

1 Timothy 2:8.

Stretched Out Hands = Surrender.

Psalm 44:20, Psalm 88:9, 1 Kings 8:22.

Raised Hands = Worship; surrender; prayer.

Psalm 28:2, 1 Kings 8:22, 1 Timothy 2:8.

Laying on of Hands = Impartation; sending off in the power of the Holy Spirit; healing.

Acts 8:17-18, Acts 19:6, 1 Timothy 4:14, 2 Timothy 1:6, Acts 6:6, Acts 13:3, Acts 9:17.

Trembling Hands = Weakness; fear; spirit of fear; awe of God's presence.

Hands Covering Face = Grief; sorrow; guilt; shame; laughter.

Jeremiah 2:37.

Hands under Thighs = Oaths.

Genesis 24:2-9, Genesis 47:29-30.

Shaking Hands = Covenant; agreement.
Proverbs 11:15, Proverbs 6:1-5, Proverbs 22:26-27, Proverbs 17:18.
Washing Hands = Declaring innocence; disassociate oneself.
Psalm 26:6, Matthew 27:24.

Hand Soap - Cleansing; conviction; forgiveness; prayer; repentance. See Bathroom.
Malachi 3:2, Jeremiah 2:22, Isaiah 1:16.

Harbor - Safe place; divine protection; a place of God's refuge; a place of anchor; comfort zone; no progress; complacency, no growth; low expectations; hides weak faith; harbors anger, resentment, bitterness.
Psalm 91:1-2, John 10:10-13, Matthew 10:16, 1 Corinthians 16:9, Ezekiel 3:14.

    Anchor = Representation of security, safety and hope; Jesus the Anchor of our soul.
    Hebrews 6:19-20.

        Trying to Secure an Anchor = Need to put things in order; need to make things more secure.
        Broken Anchor = Lost firmness; lost security.
        Weak Shaking Anchor = Need to strengthen existing security.
        Strong Firm Anchor = Security in place.
        Acts 27:29.
        Cutting off of an Anchor = Letting go of security, in self or in God.
        Acts 27:40.

Port = A place of spiritual portals; distribution; exports the spiritual to the natural; spiritual gateway; family line; prophesy, speaking into existence.
Micah 5:2, Genesis 28:12, Deuteronomy 28:12, Revelation

11:3-6, & 19, Revelation 4:1, Revelation 8:3-5, Revelation 19:10 (testifying by the Spirit within), James 5:17-18.

Harlot - Seduction; the worldly church; adultery; fornication; temptation; enticement; snare; unclean person; stubborn. See Sex.
Revelation 17:5, Ecclesiastes 7:26, Jeremiah 3:3.
 Appearance of a Harlot = Tempting situation; enticing situation.
 Negotiating with a Harlot = Handling a situation that is enticing; being seduced by an evil spirit.
 Affair with a Harlot = Succumb to fleshly desires.
 Repeated Dreams of Scenes involving Harlots = Unbroken root of desires, generational or personal; preoccupation of desires.

Harp - Praise; worship to God.
Genesis 4:21, Genesis 31:27, 1 Chronicles 15:28, Psalm 33:2, Psalm 150:3-4.
 Playing a Harp = Praise or worship to God; thankful situation.
 1 Chronicles 15:28, Psalm 33:2, Psalm 150:3-4.
 Hanging up a Harp = Situation causing one to not be able to praise God.
 Psalm 137:1-2.

Hat - Covering; protection; hope; mantle; crown; thought; attitude; activities.
Isaiah 59:17, Ephesians 6:17, 1 Thessalonians 5:8.
 Putting on a New Hat = New level of protection; new mantle; new thought life.
 Removing One's Hat = Demonstrate respect; sign of submission.
 Revelation 4:10.

Hat that does not Fit = Mantle that is not yours to carry; not suited to one's specific DNA; carrying someone else's mantle.
1 Samuel 17:38-40, Romans 15:20, 1 Corinthians 3:6-10, 2 Corinthians 10:13-16.

Hay - Preparation; bundle or gather together; unprofitable works that are burned up.
1 Corinthians 3:12-15, Jeremiah 23:28, Isaiah 5:24, Psalm 1:4, Matthew 3:12.

Hawk - Predator; sorcerer; evil spirit; a warmonger. See Bird. Acts 20:30.

Head - Authority; Jesus; husband; pastor; boss; thoughts; mind. See Forehead.
Ephesians 1:22-23, Matthew 21:42.
Anointed Head = Set apart for God's service; preparation for burial.
Mark 14:3, & 8.
Laying on of Hands on Head = Impartation of anointing of gifts and the Holy Spirit; a sending off.
1 Timothy 4:14, Acts 6:6, Acts 8:17, Acts 19:6, Acts 13:3.
Hands on Head = Grief; sorrow; guilt; shame; laughter.
Jeremiah 2:37.
Shake One's Head = Astonishment; shame; scorn; mock.
Jeremiah 18:16, Lamentations 2:15, Psalm 44:14, Psalm 109:25, Psalm 22:7, Matthew 27:39-40.
Bald Head = Uncovering; purification; petition to God; mourning; humbled; shame; judgement; natural baldness.
Acts 21:24, & 26 (See with Numbers 6:13-20, verse 18), Acts 18:18, Numbers 8:7, Job 1:20, Jeremiah 48:37-38, Isaiah 15:2, Ezra 9:3-6, Ezekiel 5:1, Ezekiel 29:18, Isaiah 22:12, Micah 1:16, Ezekiel 7:18, Jeremiah 47:5.

Healing Pool - Time of refreshing; healing when water stirred. See Pool, Water.
Acts 3:19, John 5:2-9.

Heart - Emotions; affections; motivations; will; desires; morality; courage.
Jeremiah 17:1, & 9-10, Matthew 15:18-19, Hebrews 13:9-10.

Heat - Passion; power; anger; envy; jealousy; strife; desire; lust; gossip.
Numbers 11:1, Exodus 32:19, Deuteronomy 9:19, Esther 1:12.

Hedge - Protection; shield; barrier; hidden.
Job 1:10, Zechariah 2:5.

Heel Kicking or Lifting - Threatening; betrayal; rebellion; persecution.
Psalm 41:9, John13:18, Acts 9:5, Acts 26:14.

Heifer - Rebellious woman. See Calf.
Amos 4:3, Judges 14:15-18, Hosea 4:16, Hosea 10:11, Jeremiah 50:11.

Helicopter - Ministry; individual; the Church; versatile, no forward movement; stationary; lack of progress. See Airplane, Pilot.
2 Timothy 4:2a.
> **Military Helicopter** = Powerful prayer life; challenging enemy attack.
> **Military Helicopter Fighting for One** = Powerful intercession on one's behalf.
> **Attacking War Helicopter** = Enemy forces coming against one.

Helmet - Covering; protection; inner assurance of salvation; hope; God's promise.
Isaiah 59:17, Ephesians 6:17, 1 Thessalonians 5:8.
Putting on a Helmet = Protection; evidence of salvation.
Without a Helmet in a Construction site = Not protected; exposed to danger.

Hen - Gathering; protection; gossip.
Luke 13:34.
Chicken = Fear; cowardliness.
Deuteronomy 1:29, Luke 13:34.
Chick = Defenceless.
Rooster = Bragging; proud; boasting; arrogance; sexual pride.
John 18:27, Luke 22:33-34.

High School - Moving into higher level of walk with God; high level of training and equipping; capable of giving the same to others; need to be aware of false teaching (evolution, etc).
Hebrews 5:14, Ephesians 4:11-13, Matthew 28:19-20.

Highway - Holy way; Christ; the Christian faith; truth; life; way of error.
Isaiah 35:8, John 14:6, Matthew 7:13-14, Jeremiah 6:16, Nahum 2:4, Haggai 1:5-7, Luke 15:15-17, Jeremiah 18:15-16.
Under Construction = In preparation; not ready; change; hindrance.
Crossroads = Decision; change of direction.
Jeremiah 6:16, Haggai 1:5-7.
Long Highway = Time.
Dead End = Change direction, stop and repent; certain failure.
Luke 15:15-17.
Narrow Highway = Way to life; God's way.
Matthew 7:13-14.

Broad Highway = Way of destruction; man's way.
Matthew 7:13-14.
Gravel or Stones on the Highway= Difficult way, narrow
way.
Psalm 17:5, Matthew 7:13-14.

Hill - Elevation; high; loftiness; Throne of God; Mount Zion;
pride; idolatry. See Mountain.
Isaiah 57:15, Psalm 68:15-16 (KJV), Psalm 99:9, Psalm 2:6,
Psalm 121:1-2, Isaiah 2:11-14, Jeremiah 2:20, Hosea 4:13,
Ezekiel 6:3-4, & 13, Jeremiah 17:2-3, Psalm 24:3.
Ascending a Hill = Spiritual elevation.
Psalm 24:3, Isaiah 58:14.
Descending a Hill = Be watchful to not lose spiritual
ground.
Isaiah 2:11-14, Ezekiel 6:3-4, & 13.

Hips or Loins - Mind; truth; support; joint; faith; reproduction.
1 Peter 1:13, Ephesians 6:14, Daniel 5:6, Psalm 69:23, Genesis
32:25-32, Ezekiel 47:4, Hebrews 7:10.
Exposed Hip = Seduction; enticement.
Water up to Hip Level = Faith to impart the next generation;
spiritual offspring.
Ezekiel 47:4.
Hip out of Joint = Offense between brethren.
Hip Dislocation or Replacement = turn from reliance on
self to reliance on the Lord.
Genesis 32:25-32.

Hog - Unclean; selfish; backslider; unbeliever; glutton;
fornicator; hypocrite; destroyer; devourer; idolater.
2 Peter 2:22, Matthew 7:6.
Boar = Persecutor; hostile to virtue; vicious; vengeful;
danger.
Psalm 80:13, 2 Timothy 3:2-3.

Home - Heart; identity; roots; dwelling place.
Luke 11:24, Acts 16:31, 1 Chronicles 17:5.
Door to the Home = Entrance; Christ; way; avenue; mouth.
John 10:7-9, Revelation 4:1, Colossians 4:3, Psalm 141:3, Isaiah 22:22, Revelation 3:7-8.

> **Open Door** = New opportunity; grace for progress.
> Revelation 3:8.
> **Closed Door** = Obstacle; hidden activities.
> Ezekiel 8:3-18.
> **Keys to the Closed Door** = Authority over the obstacle; authority to create opportunity; power to bind or loose; lock or unlock; wisdom; knowledge; important.
> Matthew 16:19, Isaiah 22:22, Revelation 3:7, Luke 11:52, Proverbs 4:7.
>> **To be Given Keys** = Given power and authority.
>> Isaiah 22:22.
>> **To Lose One's Keys** = Lose the power and authority one was given.

Childhood Home at Your Current Age = You are either dealing with things from your childhood that are affecting you now or there could be things your family is called to do that you will be fulfilling.

New Home = New life, salvation; new spiritual family; change; renewal; new move, natural or spiritual. See Moving Van.
2 Corinthians 5:1, &17.

Two or Three-Story Home = Multi level giftedness; multi talented family.
Acts 20:7-11.

Basement = Soul; carnal nature; lust; discouragement; depression; refuge; retreat; hidden; beneath the surface; foundational issues; forgotten; secret sin; bloodline issue; demonic realm. See Foundation.
Jeremiah 38:6, Isaiah 24:22.

Valuables in the Basement = Inherited giftedness; great potential yet to be revealed or manifested.
Fault in the Basement = Broken foundation; bloodline issue needing repentance.

Homosexuality - Unfruitful, non- evangelistic; demonic stronghold (sodomy rooted in ancient deity fertility rites); lust.
Ephesians 5:11-12, & 31-32, Jude 1:6-7, Romans 1:24-27.

Homosexual Acts - Against nature; rebellion; disobedience; fornication.
Romans 1:24-28, Leviticus 18:22, Ezekiel 16:45 & 49-50, 1 Corinthians 6:9.

Honey - Sweet; strength; the Word of God; abundance; enlightenment; wisdom.
Proverbs 27:7, Psalm 119:103, 2 Samuel 17:29, Psalm 19:9-11, Genesis 43:11, Exodus 3:8, Job 20:17; Proverbs 24:13-14, 1 Samuel 14:29, Isaiah 7:15.

Horn(s) - Source of anointed power; authority; strength; defence; power of a king; evil power.
Psalm 75:10, Psalm 118:27, Psalm 132: 17-18, 1 Samuel 2:1, Ezekiel 34:21, Revelation 17:12-14.
    Horn Anointed = Powerful authority.
    Horns Coming against One = Powers coming against one.
    Ezekiel 34:21, Revelation 17:12-14.

Horn of Plenty - Abundance without measure or limitation; goodness without end; blessing; anointing.
Deuteronomy 28:2, & 4-5, Galatians 5:22-23, Ephesians 3:20.

Hornets - Affliction; stinging; biting words; slander; strife; curse (because of sin); persecution; trouble; offense; demon spirits. See Bees.
Deuteronomy 7:20, Exodus 23:28, Joshua 24:12.

Horse - Work; flesh; the work of God's Spirit through man; spiritual warfare; one week, or another specific period of time; age; strength; power.
Jeremiah 5:8, Psalm 33:17.
Front Half of Horse = First part of time or work; beginning; ready.
Back Half of Horse = Last part of time or work; end; an offensive or obnoxious person.
Kicking Horse = Threatening; opposition.
White Horse = Righteous; true; pure; peace; conquer. See White in Part 2.
Revelation 19:11, Revelation 6:2.
Red Horse = Persecution; anger; danger; opposition; could have apocalyptic meaning. See Red in Part 2.
John 16:2, Revelation 6:4, Zechariah 1:8.
Black Horse = Famine; bad times; evil; could have apocalyptic meaning. See Black in Part 2.
Revelation 6:5, Amos 8:11.
Pale Horse = Spirit of death; pestilence. See Green in Part 2.
Revelation 6:8, Zechariah 6:3.

Horse's Rider - Nature of work or time; anxious; happy; confident.
2 Kings 4:24, Revelation 6:2, Revelation 6:8a.

Hospital - Care; church; place of healing; mercy; persons who are wounded, dying, or sick.
Luke 10:30, & 33-34, Psalm 109:22, Isaiah 53:5.

Visiting a Hospital = Welfare; healing anointing; chaplaincy anointing.
A Patient in a Hospital = Physical afflictions.
A Patient in a Mental Hospital = Spiritual affliction; emotional affliction; situation causing mental instability.

Hot or Boiling Water - Spiritual condition; anger; war; judgment. See Water, and Hot Water subheading.
Isaiah 64:2, Jeremiah 1:13-16, Ezekiel 24:3-14, Psalm 58:9.

Hotel - Church; place for rest in Christ; natural place of rest; public gathering; meeting; travel; business travel; adultery; lust; temptation.
Acts 28:15, Luke 10:34, Luke 2:7, Genesis 42:27, Genesis 43:21, Exodus 4:24.
Lodging in a Five Star Hotel = Elevation; an exalted place imminent.

Hound Dog - Strife; contention; offense; unclean spirit; obsession; guilt, shame, cowardly. See Dog.
Galatians 5:15, Proverbs 26:17, Proverbs 26:11, Luke 16:21, 2 Peter 2:22, Matthew 7:6,
2 Timothy 3:2-4, Isaiah 56:10-11, Revelation 22:15.

House - Family; an individual; Church; when naturally interpreted it means a dwelling place; heart; identity; roots.
Luke 11:24, Acts 16:31, 1 Chronicles 17:5.
Door to the House = Entrance; Christ; way; avenue; mouth.
John 10:7-9, Revelation 4:1, Colossians 4:3, Psalm 141:3, Isaiah 22:22, Revelation 3:7-8.
Open Door = New opportunity; grace for progress.
Revelation 3:8.
Closed Door = Obstacle; hidden activities.
Ezekiel 8:3-18.

Keys to the Closed Door = Authority over the obstacle; authority to create opportunity; power to bind or loose; lock or unlock; wisdom; knowledge; important. Matthew 16:19, Isaiah 22:22, Revelation 3:7, Luke 11:52, Proverbs 4:7.
> **To be Given Keys** = Given power and authority. Isaiah 22:22.
> **To Lose One's Keys** = Lose the power and authority one was given.

Childhood Home at Your Current Age = You are either dealing with things from your childhood that are affecting you now or there could be things your family is called to do that you will be fulfilling.

New House = New life, salvation; new spiritual family; change; renewal; new move, natural or spiritual. See Moving Van.
2 Corinthians 5:1, &17.

Two or Three-Story House = Multi level giftedness; multi talented church.
Acts 20:7-11.

House Trailer = Temporary relationships, place, or situations; poverty.
James 4:14.

House under Construction =Not ready to proceed with construction when incomplete; the local church body; church government; building program.
Psalm 11:3, Luke 14:29, 1 Corinthians 3:10-11, Ephesians 2:20.

Cracked Walls = Faulty defences; physical afflictions.

Leaking Roof = Inadequate spiritual coverage.

House in Bad Condition = Sin; transgression; renewal needed.
Ezekiel 36:10, 2 Chronicles 10:19.

House needing Renovation or Remodelling = Revival needed.

2 Chronicles 30:11-18, Ezekiel 37:23.
House Unpainted or Overgrown with Weeds = Untended; ignored.
Ecclesiastes 10:18, Ezekiel 36:10, 1 Kings 12:16-20.
House beyond Repair, in Ruin = Neglect; unusable; the Lord's intervention needed.
Ezekiel 37:11, Matthew 12:25-30.
Basement = Soul; Carnal nature; lust; discouragement; depression; refuge; retreat; hidden; beneath the surface; foundational issues; forgotten; secret sin; bloodline issue; demonic realm. See Foundation.
Jeremiah 38:6, Isaiah 24:22.
Valuables in the Basement = Inherited giftedness; great potential yet to be revealed or manifested.
Fault in the Basement = Broken foundation; bloodline issue needing repentance.

House Coat - Idleness; unprepared; lazy; resting; at ease.
Ecclesiastes 10:18, Luke 12:45 – 47, Revelation 16:15, Luke 12:19-20.

Hovering - No forward movement: stationary; lack of progress. See Helicopter.
2 Timothy 4:2a.

Hunting - Diligence; working for provision of food; judgement against sin; enemy pursuit; adulterous pursuit; false prophets after souls; persecution.
Proverbs 12:27, Genesis 27:30-31, Deuteronomy 14:4-6, Jeremiah 16:16-18, 1 Samuel 26:20, Psalm 140:11, Proverbs 6:26, Ezekiel 13:18-20, Micah 7:2.
Hunting Dog = Persistence; determination; pursuit; chase after; serving the Master; obsessed. See Dog.

Hurricane - Great disturbance; intense spiritual warfare; witchcraft; sudden calamity or destruction; judgement; trial; persecution; opposition; outpouring of revival; powerful move of the Spirit. See Tornado, Whirlwind.
Isaiah 25:4, Acts 27:14-15, & 18-25, 1 Thessalonians 5:3, Nahum 1:3, 2 Samuel 22:10-15, Psalm 18:9-14, Psalm 104:3, Psalm 58:9, Hosea 13:3, Zechariah 7:14.

Husband - Authority; God or Christ; a divorcee's first husband sometimes represents the world, bondage to sin before salvation; natural husband.
Genesis 3:16, Isaiah 54:5, Jeremiah 3:20, Ephesians 5:27-32, 2 Corinthians 11:2-3.
Dreaming of a Husband = Authority figure over the dreamer; literal husband.
Pursued by a Loving Kind Husband = Jesus reaching out to the person.
Ex Husband = Previous head or authority over the dreamer; something that had control over the dreamer in the past.
Husband's Sister = The Church.

Hyena - Warning of attack against the spiritually asleep; a call to stay awake and alert. See Dog.
Isaiah 52:1, Luke 22:45-46.

Ice - A move of the Holy Spirit coming later; hard saying; slippery, dangerous time.
Psalm 147:17-20, John 6:60, Psalm 73:2.

Iced Tea - Refreshing; grace; good news; salvation; soothing; time of refreshing (Tea time).
Proverbs 25:25, Isaiah 28:12, Acts 3:19.

Tea Bag = Healing.
Revelation 22:2, Ezekiel 47:12.
Hot Tea = Warmth; social gathering.

Idle or Abandoned Factory - Not busy; not reaching full potential; laziness; idleness; sloth; natural workplace when applicable. See Factory.

Illness - Iniquity or sin; corrupted environment; corruption of world systems; actual sickness that needs prayer for healing; hopelessness.
John 5:14, Luke 5:18-25, & 31-32, James 5:14-16, Isaiah 1:5-6, Matthew 4:24, Matthew 8:16-17, Proverbs 13:12.

Incense - Prayer; intercessions; worship.
Psalm 141:2, Revelation 5:8, Revelation 8:3-4.

Incest - Inordinate affection: Improper relationship; impure attraction towards normal kin or brethren.
Leviticus 18:6-18, Leviticus 20:17-21, Ezekiel 22:11, Deuteronomy 27:22.

Incubation - Initiation; cleansing, preparation, training and empowerment.
Leviticus 8:33-35.
> **Initiation** = Practices or trials, that causes one to die to or put off the old self, and be regenerated into, to put on the new self in Christ.

Indian, Native American - Flesh, the old man; firstborn; chief; fierce; savvy; native.
Colossians 3:5-10, Genesis 49:3, Acts 15:22.

Indy Race Car - Acceleration into the new season and ministry. See Car.

Keys = Authority; power to bind or loose; lock or unlock; wisdom; knowledge; important.
Matthew 16:19, Isaiah 22:22, Revelation 3:7, Luke 11:52, Proverbs 4:7.
> **To be Given Keys** = Given power and authority.
> Isaiah 22:22.
> **To Lose One's Keys** = Lose the power and authority one was given.

Insects - Plague (plagues of Egypt); pest; small; problem; trouble; annoyance; religious spirit (bad-mouthing those led by the Spirit); broken (there's a bug in this); spying device.
Exodus 5:3, Exodus 8:16-18, & 21-24, Psalm 78: 45-46, Psalm 105: 31, & 34, Isaiah 7:18, Matthew 23:24, Luke 18:5, John 7:12, John 9:16, Isaiah 1:14, Luke 18:5, John 9:16.
> **Ant** = Industrious; wise; diligent; prepared for the future; nuisance, stinging or angry.
> Proverbs 6:6-8, Proverbs 30:25.
> > **Invasion of Large Numbers of Ants** = Challenging or dangerous situation; overwhelming situation; onslaught of the enemy.
> > **Fire Ant** = Fiery, angry words; attack of the enemy; volatile, dangerous situation.
> > James 3:6, Proverbs 16:27.
> > **Stung or Bitten by Ants** = Attacking words; stinging words; dangerous situation; attack of the enemy; strife.
> > Proverbs 26:20-21.
> **Bees** = Chastisement; judgement; offense; stinging words; affliction; busybody; gossip; busy.
> Deuteronomy 1: 44, Psalm 118:12, Judges 14:8, 1 Timothy 5:13.
> **Hornets or Wasps** = Affliction; stinging; biting words; slander; strife; curse (because of sin); persecution; trouble; offense; demon spirits.
> Deuteronomy 7:20.

Spider = Evil; sin; false doctrine; temptation; deceiver; difficult escape from entanglement; conflict; stronghold; threatening issue with danger of entanglement or possibly death; false trust; tenacious; clever; evil spirit; religious spirit; predatory person.
Proverbs 30:24, & 28, Proverbs 7:22-23, Isaiah 59:5-6, Genesis 31:27, 2 Corinthians 10:4-5, Acts 4:17, 21, & 29, 1 Peter 2:23, Job 8:13-15, 1 Timothy 6:9, 2 Timothy 2:26, Matthew 23:27-28; Psalm 91:3, Psalm 124:7, Hosea 9:8.
Black Widow = Great danger; deadly; life-threatening; evil; slander.
James 3:8.
Fangs = Evil intent or motive: poisonous; great danger.
Psalm 57:4, Psalm 58:6, Proverbs 30:14, Daniel 7:5-7, Revelation 9:8.
Spider Web = Snare; lies and deception; scheme; trap; ruin; internet.
Ecclesiastes 7:26, Isaiah 59:5-7; Psalm 91:3, Psalm 124:7, Ecclesiastes 9:12; Psalm 140:5, Psalm 119:110, Psalm 141:9.
Flea = Insignificant; nuisance; irritant; hunted; elusive.
1 Samuel 24:14, 1 Samuel 26:20.
Lice = Condemnation; accusation; shame; guilt; affliction.
Exodus 8:16-17, John 8:6, & 9.
Tick = Hidden unclean spirit; oblivious to one's true self, self-justification and self-righteousness; parasite; life-stealing; draining; pest.
Leviticus 5:2, Jeremiah 17:9.
Flies = Beelzebub "Lord of the flies" is a reference to the devil. Evil spirits; Satan; doctrines of demons (fly in the cup); unclean; corruption; curse; nuisance; foolishness destroying ones' reputation.
Exodus 8:21-31, Matthew 12:24, &26-27, 1 Corinthians 10:21, 2 Corinthians 6:15-17, Ecclesiastes 10:1, Isaiah 7:18.

Covered by Flies = Corruption that breeds unclean spirits.

Fly Screen = Covering; protection from demonic attacks.

Ecclesiastes 10:1(See with Ecclesiastes 9:18).

Cockroaches = Unclean; infestation; crept in; defiled; hidden sin; in darkness; lies.

Leviticus 5:2, Leviticus 11: 31, & 43, 2 Corinthians 7:1; 2 Timothy 3:6, Jude 1:4,

1 Corinthians 4:5, 1 John 1:6.

Mosquito = Parasite; evil spirit; unseen attack sapping the life out of another; stealing of finances; irritation.

John 12:6, John 10:10, Deuteronomy 25:18, Micah 7:2-3, Matthew 27:6 (See with Exodus 21:30, Leviticus 17:11).

Grasshoppers = Small; very little; insignificant; many together can destroy crops; instrument of judgement.

Numbers 13:33, Isaiah 40:22, Amos 7:1-2.

Locusts = Judgement; famine; death; devourer; pestilence; plague; demonic spirits; oppressive multitude; invades their enemy in military order (like a swarm of locusts); weak when alone; flighty; restoration possible.

Exodus 10:4-6, 14-15, &17-19, Deuteronomy 28:38, & 42, 2 Chronicles 7:13, 1 Kings 8:37, Psalm 78:46, Psalm 105:34-35; Joel 1:4, Revelation 9:3-10, Psalm 109:22-24, Joel 2:7-9, Nahum 3:15-17, Joel 2:25.

Slug or Snail = Slowly eats away the truth of the word of God; corruption of injustices; unclean issues; lawlessness.

2 Timothy 2:17, Nahum 3:15, James 5:3, Leviticus 11:29-30, & 41-45, Leviticus 22:5-6, Habakkuk 1:14.

Worm = Corruption; weak; insignificant; filthiness of the flesh; evil; eats from the inside; pride; transgressor; death; rotten motives; bitter; temptation leading to sin; fearful; reproached; despised.

Job 17:14, Job 25:6, Job 7:5, Isaiah 14:11, Isaiah 66:24, Proverbs 5:4, Mark 9:43-50, Isaiah 41:14, Psalm 22:6.

Maggot = Corruption; filthiness of the flesh; despised; decay; evil; death; judgement; rotten motives.
Job 17:14, Psalm 22:6, Exodus 16:20, Acts 12:23, Deuteronomy 28:39, Job 24:20.
Leech = Sucks the life out of another; a sponge; soaks up others' resources and strength; insatiable appetite to steal the life of others.
Proverbs 30:15 (See with Habakkuk 2:5, Proverbs 27:20).
Termites = Corruption; hidden destruction; secret sin; deception; demons; unclean spirits.
Psalm 11:3, Haggai 1:6.
Moth = An insect of darkness; loss through deceit; secret or undetected trouble; rotten; corruption; riches eaten up; destruction; chastisement.
Hosea 5:12, Job 13:28, Isaiah 50:9, Isaiah 51:8, Matthew 6:19-20, James 5:2,
Job 4:19, Psalm 39:11.
Butterfly = Freedom; new believer; new creation; beauty; fragile flighty or flitting about; temporary glory.
2 Corinthians 5:17, John 3:3, 1 Peter 1:23-25, Isaiah 41:14, & 16 (See with Genesis 32:28).

Insurance - Faith; protection; prepared; safe; covered; Holy Spirit; salvation.
2 Samuel 22:3; 2 Corinthians 1:22, Ephesians 1:13-14, 2 Corinthians 5:1-3.

IPod - Recorded music; record of memories; praise and worship; celebration; reliving past memories.
Mark 14:72, Luke 15:25.
    Listening to Music on an IPod = Reliving memories of praise and worship; reliving time when music was played.

Iron - Strength; powerful; invincible; stronghold; stubborn; judgement from sin

Daniel 2:40a, Isaiah 48:4, Deuteronomy 28:48, Daniel 4:15.
Broken Iron Bars = Deliverance; broken limitations.
Isaiah 45:2, Psalm 107:16.

Ironing - Correction; God's discipline; pressure; repentance; sanctification; exhortation; reconciliation.
Ephesians 5:27.

Island - Something related to the Island; what the Island is known for or its name. See Nation.
Revelation 1:9, Acts 13:6, Acts 28:11, Isaiah 23:2-6.

Israel - Jewish people; God's chosen people; remnant; persecuted; wrestles with God; shrewd business dealings. See Jerusalem, Krav Maga.
Genesis 12:1-3, Genesis 22:17-18, Numbers 6:22-27, Exodus 3:9-15, Isaiah 12:2-6, 2 Chronicles 6:5-6, Luke 1: 68-75, Genesis 32:24-28.

Jackass - Obnoxious; self-willed; bragging, if braying; stubborn; unyielding; tenacious.
Proverbs 26:3, Numbers 22:25, 2 Peter 2:16.
 Mule = Stubborn; self-willed; rebellious; tenacious; strong; unbelief.
 Psalm 32:9, Zechariah 7:11.

Jack-O-Lantern - Witchcraft; deception; snare; appeasement; trickery.
2 Kings 21: 7, 2 Chronicles 33: 7, Isaiah 8:19-20, Judges 18:17-20, Acts 8:9-11.

Halloween = A satanic holiday; a high offering day for witches, sorcerers, occultists and Satanists, to demonic spirits; a celebration of death.
Deuteronomy 18:10-12, 2 Kings 21:6-7, 2 Chronicles 33:6-7, Micah 5:12, Acts 8:9-11, Isaiah 8:19-20, Mark 12:26-27.

Jail - Bondage; rebellion; strong emotion; addiction; sin; persecution.
Luke 4:18, Hebrews 2:15, 2 Peter 2:14, 2 Timothy 2:25-26, Jeremiah 38:6, Zechariah 9:12a. See Cage.
Prisoners = Lost Souls; stubborn; sinners; persecuted saints.
Luke 4:18, Hebrews 2:15, 2 Peter 2:14, 2 Timothy 2:25-26, Jeremiah 38:6, Zechariah 9:12a.
Death Row = Death sentence; cursed; judgement; certain death of something if unrepentant; in need of the Lord's intervention.
Genesis 20:3, Ezekiel 33:14, Luke 13:3-5.
Broken Iron Bars = Deliverance; broken limitations.
Isaiah 45:2, Psalm 107:16.

Jam - Sticky situation; trouble; tight spot.
Job 3:26.

Jell-O - Unstable; shaky; fearful; trembles.
Genesis 49:4, James 1:6-8, 2 Peter 2:14, 2 Peter 3:16.

Jet - Ministry or Minister; powerful, fast, effective. See Airplane.
Genesis 41:43, 2 Kings 10:16.

Jerusalem - Establishment of peace; chosen place by God; the city of God. See Israel.
Genesis 14:18, Psalm 76:2, Hebrews 7:1-2, 2 Chronicles 6:6, Zechariah 8:3, Revelation 3:12, Revelation 21:2.

Jewelry - Treasure; precious; God's gifts; desire; idolatry; self-glorification; pride; not to be given to those who won't value it.
Matthew 13:44-46, Proverbs 8:11, Job 28:15-19, Proverbs 17:8, Isaiah 3:16-22, James 2:2, Proverbs 11:22, Matthew 7:6.

Jewels - People of God; precious person; gifted person; knowledge; truth.
Malachi 3:16-18, Proverbs 20:15.

Jigsaw Puzzle - Riddle; parable; mystery; the body of Christ.
Numbers 12:8, Ezekiel 17:2, Judges 14:12-19, 1 Corinthians 13:12, Hosea 12:10, 1 Corinthians 14:2, 1 Corinthians 12:12-28, Ephesians 4:16, Colossians 2:19.
Puzzle Pieces = Individual members of the body of Christ; individuals' purposes; innovation; a collective idea.
1 Corinthians 12:12-28, Psalm 139:15-16, Romans 12:4-11.
Puzzle Pieces Joined Together = Working together in unity; edifying one another.
Ephesians 4:16, Colossians 2:19, Romans 12:4-11.
Putting Puzzle Pieces together = Alignment of the Body of Christ; problem solving; bringing together new solutions or ideas.
Scattered Puzzle Pieces = Disunity; working in one's own strength; independent spirit; one one's own; vulnerable; unprotected; unfruitful.
Amos 3:3, Ecclesiastes 4:9-12, Psalm 119:176, Luke 10:1.
Breaking apart Puzzle Pieces = Destroying what God has put together.
Putting Back Together according to one's own Preference = Taking things into one's own hands; partiality; acting out in presumption.
Light or Colorful Puzzle = Heavenly realm; spiritual angelic atmosphere.

Shady or Dark Color Puzzle = Earthly realm; physical human atmosphere; demonic realm.
Two Puzzles, One Light and One Dark = Duality of the heavenly, angelic realm and the earthly physical human realm.

Jogging - Striving; working out one's salvation; faith; trial. 1 Corinthians 9:24-27, Jeremiah 12:5.

Joint - Difficult to separate, except by the word of God. Hebrews 4:12.

Joker - Mocker; foolish person. See Clown. Proverbs 14:9.

Journal - A record of life; records of encounters with God; a record of God's righteous dealings on one's behalf; recorded thoughts of God's power, omniscience, justice, goodness, mercy, peace and truth.
Malachi 3:16, Job 19:23-25, Psalm 56:8.

Judge - Authority; God; conscience; See Courthouse, Lawyer. Psalm 75:7, James 5:9, 1 Corinthians 11:31.
Fair and Just Judge = Rule of God.
Unjust Judge = Prejudiced; verdict already decided before hearing the defence.
Proverbs 18:13, John 7:51, Luke 18:2-6.
Evil Judge = Satan; evil authority.
Psalm 94:20, Matthew 5:25-26, Luke 12:58-59.
Before an Unfair or Evil Judge = Evil powers' influence over one's situation.

Judo - Spiritual warfare; deliverance ministry; self-defence. Ephesians 6:12, 1 Timothy 6:12.

Junkyard - Ruined; waste; wrecked; lost souls; the lost world; corruption; destruction. See Garbage Dump.
Psalm 9:17, Proverbs 9:18, Isaiah 5:14.
Vehicle in Junkyard = Abandoned ministries; ministries need repair.

Junior High School - Medium level of equipping; foundational level in Christianity; ready for discipleship; intermediate stage of situation.
Luke 2:46-52.

Juniper Tree - One who provides just enough shade, or rest from the desert experience. See Trees.
1 Kings 19:4-5.

Kangaroo - Predisposition; prejudiced; based on lies; to rush to a conclusion; Australia.
Proverbs 18:13, Deuteronomy 13:14, Daniel 6:9-14.
Kangaroo Court = Prejudiced; verdict already decided before hearing the defence.
Proverbs 18:13, John 7:51.
Before a Kangaroo Court = Unfair judgement at hand or imminent.

Karate - Spiritual warfare; deliverance ministry; self-defence.
Ephesians 6:12, 1 Timothy 6:12.

Keys - Authority; power to bind or loose; lock or unlock; wisdom; knowledge; important. See Vehicle, House.
Matthew 16:19, Isaiah 22:22, Revelation 3:7, Luke 11:52, Proverbs 4:7.

To be Given Keys = Given power and authority.
Isaiah 22:22.
To Lose One's Keys = Lose the power and authority one was given.

Kick - Rebel; resist; persecute; driven.
Acts 9:5, Acts 26:14.

Kicking Lifting Heel - Threatening; betrayal; rebellion; persecution.
Psalm 41:9, John13:18, Acts 9:5, Acts 26:14.

Kid(s) - Similar characteristics or behavior of oneself; someone they remind the dreamer of; innocence; purity; humble; trusting; new believer; immaturity; undisciplined; disobedient.
Ezekiel 16:44, Isaiah 3:4, & 12a, Matthew 18:3-6, 1 John 2:12-14, 1 Corinthians 13:11, Hebrews 12:8, Ephesians 5:6, Colossians 3:6.
Many Kids = Future children of God; the church.
Jeremiah 31:17, John 1:12.

Killing or Murder - Operating under spirit of death, anger, hatred and rage.
Genesis 4:8, Psalm 10:8, Psalm 94:6, Jeremiah 7:9, Hosea 6:9, Matthew 5:21-22.

Kind Stranger - Jesus; a minister of mercy; helper, angel.
John 20:14, Luke 24:15-16, John 21:4, Matthew 2:13, Luke 10:33, Hebrews 13:2.

King - Jesus; dominion; authority; ruler; power.
Revelation 1:5-6, Revelation 19:16, Proverbs 8:15-16, Daniel 7:14, Isaiah 33:22, Psalm 72:1-2, & 7-11, Psalm 20:9, Genesis Chapter 14, Psalm 2:1-12, Daniel 2:21, Daniel 5:18-23.

King of Sodom = Principality; against the king of Salem, peace; enemy of the Prince of Peace.
Genesis 14:17-24, Psalm 110:2-6, Ephesians 6:12.
Prime Minister = Christ Jesus; a senior minister; literal Prime Minister.
Hebrews 3:1-5, 1 Timothy 1:12, Acts 20:28, 1 Peter 5:1-4, 1 Timothy 2:1-2, Romans 13:1-7, 1 Peter 2:13-17.
President = Christ Jesus; literal President; head of a company.
Psalm 45:1-17, Romans 13:1-7, 1 Timothy 2:1-2, 1 Peter 2:13-17.

Kiss - Agreement; covenant; enticement; seduction; betrayal; deception; friend.
Psalm 2:12, 2 Samuel 20:9-10, Proverbs 7:10-13, Luke 22:48, Proverbs 27:6.
To be Kissed = Agreement; romance; enticement.

Kitchen - Heart; intent; motive; plans; preparation; hunger for the word of God; nourishment; passion; ambition; affliction.
Hosea 7:6, Psalm 139:2, Jeremiah 17:10, Hebrews 4:12.
    Refrigerator = Heart; motive; attitude; thoughts.
Matthew 12:35, Mark 7:21-22.
        Stored Food = Memories.
        Spoiled Food = Harboring a grudge; unclean thoughts.
Freezer = Stores spiritual food for the future; preservation of life.
Psalm 12:6-7, Genesis 45:5-7, Psalm 31:23, Psalm 37:28, Psalm 121:8, Psalm 145:20, Psalm 116:6, John 10:28-30, 2 Timothy 4:18, 1 Thessalonians 5:23.
        Discover Food in the Freezer = Recovery of the reward of one's labor.
        Spoiled Food in the Freezer = Must leave past hurts and losses behind.

Microwave Oven = Instant; quick work; sudden; impatient; convenience; easy option.
Romans 9:28.
Oven = Heart; intense; fervency; passion; meditation; imagination; judgement.
Hosea 7:4-7, 1 Corinthians 7:9, Psalm 21:9.
Baker = Instigator; one who originates sin; anger; mischief in one's heart; Satan; minister; self.
Hosea 7:4-7, Genesis 40:1-2, & 16-19.

Kitten - Precious gift; helpless; must be attended to.
1 Corinthians 12:4, 1 Timothy 4:14.

Knees - Reverence; honor; humility; service; supplication; prayer; submission; growth in the faith.
Psalm 95:6, Isaiah 45:23, Romans 14:11, Philippians 2:10, Romans 11:4, Ephesians 3:14, Ezekiel 47:4.
Kneeling = Surrender; praying; serving; submitting.
John 13:5, 1 Kings 8:54, Daniel 6:10, Luke 22:41, Acts 21:5.
Weak Knees = Waver; bereavement; faint; illness.
Job 4:4, Psalm 109:24, Isaiah 35:3, Hebrews 12:12.
Shaking Knees = Fear; terror.
Daniel 5:6, Nahum 2:10.

Knife - Words; revelation; truth; sharp, angry rebuke; accusations; gossip. See Sword, Machete; Arrows.
Acts 7:54, Psalm 52:2, Titus 1:13.
Pocket Knife = Personal revelation of practical use.
To be Pursued with a Knife = Being chased by the word of God; being chased by false accusations.
To be Stabbed = Attacking words; accusation.
Stabbed in the Back = Betrayal; slander.

Krav Maga - Severe spiritual warfare; powerful deliverance ministry; spiritual combat; self-defence; originated from the IDF.
Ephesians 6:12, 1 Timothy 6:12, 2 Corinthians 10:3-6.

L

Ladder - Change in spiritual position; entrance; way of escape.
Genesis 28:12-13, John 3:13, Romans 10:6-7.
Finding it Hard to Climb a Ladder = Struggles in the spirit realm.
Fireman's Ladder = Rescue; help.
Psalm 27:10.
Climbing a Ladder = Going higher in the Spirit; taking steps to a promotion.
Psalm 24:3.
Angels on the Ladder = Divine messengers bring blessings down from heaven; divine messengers take prayers up to heaven.
Genesis 28:12-13, John 1:51.

Lamb - Humility; gentleness; traceableness; the Church; Christ; blamelessness; sacrifice; trusting; vulnerable.
Revelation 5:12, John 1:29, 1 Corinthians 5:7, Genesis 22:7-8, Luke 10:3.
Sheep = Innocent; saints; unsaved persons.
Matthew 10:16, Psalm 44:11, 2 Samuel 24:17, Matthew 25:33, Isaiah 53:6, Matthew 10:6, Luke 15:3-7.

Lamp - Manifest; revealed; illuminated; knowledge of the word; exposed.
Psalm 27:1, Psalm 119:105, John 8:12, John 3:19-21, Ephesians 5:13.

Small Lamp = Personal knowledge or understanding; guidance.
Psalm 119:105, Ephesians 5:13, John 3:21.
Dim Lamp = Without full understanding or manifestation; partial knowledge of the word.
Lamp Turned Off = Hidden; without understanding or manifestation; without knowledge of the word.
John 3:19-20, Romans 1:21, Ephesians 4:18, Ephesians 5:11-14, Job 18:6, Isaiah 8:20.

Lampstand - See Candlestick.

Large Vehicle - Large ministry or church; influence large people groups; clunky and burdensome; costly to power; prideful. See Vehicle or Truck.

Las Vegas - Gambling; prostitution; sin; lust; debauchery.
Jude 1:7.

Lawnmower - Source of discipline; to bring to obedience; to chastise; source of illness; source of financial loss; to depress; source of anguish.
Amos 7:1-2, Psalm 37:2, Psalm 72:6, 1 Corinthians 11:27-32.

Lawyer - Advocate; Christ; a legalistic minister. See Courthouse.
1 John 2:1, Luke 11:46, Revelation 12:10.
   Evil Lawyer = Devil's advocate; the accuser of the brethren. Revelation 12:10.

Lead - Weight; wickedness; sin; burden (cares of the world); judgment; fool, foolishness.
Zechariah 5:8, Exodus 15:10, Proverbs 27:3, Hebrews 12:1.

Leather - Covering; the Lord's glory, salvation, protection. See Coat, Clothing.
Genesis 3:21, Isaiah 61:10, 2 Corinthians 5:2-4, Romans 13:14.

Leaven - Religious doctrine; imposed legalism; hypocrisy; pride; sin; corruption; the kingdom of heaven.
Matthew 16:12 (See with Matthew 23:13-28), Luke 12:1, Mark 8:15, 1 Corinthians 5:6-8, Galatians 5:9, Matthew 13:33, Luke 13:20-21.

Leaves - First manifestation; medicine; healing; self justification; temporary.
Psalm 1:3, Jeremiah 17:8, Ezekiel 47:12, Revelation 22:2, Genesis 3:7, Isaiah 1:30, Jeremiah 8:13, Isaiah 64:6.
  Fig Leaves =Self-atonement; self-made covering; profession of religion but bearing no fruit; broken promise of fruit (figs come before the leaves); barren.
  Genesis 3:7, Matthew 21:19.

Leech - Sucks the life out of another; a sponge; soaks up others' resources and strength; insatiable appetite to steal the life of others. See Insects.
Proverbs 30:15 See with Habakkuk 2:5, Proverbs 27:20.

Left - Spiritual; weakness (of man), and therefore God's strength or ability demonstrated through man's weakness; rejection.
2 Corinthians 12:9a, & 10b, Judges 3:20-21, Judges 20:16, Matthew 24:32-33.

Left Turn - Spiritual change.

Legs - Man's walk; man's strength; support; spirit of man. See Run, Marching.

Psalm 147:10, Song of Solomon 5:15, Proverbs 26:7, Proverbs 18:14.

Female Legs = Seduction.

One Leg In = Indecision; wanting the best of both worlds; not firm; greed.

Lemon – Something gone sour; bitter doctrine; hard to accept teaching; bad deal; problems.

Hosea 4:18, Acts 8:23, Job 20:14, Matthew 27:34.

Vehicle Breakdowns (a Lemon) - Problems; sicknesses; spirit of poverty; demonic attacks; hindrances to one's life, ministry, career, livelihood.

1 Thessalonians 2:18, Acts 16:6-7.

Leopard - Powerful leader, good or evil; predator; permanent; unchanging evil person; danger. See Lion.

Jeremiah 5:6, Jeremiah 13:23.

Fangs = Evil intent or motive: danger.

Psalm 57:4, Psalm 58:6, Proverbs 30:14, Daniel 7:5-7, Revelation 9:8.

Letter - Important message from God; prophecy; personal instructions.

Job 33:14-16, Deuteronomy 29:29.

Envelope = Important message from God; prophecy; personal instructions.

Job 33:14-16, Deuteronomy 29:29.

Sealed = Prophecy un-interpreted; message or instruction not revealed.

Daniel 8:26, Daniel 9:24, Daniel 12:4, & 9.

Opened = Prophecy interpreted; message or instruction revealed.

Revelation 22:10.

Postage Stamp = Seal; authority; authorisation; empowerment; small but powerful. Esther 8:8, 2 Timothy 2:19.

Leviathan - Satan; high level demonic spirit against the Government of God; global level of wickedness; division; confusion; twists the Word of God, and the words of spiritual leaders; causes miscommunications between believers; instigator of overwhelming situations or tribulation; extremely strategic level of spiritual warfare needed. See Snake. Isaiah 27:1-3, Psalm 74:13-14, Ezekiel 29:3, Ezekiel 32:2, Job Chapter 41, Ephesians 6:12, & 16, Genesis 3:1, Matthew 4:6, Romans 8:35-39, Matthew 24:6-13, Revelation 20:2.

Liberty Bell(s) - Announcement of physical and spiritual freedom; Salvation; deliverance; healing; freedom in Christ; new day or era on the horizon; approaching jubilee. 2 Corinthians 3:17, Isaiah 61:1, Luke 4:18-19.

Library - Knowledge; education; intellectualism; learning; research; distraction, when noisy. See Book, Noise. 2 Timothy 2:15, Ecclesiastes 12:12.
> **Going to a Library** = Coming to a season of knowledge; inquisitiveness.
> **Finding a Book at a Library** = Knowledge becoming available.
> **Not Finding the Required Book** = Not correctly positioned to obtain the required knowledge.

Lice - Condemnation; accusation; shame; smear campaign; guilt; affliction. Exodus 8:16-17, John 8:6, & 9.
> **Lice on the Head of a Person** = Pathological liar; untrustworthy.

Lifted Hands - Worship; surrender; prayer. See Hand.
Psalm 28:2, 1 Kings 8:22, 1 Timothy 2:8.

Light - Manifest; revealed; illuminated; knowledge of the word; exposed.
Psalm 27:1, Psalm 119:105, John 8:12, John 3:19-21, Ephesians 5:13.
　　Candle = Word of God; Jesus; spirit of man.
　　Zephaniah 1:12, Psalm 132 :17, 2 Samuel 22:29, Psalm 18:28, Job 29:3, Proverbs 20:27, Matthew 25:1-12, Proverbs 13:9.
　　Unlit Candle = Lack of God's presence; the wicked; unbeliever.
　　Matthew 25:8, Proverbs 20:20, Proverbs 24:20, Job 18:5-6, Job 21:17.
　　Small Lamp or Flashlight = Personal knowledge or understanding; guidance.
　　Psalm 119:105, Ephesians 5:13, John 3:21.
　　Dim Light = Without full understanding or manifestation; partial knowledge of the word.
　　Light Turned Off = Hidden; without understanding or manifestation; without knowledge of the word.
　　John 3:19-20, Romans 1:21, Ephesians 4:18, Ephesians 5:11-14, Job 18:6, Isaiah 8:20.

Lighthouse - Spiritual guidance or light; keeps one from danger.
Psalm 27:1, Psalm 84:11, Isaiah 60:1-3.

Lightning - Power; God's voice; instantaneous miracle; enlightenment through His sent ones; judgment; instantaneous destruction; swift intervention.
Isaiah 30:30, Psalm 144:6, Job 36:32, Luke 10:17-18, Psalm 97:4, Psalm 77:18, Zechariah 9:14, 2 Samuel 22:14-15, Psalm 18:13-14.

Lily - Death; funeral; mourning.
Song of Solomon 2:1.

Limousine - High call of God; pride; exhibitionism.
Philippians 3:14, Hebrews 3:1, 1 Corinthians 10:12, 1 Corinthians 4:6-8, Esther 6:6-12.

Lion - Dominion; Christ; king; regal; bold; power; strength; conqueror; lust; fornication; Satan; religious tradition; powerful destroying spirit. See Leopard.
Revelation 5:5, Proverbs 30:30, Proverbs 28:1, 1 Peter 5:8, Colossians 2:8.
Fangs = Evil intent or motive: danger.
Psalm 57:4, Psalm 58:6, Proverbs 30:14, Daniel 7:5-7, Revelation 9:8.
Head of a Lion without a Body = Jesus Christ.
Lion Cubs = Christians.

Lips - Words; word of God; testifying; speech; falsehood; accusation; seduction.
Proverbs 8:6-8, Job 33:3, Proverbs 10:19, Proverbs 7:21.

Liquor, Strong Drink or Wine - Intoxicated emotions; spiritual dissipation; toxic; spirit of man; counterfeit spirit; witchcraft; delusion; mocker; spirit of joy; Spirit of God; revelation; teaching truth; blessing.
Ephesians 5:18, Proverbs 31:6, Deuteronomy 32:32, Proverbs 4:17, Acts 2:13-17, Proverbs 20:1, Luke 5:37-38, 1 Corinthians 10:16, Titus 2:3, Deuteronomy 11:14.
Wineskins = Human body as a vessel; the church; believers.
Luke 5:37-38.
Winepress = True doctrine; spiritual birthplace.
Matthew 21:33, Isaiah 5:1-2, Mark 12:1.

Drink Wine in Moderation = Representative of healing in certain circumstances; giving into temptation if one had a previous bondage.
1 Timothy 5:23, Proverbs 23:29-32.
Drinking Wine with Another = Representative of communion; spiritual fellowship.
1 Corinthians 10:16.

Living Room - Revealed; personality; everyday or current affairs; that which is manifest; truth exposed; without hypocrisy; family; relational; fellowship; community.
Mark 2:4-5.
Stains on the Walls = Impure personality issues.
Repainting the Walls = Rebuilding public image.

Loch Ness Monster - Leviathan spirit; Satan; world power; extremely strategic level of spiritual warfare needed. See Snake.
Isaiah 27:1, Job 26:13, Psalm 74:13-14, Isaiah 51:9, Revelation 12:3-17, Ezekiel 29:3.

Lock Washer - Secure; unmovable; unyielding.
Nuts and Bolts = Essential; the bottom line; indispensible; wisdom; to fasten.
Proverbs 4:7.

Locusts - Judgement; famine; death; devourer; pestilence; plague; demonic spirits; oppressive multitude; invades their enemy in military order (like a swarm of locusts); weak when alone; flighty; restoration possible. See Grasshoppers.
Exodus 10:4-6, 14-15, &17-19, Deuteronomy 28:38, & 42, 2 Chronicles 7:13, 1 Kings 8:37, Psalm 78:46, Psalm 105:34-35; Joel 1:4, Revelation 9:3-10, Psalm 109:22-24, Joel 2:7-9, Nahum 3:15-17, Joel 2:25.

Lost - Truth lost through tradition; gift lost through neglect; soul lost through sin. See Found.
Colossians 2:8, John 6:12.

>   **Lost in Finding a Destination, Directions** = Inner confusion; lack of guidance, bad directions; directions twisted by the enemy; misinterpretation of a prophetic word, resulting in misapplication or wrong timing; indecision.
>   Psalm 119:176, Ezekiel 34:16, Micah 4:6.
>
>   **Found what was Lost** = Understanding; revelation; knowledge; sound direction; proper application and timing of a prophetic word; decisive; gift of God.
>   Jeremiah 15:16, Ezekiel 3:1-3, Luke 15:4-10.

Lumber - Life; humanity; spiritual building material; temporary; flesh; carnal. See Trees.
Jeremiah 5:14, Proverbs 26:20-21, 1 Corinthians 3:12.

M

Machete - Slicing words; sharp rebuke; harsh accusations; gossip; clears a path for the righteous.
Acts 7:54, Psalm 52:2, Titus 1:13, Isaiah 41:15, Habakkuk 3:12.

>   **To be Pursued with a Machete** = Being chased by false accusations.
>   **To be Wounded by a Machete** = Harsh attacking words; sharp accusation.
>   **Attacked from Behind** = Betrayal; slander.

Machine(s) - Power of God for the work of God; productive; motion. See Factory.
Ecclesiastes 7:29, Romans 7:5-6.

Idle Machine = Unproductive; motionless.

Maggot - Corruption; filthiness of the flesh; despised; decay; evil; death; judgement; rotten motives. See Insects.
Job 17:14, Psalm 22:6, Exodus 16:20, Acts 12:23, Deuteronomy 28:39, Job 24:20.

Male Deer - Regal; rule; authority; strength; power.
Psalm 42:1-2, Song of Solomon 2:9, & 17, Song of Solomon 8:14, Isaiah 35:6.
Deer = Graceful; divine enabling, swift; sure-footed; agile; spiritual longing; provision; timid; skittish.
2 Samuel 22:34, Psalm 18:33, Habakkuk 3:19, Psalm 42:1-2.

Man (Unknown) - Angel, oneself, or a demon: God's messenger; Jesus; person with evil intent; danger.
Matthew 2:13, Hebrews 13:2, Job 4:13-16, Luke 10:33, John 20:14, Luke 24:15-16, John 21:4, John 10:5.

Manna - God's miraculous provision; glory of God; bread of life; spiritual nourishment direct from God; angel's food.
Exodus 16:4-15, John 6:31-35, & 48-51, 1 Kings 19:5-8.

Map - Seeking directions; word of God; correction; advice; Holy Spirit guidance; seeking progress; territory.
Jeremiah 6:16, Psalm 119:105, Proverbs 6:23; Jeremiah 21:8, John 16:13, Deuteronomy 11:24-25, Joshua 1:3-4, Joshua 14:9.

Marble - Strong; beautiful; precious; majesty of God.
1 Chronicles 29:2, Ezra 5: 8, Ezra 6:4, Esther 1:6, Revelation 18:12, 1 Corinthians 3:12, Song of Solomon 5:15.

Mark - Distinguishing symbol; set apart; mark of God; mark of the devil.
Genesis 4:15, Ezekiel 9:4, 2 Timothy 2:19, Revelation 7:2-3, Revelation 14:1, Revelation 20:4, Revelation 13:16-17.

Marching - Relentless pursuing all in rank and file, in precise order. See Legs.
Joel 2:7.

Marriage - Covenant; the Church as the Bride of Christ; agreement; joined; natural marriage. See Bride, Groom.
Ephesians 5:31-32, see Nehemiah 13:27 with Exodus 23:32 and 2 Corinthians 6:14.
Getting Married = Going higher with Jesus.
Issues Arising during Marriage = Hindrances coming against one's effort to go higher with Jesus.
Soiled Marriage Clothes = Life issues hindering the ability of intimacy with Jesus.
Sexual Intimacy = One in agreement.
Interruption of Intimacy = Interference or trouble in the marriage or covenant relationship.

Marsh - Stagnant in the flow of the Holy Spirit; illness; blocked flow due to neglect or perversion of the gospel; rejection of the gospel; bitter; spiritually dead.
Ezekiel 47:11, Exodus 15:23, Mark 12:1-12, Isaiah 42:15, Isaiah 50:2, Psalm 107:33-35.

Martial Arts - Spiritual warfare; deliverance ministry; self-defence.
Ephesians 6:12, 1 Timothy 6:12.

Mask - Hypocrisy; falsehood; deception; hiding one's true identity; two-faced.
Matthew 23:27, Genesis 38:14-16, Psalm 10:11, Galatians 2:11-12.

Costume = Change of one's appearance; wanting to be someone else; hiding true identity; to feel the need to be someone else; false Christian.
1 Samuel 21:13, Romans 7:18-19, Genesis 27:15-16, Proverbs 6:19, Galatians 2:4.

Maze - Trying to find one's way through a complicated situation; complicated assignment, needing God's constant direction; crooked ways in need of straightening out; wicked; perverse; close walk with God to make it through.
Exodus 33:13, Luke 3:4-5, Hebrews 12:13, Jeremiah 10:23, Proverbs 20:24.

Lost = Truth lost through tradition; gift lost through neglect; soul lost through sin.
Colossians 2:8, John 6:12.

Lost in Finding a Destination, Directions = Inner confusion; lack of guidance, bad directions; directions twisted by the enemy; misinterpretation of a prophetic word, resulting in misapplication or wrong timing; indecision.
Psalm 119:176, Ezekiel 34:16, Micah 4:6.

Found what was Lost = Understanding; revelation; knowledge; sound direction; proper application and timing of a prophetic word; decisive; gift of God.
Jeremiah 15:16, Ezekiel 3:1-3, Luke 15:4-10.

Measure or Measuring - Determining one's faith and growth; time; distance; decision; precision; reciprocity; judgement; the heart receiving by hearing.

Romans 12:3, Ephesians 4:13, Psalm 39:4, Joshua 3:4, Deuteronomy 21:2, Job 28:25, Isaiah 40:12, Luke 6:38, Matthew 7:1-2, Isaiah 65:7, Daniel 5:27, Mark 4:24.

Tape Measure = Measure for service; boundaries of one's service; fitting preparation; preparation for expansion; change of heart to enter in.
Ephesians 4:13-16, 2 Corinthians 10:12-16, 1 Samuel 2:19, Isaiah 54:2, Mark 12:34.

Precise Measurement = Diligent study of the Word; possible confirmation of a future event.
2 Timothy 2:15, Zechariah 2:1-5, Ezekiel 40:2-4.

Balances = Justice; judgement; business; falsehood; deceitful; divide; purchase; integrity; make judgement before hearing the matter; vanity. See Business, Merchant.
Proverbs 16:11, Ezekiel 45:10-12, Daniel 5:27, Proverbs 20:23, Proverbs 11:1, Deuteronomy 25:13-15, Leviticus 19:35-36, Hosea 12:7, Micah 6:10-11, Ezekiel 5:1, Jeremiah 32:9-10, Job 31:6, Job 6:2, Proverbs 18:13, John 7:51, Psalm 62:9.

Measuring of Oneself = Pondering truth; considering one's ways; looking at one's progress of ridding oneself of sins; natural concern for health; obsession of appearance.
2 Timothy 2:15, 1 Corinthians 14:29, 1 Thessalonians 5:21, Hebrews 12:1-3, 2 Corinthians 10:7, 12, & 17, 1 Corinthians 1:26-31, 1 John 2:16.

Meat - Solid food; work of God; spiritually mature; strong doctrine.
Hebrews 5:12-14, Job 12:11, John 4:32-34, John 6:27-29, & 52-56, 1 Corinthians 10:3, 1 Corinthians 3:2.

Chewing Meat = Meditating; gaining understanding; deep things of God.
1 Timothy 4:15-16, Psalm 119:97-100.

Hard to Chew Meat = Doctrine difficult to understand.
2 Peter 3:16.
Rotten Meat = Harboring a grudge; unclean thoughts or desires.
Mark 7:21-22.
Blood of Meat = Life of the flesh; covenant; murder; defiled; unclean; pollution; purging; testimony; witness; guilt.
Leviticus 17:11, Deuteronomy 27:25, Psalm 106:38, Ezekiel 33:8.

Mechanic - Minister; Christ; prophet; pastor; counsellor; need for adjustment in theology, attitude, relationship.
Exodus 31:3-4, 2 Timothy 3:16.
Mechanic's Tools = Word of God: Gifts of the Spirit; wisdom; knowledge.

Medicine / Drugs - Regulate body systems; relief of symptoms; healing; influence; spell; sorcery; witchcraft; control.
Revelation 22:2, Ezekiel 47:12, Galatians 5:20-21, Acts 8:9-11, Acts 13:6-8, Deuteronomy 18:10-11, Galatians 3:1.

Menorah - Light bearer. See Candlestick.

Merchant - Trading; Traffic; gain; wealth; tribute; barter; export; worldly business; demonically influenced; demonic oppression; sale of indulgences; judgement; covenant breaker; filthy lucre at the expense of the Lords' business. For normal business practices, see Business, Balances.
Ezekiel 27:12-24, Revelation 18:11-19, 2 Peter 2:3, Ezekiel 28:5, & 14-16 (See with Psalm 89:39), John 2:16 (The sellers, admitted by the chief priests, into the Gentile court, distracted the Gentiles in their worship, or coming to God, for money; the sellers' rents, no doubt, being a considerable revenue).

Mice or Mouse - Curse; judgement; plague; unclean; hidden; small; insignificant; timid.
1 Samuel 6:4-5, Leviticus 11:29, Isaiah 66:17 (See with Ezekiel 8:10-12); Malachi 3:11a, Judges 6:15, 2 Timothy 1:7.

Microphone - Voice; authority; preaching anointing; prophetic ministry; ability to influence many people.
Matthew 10:27, Acts 5:20.
Using a Microphone = Supernatural ability to influence people.
Using a Faulty Microphone = Not having the influence or anointing to impart message.

Microscope - Close examination; self-examination; careful observation; discernment.
1 Corinthians 11:28, 2 Corinthians 13:5, Psalm 26:2.
Presence of a Microscope = The dreamer is being scrutinized; scrutinising imminent.
Using a Microscope = Process of verification; concerned about the details.

Microwave Oven - Instant; quick work; sudden; impatient; convenience; easy option.
Romans 9:28. See Kitchen.

Middle School - Medium level of equipping; foundational level in Christianity; ready for discipleship; intermediate stage of situation.
Luke 2:46-52.

Midget - Made small by comparison.
Psalm 119:141, Numbers 13:33, 1 Samuel 17:42.

Military Self-defence - Severe spiritual warfare; powerful deliverance ministry; spiritual combat; self-defence. Ephesians 6:12, 1 Timothy 6:12, 2 Corinthians 10:3-6.

Milk - Word of God; foundational truth, elementary teaching. See Food, Eating.
1 Peter 2:2, Hebrews 5:12-13, Exodus 23:19.

Minister - Showing or confirming a calling as to the type of ministering shown in the dream; message from God.
Acts 9:1-16, Acts 26:16, Acts 16:9, Galatians 1:15-16, Romans 10:14-15, Jeremiah 1:4-10.

Mirror - God's word; Moses' Law; heart: reflection; memory; past; self-consciousness; vanity; obsession.
1 Corinthians 13:12, 2 Corinthians 3:18, James 1:23-24, Proverbs 27:19, 2 Samuel 14:25, Proverbs 31:30.
Clear Mirror = Word of God bringing clarity on something.
Darkly Stained Mirror = Poor perception; spiritual mysteries; prophetic word not yet fully understood.
1 Corinthians 13:12.
Image in a Mirror not what is Expected = Disparity between reality and perception.
Rear-view Mirror - Looking back; obsessed with the past; lack of forward focus or looking ahead.
Genesis 19:26.

Miscarriage - New ministry destroyed; promise lost or robbed; failure; judgment; injustice (miscarriage of justice); lacking spiritual strength; repentance.
Acts 7:19, Matthew 2:16-18, Hosea 9:11- 16, Job 21:10, Isaiah 59:4, Isaiah 37:3,
Hosea 13:13, 2 Kings 19:1-4. See Baby.
Experiencing a Miscarriage = Termination of ministry, plan or promise; experiencing an injustice.

Premature Delivery = Supernatural intervention; divine acceleration; presumptuous situation running ahead of the scheduled time.

Missile - Powerful ministry; all-powerful word of God; swift progress; spiritual warfare; powerful words of destruction; swift destruction; sudden, unexpected attack, judgement. Psalm 64:7, Hebrews 4:12, Isaiah 55:11, Proverbs 6:15, Proverbs 29:1, Isaiah 54:17, Ezekiel 39:3, 2 Samuel 22:14-15, Psalm 18:13-14.

Money - Wealth; spiritual riches; provision; natural talents and skills; power; strength of man; greed; covetousness. Deuteronomy 8:18, Ecclesiastes 7:12, Matthew 17:27, Luke 16:11, Genesis 31:15, Ezekiel 22:12, 1 Timothy 6:10, James 5:1-4.

Getting Money = Literal financial increase; increase in favor. Matthew 17:27.

Bundle of Money = Season of abundance of money or favor.

International Currency = Privilege or favor from that country.

Short of Money = Season of a lack of money or favor.

Monkey - Foolishness; clinging; mischief; dishonesty; addiction; holds onto security; clings to someone or something trusted and known. Proverbs 27:22, Proverbs 23:35, Mark 7:8, Revelation 12:11(AMP/AMPC), John 20:17 (NKJV, AMP/AMPC), John 17:20 (AMP/AMPC).

Moon - Rules the night, darkness; apostate church; reflects the Sun's light; true church.
Genesis 1:16, 2 Kings 23:5, Jeremiah 8:2, 1 Corinthians 15:41, Isaiah 30:26.
> **Moon in a Dream** = Lordship of God in a dark season; dawn of light in an otherwise dark season.
> **Blood Moon** = Persecution; judgement; a sign.
> Revelation 6:12, Joel 2:30-31, Acts 2:19-20.

Morning - Light of God after a dark season; joy after sorrow and trouble; beginning.
Psalm 30:5, Hosea 6:3, Isaiah 33:2, Psalm 143:8, 2 Samuel 23:4.
> **Morning in a Dream** = Solution coming to the problem; beginning of God's intervention; beginning of a pleasant season.
> Psalm 59:16, 2 Samuel 23:4.

Mosquito - Parasite; evil spirit; unseen attack sapping the life out of another; stealing of finances; irritation. See Insects.
John 12:6, John 10:10, Deuteronomy 25:18, Micah 7:2-3, Matthew 27:6 (See with Exodus 21:30, Leviticus 17:11).

Motel - Church; place for rest in Christ; public gathering; natural place of rest; travel; business travel; adultery; lust; temptation.
Acts 28:15, Luke 10:34, Luke 2:7, Genesis 42:27, Genesis 43:21, Exodus 4:24.

Moth - An insect of darkness; loss through deceit; secret or undetected trouble; rotten; corruption; riches eaten up; destruction; chastisement. See Insects.
Hosea 5:12, Job 13:28, Isaiah 50:9, Isaiah 51:8, Matthew 6:19-20, James 5:2, Job 4:19, Psalm 39:11.

Mother - Church; spiritual or natural mother; Jerusalem; love; kindness; if negative, then legalistic church.
Genesis 3:20, Psalm 87:5-6.
Mother-in-law = A church that is not the dreamer's church; legalistic church; meddler; trouble.

Motor - Power; motive; motivation; anointing.
Acts 10:38.

Motorcycle - Personal ministry; independence; rebellion; selfish; pride; swift progress.
Acts 8:4-7, & 26-39, 1 Corinthians 3:4-5, 1 Corinthians 12:14-16, & 20-21, 1 Samuel 15:23a.
Trail Motor Bike = Independent ministry; pioneering spirit; trail blazer.
2 Samuel 22:34, Psalm 18:33, Habakkuk 3:19.
Keys = Authority; power to bind or loose; lock or unlock; wisdom; knowledge; important.
Matthew 16:19, Isaiah 22:22, Revelation 3:7, Luke 11:52, Proverbs 4:7.
>**To be Given Keys** = Given power and authority.
>Isaiah 22:22.
>**To Lose One's Keys** = Lose the power and authority one was given.

Stalled Motorcycle = Ministry on hold; operation in one's own strength; need to take authority; hindrance by Satan; opposition.
Isaiah 49:2, Exodus 14:13-16, Galatians 5:7-12, Nehemiah 4:1-18, 1 Thessalonians 2:18.
Motorcycle Breakdown = Problem; sickness; spirit of poverty; demonic attack; hindrance to one's life, ministry, career, livelihood.
1 Thessalonians 2:18, Acts 16:6-7.
Motorcycle Crash = Strife; contention; conflict; confrontation; calamity; offense; mistake or sin in ministry;

failure; personal disaster (failed marriage, business venture, ministry, project etc.); end of one phase (for whatever reason unbeknownst to the dreamer).
Nahum 2:3-4, 2 Corinthians 11:25-27, 1 Timothy 1:19-20.

Mouldy Bread - Unfit; tradition; old revelation; stale; defiled.
Joshua 9:5b, Malachi 1:7, 1 Corinthians 5:8, Matthew 15:2-3, & 6, Exodus 16:20.

Mountain - Exalted; Kingdom; authority; rule; dominion; government; dignity; permanence; obstacle; difficulty; challenge. See Hill.
Luke 9:27-35, Matthew 17:20, Revelation 21:10, Zechariah 8:3, Joshua 14:12, Psalm 30:7a, Revelation 6:14, Matthew 21:21.
> **Ascending a Mountain** = Spiritual elevation.
> Psalm 24:3, Isaiah 58:14.
> **Descending a Mountain** = Be watchful to not lose spiritual ground.
> Isaiah 2:11-14, Ezekiel 6:3-4, & 13.
> **The Mountain of the LORD** = The Chief of the Mountains; Mount Zion; the governing mountain above all other mountains and hills; kingdom cultural influence (equity and justice) over the 7 mountains of society.
> Micah 4:1-2, Isaiah 2:2-3, Zechariah 8:3, Amos 4:13, Psalm 2:6.

Movie - Story; one's life (Book of Life); history; legacy; memory; entertainment.
Philippians 4:3, Revelation 3:5, 1 Timothy 6:12, John 21:25 (see with Hebrews Chapter 11), 2 Corinthians 3:1-3, 1 Thessalonians 1:7-9, Romans 1:8, 1 Corinthians 10:6-7, & 11, Revelation 20:12.
> **From 2D to 3D** = Breaking out of the mold; breaking free of restraints; getting out of the box; moving into all the fullness of God.

From SD to HD = Moving to the next level; better clarity; greater influence.

Movie Camera - Focusing; recording; memories; publishing; fame; reliving memories; seeing the promises of God.
Hebrews 12:1-2, Mark 5:20, Mark 7:36, Matthew 26:13, John 21:25, 1 Corinthians 2:9-10.
Movie Camera Operator = Seer; prophet; one with clear focus.
Numbers 24:4, & 16, 2 Samuel 18:24, Acts 10:10-20.

Moving - Spiritual change; emotional change; situational change.
Ezekiel 12:3.

Moving Van - Geographical move, natural or spiritual, (house, area, church, including change of affiliations, denominations); relocation. See Vehicle.
Ezekiel 12:2-3.

Mud - Weakness of man; stuck; those who reject, neglect, or pervert the gospel; backslide into past sins; slander (mudslinging).
Psalm 69:2, Isaiah 57:20, Jeremiah 38:6, &22, Ezekiel 47:11, 2 Peter 2:20-22, Psalm 69:14, Ecclesiastes 7:21-22.

Muddy Road - Man's way; difficulty (caused by weak flesh); not clear; uncertain; offense; lust; passion; strife; sin; temptation.
Psalm 69:2, Isaiah 57:20, Jeremiah 18:15-16.

Muddy or Dirty Water - Corrupted spiritually; causing strife; bitter words; unstable hypocrite; sin; false doctrine; unattractive or too common to the proud.
Ezekiel 32:2, Ezekiel 34:18-19, Isaiah 57:20, Exodus 15:23-24, Job 8:11, 2 Kings 5:12, Ezekiel 47:11.

Mule - Stubborn; self-willed; rebellious; tenacious; strong; unbelief.
Psalm 32:9, Zechariah 7:11.
Donkey = Obnoxious; self-willed; bragging, if braying; stubborn; unyielding; tenacious.
Proverbs 26:3, Numbers 22:25, 2 Peter 2:16.

Murder - Operating under spirit of death, anger, hatred and rage.
Genesis 4:8, Psalm 10:8, Psalm 94:6, Jeremiah 7:9, Hosea 6:9, Matthew 5:21-22.

Mushroom - Sudden growth; unexpected appearance; fragile; deadly poison.
Jonah 4:10, Isaiah 48:3, 2 Kings 4:39-41.

Music - Praise and worship, to God or idols; activity from the heart; message.
2 Chronicles 29:25, Psalm 68:25, Psalm 81:2-3, Psalm 92:3, Ezekiel 33:32, Daniel 3:5.
   Playing Instruments = Ministering in the gifts of the Spirit; prophesying; praising; worshipping.
   Psalm 150:3-5, Psalm 33:2-3, Psalm 149:3.
   Title or Words of the Music = Divine message in the revelation.
   Type of Music = Season of life associated with the song.

Mustard Seed - Faith; sowing by faith; progress of the Gospel; growth of the church; God's promise.
Luke 17:6, Matthew 17:20, Matthew 13:31-32, Mark 4:30-32, Luke 13:19.

Myrtle Tree - The Hebrew name *Hedassah,* is the original name of Esther, therefore, a type of the Christian church or person, lowly, though beautiful, fragrant. See Trees.
Isaiah 55:12-13, Isaiah 41:19.

N

Nail - Permanence; secure; the way Jesus dealt with the sins of humanity; word of God.
Colossians 2:14, Isaiah 41:7, Ecclesiastes 12:11.

Name - Identity; authority; status; reputation.
Philippians 2:9-11, Hebrews 1:4, Isaiah 62:2-4, Genesis 32:28, Revelation 2:17, Revelation 3:12, Hosea 1:9.
> **Called by a Name Different from One's Real Name** = New identity given by God; disparity between reality and perception.
> Isaiah 62:2-4, Genesis 32:28.

Nation or Nationality - That for which the people are generally known; may represent the actual nation in the natural.
1 Kings 9:7.
> **Country** = Offspring; a move to another country; characteristics of the specific country representative to the dreamer; entering our heavenly country.
> Genesis 10:20, & 31, Genesis 12:7a, Genesis 11:1-9, Joshua 1:11, John 3:5, Hebrews 11:14-16. Some examples below:
> > **Israel** = Inventions; innovation; prudent entrepreneurship; humanitarian; chosen; prince of God; warfare. See Krav Maga.
> > Psalm 46:6-11, Genesis 32:24-28, Luke 21:9-10.
> > **Germany** = Industrious; hardworking; world war.

China = Industrious; global economic dominance; power; influence; world dominance; communist; antichrist, the Dragon is China's national symbol; underground church; persecution.
Revelation 16:12-16, Isaiah 49:12, Acts 19:22-31.
France = Romance; tourism; arrogant, surrender.

Native American or Indian - Flesh, the old man; firstborn; chief; fierce; savvy; native.
Colossians 3:9, Genesis 49:3, Acts 15:22.

Near-sightedness - Sees only one's own church or denomination; eyes only on the present rather than on the future; vision too small; limited spiritual insight; lack of foresight; vulnerable to the attacks of the enemy. See Blind.
2 Peter 1:9, Judges 9:36.
> **Squinting** = Straining to see further ahead; hindrance to spiritual insight.
> Mark 8:24, 1 Corinthians 13:9-12.

Neck - Self-willed; stubborn; strong-willed; unbelief; authority; rule.
Jeremiah 17:23, Genesis 41:42-43.
> **Stiff Necked** = Rebellious.
> **Long Neck** = Nosy; inquisitiveness.

Net - Evangelize; ministry; the kingdom of heaven; trap (including the internet); snare; justice; seductive heart; death.
Matthew 4:19, Matthew 9:16, Matthew 23:15, Matthew 13:47, Psalm 140:5, Proverbs 29:5, Psalm 57:6, Psalm 141:9-10, Ecclesiastes 7:26, Ecclesiastes 9:12.
> **Using a Net** = Means of reaching lost souls; something that could ensnare others.
> **Held Back by a Net** = Ensnaring situation.

New - New condition; new way; the old gives way to the new. Hebrews 8:1-13, Hebrews 9:1-28, Hebrews 10:1-20.

New House - New life, (salvation); change; renewal; new move, natural or spiritual. See House, Moving Van. 2 Corinthians 5:1, &17.

News - The Gospel; prophecy; report; important events; making headlines; mass exposure; sudden exposure. Isaiah 61:1, Romans 10:15, Luke 1:19, Luke 2:8-10, Acts 11:20-22, Amos 1:1, John 13:19, John 14:29, Isaiah 52:7, Matthew 24:30, Matthew 26:64, Genesis 45:13, 1 Samuel 4:14, Acts 22:17-18.

News Paper - Proclamation; prophetic utterance; bring something to the public.

Night or Darkness - Ignorance; hidden; unknown course of action; sin; power of evil; stealth (under cover of darkness). John 11:10, John 12:35, 1 Thessalonians 5:7, Luke 22:53, Jude 1:4, Matthew 13:25, Galatians 2:4, 2 Timothy 3:6.

Noise - Disturbance; intrusive irritation; interference; draws attention. Exodus 32:17, Proverbs 21:19, 1 Kings 1:39-41.
    Loud Noise = Alarm; sudden fright.
    Judges 7:20-22.

North - Spiritual; judgment; heaven or heavenly; spiritual warfare (taking your inheritance). Proverbs 25:23, Jeremiah 1:13-14, Deuteronomy 2:3.

Nose - Discernment; offence; pride; relentless; busybody, nosey.
Job 27:3 (KJV), Ezekiel 23:25, Psalm 115:6, Isaiah 37:29, Isaiah 65:5, Job 41:2, 1 Peter 4:15, 2 Thessalonians 3:11, 1 Timothy 5:13.
Big Nose = Great discernment.
Nosebleed = Strife; wounded by strife; weak discernment.
Proverbs 30:33.

Nuclear Bomb - Power; Holy Spirit outpouring; miracle power; sudden destruction; destroying words; ultimate judgement; can have apocalyptic meaning.
Acts 1:8, Acts 2:17 - 19, 2 Peter 3:7, & 10-12, 1 Thessalonians 5:3, Luke 17:27-29, Zechariah 14:12. See Stealth Bomber.

Nudity - Uncovered; fleshly; impure; self-righteousness; self-justification; exhibitionism; exposed; vulnerable; innocent, like a baby.
Revelation 3:17, Revelation 16:15, 1 Samuel 19:24, Genesis 2:25.

Nuts and Bolts - Essential; the bottom line; indispensible; wisdom; to fasten.
Proverbs 4:7.
Lock Washer = Secure; unmovable; unyielding.

Oak Tree - Great strength; durable; righteousness; elder; unmovable; shelter. See Trees.
Amos 2:9, Joshua 24:26, Isaiah 6:13, Ezekiel 6:13, Hosea 4:13.

Ocean - Very large groups, humanity, mission, or travel to distant shores; great anointing; covering of the earth;

innumerable; an awesome amount or expanse; very large move of the Spirit. See Water.
Isaiah 60:5, Psalm 68:22, Isaiah 24:14-15, Psalm 98:7-9, 2 Corinthians 11:25-28, Acts 27:1-44.
On the Ocean = Influencing the nations; imparting great numbers of multitudes.
Acts 27:1-44, 2 Corinthians 11:25-28.

Octopus - Mind control; fleshly control or influence (tentacles "tongue") by words; controlling spirit; soul-tie stronghold (on head); in need of deliverance; need spiritual warfare and prayer coverage. See Eight in Part 2.
Exodus 2:14, Proverbs 6:5, Galatians 2:4, 1 Kings 21:7-10, 2 Corinthians 10:4-5.

Ogopogo - Leviathan spirit; Satan; world power; extremely strategic level of spiritual warfare needed. See Snake.
Isaiah 27:1, Job 26:13, Psalm 74:13-14, Isaiah 51:9, Revelation 12:3-17, Ezekiel 29:3.

Oil - Anointing; Holy Spirit; grace; mercy; medicine; prosperity; smooth, deceptive speech.
Psalm 23:5, Deuteronomy 33:24, Matthew 25:4, James 5:14, Job 29:6, Psalm 55:21, Proverbs 5:3.
   Clean Oil = Holy Spirit anointing; healing.
   James 5:14.
   Oil on the Head = Impartation; confirmation of authority.
   Exodus 29:7, 2 Kings 9:3.
   Oil on the Feet = Prosperity; anointing.
   John 12:3.
   Dirty Oil = Unclean spirit; smooth, deceptive speech; slick; lust; hate.
   Psalm 55:21, Proverbs 5:3.

Old - Past; memories; old ways; the old gives way to the new. Deuteronomy 32:7-8, Psalm 119:52, 2 Corinthians 5:17, Isaiah 43:18-19, Hebrews 8:1-13, Hebrews 9:1-28, Hebrews 10:1-20.

Old House - Past; inheritance; established traditions; grandparent's religion; grandparent's ways; grandparent's temperament. See Grandparents. Genesis 12:1, Jeremiah 6:16, Numbers 17:2-3, Matthew 12:25-30.

Old House in Good Condition = God's ways. Jeremiah 6:16.

Old House in Bad Condition = Generational sins; personal sins; renewal needed. Ezekiel 36:10, 2 Chronicles 10:19.

Old House needing Renovation or Remodelling = Revival needed. 2 Chronicles 30:11-18, Ezekiel 37:23.

Old House Unpainted or Overgrown with Weeds = Untended; ignored. Ecclesiastes 10:18, Ezekiel 36:10, 1 Kings 12:16-20.

Old House beyond Repair, in Ruin = Neglect; unusable; the Lord's intervention needed. Ezekiel 37:11, Matthew 12:25-30.

Basement = Soul; Carnal nature; lust; discouragement; depression; refuge; retreat; hidden; beneath the surface; foundational issues; forgotten; secret sin; bloodline issue; demonic realm. See Foundation. Jeremiah 38:6, Isaiah 24:22.

Valuables in the Basement = Inherited giftedness; great potential yet to be revealed or manifested.

Fault in the Basement = Broken foundation; bloodline issue needing repentance.

Old Man - Wisdom if he is white-headed; wisdom gained from living a long life; weak (from age); carnal, as in put off the old man. See Grey Hair, White Hair.
Job 32:6-7, & 9, Leviticus 19:32, Proverbs 16:31, Romans 6:6.

Olive Tree - Anointing oil; anointing of God; Israel; church; peace. See Trees.
Psalm 52:8, Genesis 8:11, Isaiah 41:19.

Orangutan - Stronghold; defiant; strong man; strength; valiant; affluence; mammon.
1 Samuel 17:4, & 23-25, Matthew 12:29, Luke 11:21-22, 1 Samuel 14:52, Psalm 19:5, 2 Chronicles 9:21, 1 Kings 10:22.

Orchard - Fruit producing; God's farmer; cultivable.
Matthew 7:16-17, 1 Corinthians 3:6-9, John 15:2b.
  Well tended and productive Orchard = Fruitful.
  Matthew 7:16-17, John 15:5.
  Untended or Unproductive Orchard = Unfruitful; needs repentance and sanctification.
  John 15:2, Matthew 7:16-17.

Ostrich - Denial; fear; careless; cruel, hardened heart, lacks wisdom and understanding. See Bird.
Lamentations 4:3, Job 39:13-17.

Oven - Heart; intense; fervency; passion; meditation; imagination; judgement. See Kitchen.
Hosea 7:4-7, 1 Corinthians 7:9, Psalm 21:9.
  Baker = Instigator; one who originates sin; anger; mischief in one's heart; Satan; minister; self.
  Hosea 7:4-7, Genesis 40:1-2, & 16-19.

Overslept - Miss divine appointment; behind schedule; overindulgence; fatigue.
1 Thessalonians 5:6-8, Matthew 26:40-45.

Owl - Circumspect (looking around); wisdom; contemplator; demon; curse; spirit of craftiness.
Ephesians 5:15, Exodus 23:13a, Isaiah 34:13.

Oyster - A situation that may produce a spiritual blessing. See Pearl.
Matthew 13:45-46.

P

Paint - A covering; love; doctrine.
1 Peter 4:8, Psalm 32:1, Proverbs 10:12, James 5:20.

Painting = Creating a new image; recovering image; regenerating; renewal; preaching; covering up sin; exaggerating.
Psalm 51:10, Titus 3:5, Colossians 3:10, Ephesians 4:23, Matthew 23:27-28, Acts 23:3.

House Painter's Brush = Ministry; minister.
James 5:20.

Artist's Painting = Illustrative message; eloquent words; articulate; humorous.
Acts 18:24.

Pale Horse - Spirit of death. See Horse, and Green in Part 2.
Revelation 6:8, Zechariah 6:3.

Palm Tree - Fruit producing leader; righteous flourishing. See Trees.
Judges 4:5, Psalm 92:12.

Pan - Vessel; doctrine; tradition; a determination or resolve; form of the truth; a person.
Romans 2:20, Exodus 25:29, Isaiah 28:9-10, Jeremiah 1:13, 2 Kings 21:13, 1 Thessalonians 4:3-5.
God's wrath, judgement and plagues.
Revelation 15:7, Revelation 16:2-21, Revelation 17:1, Revelation 21:9.

Pant - Desire; diligent pursuit; work; tired; thirsty.
Psalm 42:1, Psalm 63:1-2.

Pants - Covering; work. See Clothing.
Luke 7:25.

Paper - Record; decree; instructions; plans; notes; information; contract; certificate. See Letter.
Esther 6:1-2, 1 Chronicles 28:11-12, Matthew 19:4-9.
   Crumpled Paper = Plans that failed; canceled contract.
   Colossians 2:14-15.
   Torn Paper = Severance of a contract; disunited; rent by factions.
   1 Samuel 15:27-28, Matthew 12:25, Mark 3:23-26.

Parachute - God's promises; salvation; faith.
Romans 13:14, Galatians 3:27.
   Parachuting = Bail out; escape; flee; saved.
   Joshua 2:15-18, 1 Samuel 19:11-12, Acts 9:24-25, 2 Corinthians 11:33.
   Parachute Difficult to Open = Dangerous complication.
   Faulty Parachute = Presumption; tempting God or another.
   Matthew 4:5-7, Luke 4:9-12.

Parents - Authority; nurture; instruct; inheritance. See Father, Mother.
1 Thessalonians 2:11, 1 Corinthians 4:14-15, 2 Timothy 1:5, Proverbs 19:14, 2 Corinthians 12:14.

Parasites - One who lives by taking from the life of another; one along for the ride for what they can get out of it.
Proverbs 30:15 (See with Habakkuk 2:5, Proverbs 27:20), John 12:6.

Park - Rest; peace; God's blessing; God's provision (the Garden of Eden); leisure; bounty; vagrancy.
Isaiah 58:11.

Parrot - Mimic; copy; mock; repeat. See Echo, Bird.
2 Kings 2:23, Luke 23:21.

Passenger - Church member; family member; self.

Passenger Jet - The Church. See Airplane.
Jeremiah 3:15, Jeremiah 23:1, 2 Corinthians 11:13.
　PTO (Aircraft Power Take-off Systems) = Empowerment through the Word of God; divine boldness; impartation of anointing from one to another; given miraculous ability to further the kingdom of God; manifest presence of God.
Acts 4:29-31, Acts 10:37-38, Romans 15:19, Acts 1:8, Luke 9:1, John 20:21-23, Mark 9:1, 1 Corinthians 4:20, 1 Thessalonians 1:5.
　Black Box = Record of conversations; to investigate; search out the answers; find evidence.
Genesis 18:21, Exodus 2:11-14, Mark 14:72, John 21:24-25, 1 Corinthians 2:9-10.
　Flying Too Low = Insufficient power, prayer, preparation, or training; only partially operating in the spirit; not following, being led by the Spirit.

Flying High = Fully empowered by the Spirit.

Soaring Aircraft = Deep in the Spirit; moving in the deep things of God.

Supersonic Flight = Fast; powerful; soaring in the Spirit; fully empowered by the Spirit; deep in the Spirit; moving in the deep things of God.

2 Kings 2:9-11, Psalm 104:3-4.

Mechanical Failure = Problem; sickness; spirit of poverty; demonic attack; hindrance to one's life, ministry, career, livelihood.

1 Thessalonians 2:18, Acts 16:6-7.

Crash = Strife; contention; conflict; confrontation; calamity; offense; mistake or sin in ministry; failure; church split; apostasy; personal disaster (failed marriage, business venture, ministry, project etc.); end of one phase (for whatever reason unbeknownst to the dreamer).

Nahum 2:3-4, 1 Timothy 1:19-20.

Path - Way; Christ; the Christian faith; truth; life; way of error.
Isaiah 35:8, John 14:6, Matthew 7:13-14, Jeremiah 6:16, Nahum 2:4, Haggai 1:5-7, Luke 15:15-17, Psalm 69:2, Isaiah 57:20, Jeremiah 18:15-16.

Under Restoration or Repair = In preparation; not ready; change; hindrance.

At a fork or adjoining Path = Decision; change of direction. Jeremiah 6:16, Haggai 1:5-7.

Long Path = Time.

Dead End = Change direction, stop and repent; certain failure.

Luke 15:15-17.

Narrow Path = Way to life; God's way.

Matthew 7:13-14.

Broad Path = Way of destruction; man's way.

Matthew 7:13-14.

Crooked Path = Trouble; difficulties; lack of clarity.
Isaiah 42:16, Isaiah 45:2.
Make the Path Straight = Bring correction; clarified; the right way.
Matthew 3:1-3, Luke 3:4-5, Isaiah 40:3.
Gravel or Stony Ground = Difficult way, narrow way.
Psalm 17:5, Matthew 7:13-14.
Muddy Path = Flesh: man's way; difficulty (caused by weak flesh); not clear; uncertain; offense; lust; passion; strife; sin.
Psalm 69:2, Isaiah 57:20.
Ruts in the Path = Habits or addiction; traditions of men.
Jeremiah 18:15-16, Isaiah 62:10.

Pastor - Messenger; shepherd; God's representative; Christ; spiritual authority, good or evil; deception.
Jeremiah 3:15, Ephesians 4:11, Luke 4:18, 1 Peter 5:1-3, Jeremiah 23:1, 2 Corinthians 11:13.

Pastor's Wife - Church.

Peacock - Pride; pious; beauty. See Bird.
Job 39:13, 1 Kings 10:22, 2 Chronicles 9:21.
White Peacock = Purified. See White in Part 2.

Pearl - Treasure; established truth of God; glory of heaven; precious. See Oyster.
Matthew 13:45-46.
Find a Pearl = Discover something of value; discover truth.
Given a Pearl = Divine provision of something valuable, salvation, blessings, or spiritual gifts.

Pen or Pencil - Tongue; written words; agreement; covenant; contract; publish; record; gossip.
Psalm 45:1, Jeremiah 8:8, Judges 5:14, Isaiah 10:1-2, Jeremiah 17:1, Job 19:23-24, Job 13:26.

Penguin - Specialized; graceful in water; awkward on land; vigilantly watches out for its natural predator, sharks.
1 Corinthians 7:20, 1 Peter 5:8.
Out of Water = Out of its natural element.

Perfume - Influence; Holy Spirit; aroma; anoint; seduction; temptation; persuasion.
Ephesians 5:2, 2 Corinthians 2:14-16, Psalm 45:8, Song of Solomon 4:13-14, Mark 14:3, John 12:3, Proverbs 7:17, Isaiah 57:9.
Buying Perfume = Increase in one's anointing; new dimension of one's anointing or acceptance.
Contaminated Perfume = Interference of one's anointing or acceptance.

Pet, Personal - Something precious: friend.

Phantom - Spirit; the Holy Spirit; angel; appearance of reality; imaginary.
Job 4:15-16.

Physician - Healer; authority; Christ; preacher; medical doctor; illness.
Mark 2:17, Mark 5:26, 2 Chronicles 16:12, 1 Corinthians 11:30-32.

Pick-up Truck - Personal ministry or work in the natural; dependable; humble. See Truck.
1 Chronicles 13:7, Genesis 45:27, Galatians 6:5.
Large Pick-up Truck = Larger ministry or church; influence large people groups; clunky and burdensome; costly to power; prideful.
1 Chronicles 13:7, Genesis 45:27, Galatians 6:5.
Pick-up Truck Box or Canopy = Heart; baggage.
Proverbs 14:14, Hebrews 13:9 (KJV), Luke 11:46, Matthew 23:4, Acts 15:28.

Picture - Memory; conscience, past experience; circumstance; imagination; message within itself.
Numbers 33:52, Hebrews 9:14.
Picture Taken with Important Person = Honor; promotion.
Frames = Mindset; mentality.
Golden Frame = Divine seal.
Unusual Picture Frame = Peculiar mindset; peculiar mentality.
Titus 2:14, 1 Peter 2:9.
Old or Antique Frame = Past memories; outdated.

Pig - Unclean spirit; spirit of religion; untrustworthy; selfish; backslider; unbeliever; glutton; fornicator; hypocrite; destroyer; devourer; idolater.
2 Peter 2:22, Matthew 7:6.
Pig in the Room = Religion blinding true spirit of another.
Boar = Persecutor; hostile to virtue; vicious; vengeful; danger.
Psalm 80:13, 2 Timothy 3:2-3.

Pillar - Main support in the church; main support of a ministry; foundational truths.
Habakkuk 2:11.

Pilot - One in control; self; Christ; pastor; teacher; Satan; the emphasis may be on the nature of the pilot (Confident, kind, careful, frantic, careless, selfish, rude ...). See Airplane, Captain.
2 Samuel 22:11, Psalm 18:10, Acts 8:39.

Pine Tree - Enduring; faithful; has staying power; does not bend to circumstances. See Trees.
Isaiah 60:13, Isaiah 41:19.

Ping Pong - Reciprocal exchange; verbal discourse; indecisive. Ephesians 4:14, James 1:6-8.

Pipe Smoking - Intellectual pride. Isaiah 65:5, Proverbs 21:24, 1 Corinthians 8:1, Deuteronomy 29:19-20.

Pistol - Words; accusations; slander; gossip; power. 2 Samuel 11:24, Psalm 64:4, Luke 11:21-22.

Being Shot by a Pistol = Powerful words coming against a person; curses; attacks.

Holding a Pistol = Equipped with authority or ability; power; unhindered.

Broken or Inoperative Pistol = Without authority or ability; without power; hindered.

Smaller Calibre = Weak or ineffective weapon; without power; lack of prayer and fasting. Revelation 3:8.

Larger Calibre = Powerful; spiritual power through acceptable service; covenant; effective; the power of evil working through agreement (acquiescence) or conquest (our defeat). 2 Corinthians 10:4.

Pit - Trap; snare; enticement; hell. Job 6:27, Genesis 37:20-24, 2 Samuel 18:17, Proverbs 22:14, Proverbs 23:27, Psalm 35:7, Job 17:16, Numbers 16:30-33.

Pit in One's Path = A trap or snare ahead.

Fallen in a Pit = Trapped; ensnared. Genesis 37:20-24, 2 Samuel 18:1 7.

Plane or Aircraft - Person or work; the Church; ministry; oversight. See Pilot. Habakkuk 1:8, Judges 13:25.

PTO (Aircraft Power Take-off Systems) = Empowerment through the Word of God; divine boldness; impartation of anointing from one to another; given miraculous ability to further the kingdom of God; manifest presence of God. Acts 4:29-31, Acts 10:37-38, Romans 15:19, Acts 1:8, Luke 9:1, John 20:21-23, Mark 9:1, 1 Corinthians 4:20, 1 Thessalonians 1:5.

Black Box = Record of conversations; to investigate; search out the answers; find evidence. Genesis 18:21, Exodus 2:11-14, Mark 14:72, John 21:24-25, 1 Corinthians 2:9-10.

Flying near Electrical Power Lines = Caution; danger; need for prayer.

Flying Too Low = Insufficient power, prayer, preparation, or training; only partially operating in the spirit; not following, being led by the Spirit.

Flying High = Fully empowered by the Spirit. 2 Kings 2:9-11, Psalm 104:3-4.

Soaring Aircraft = Deep in the Spirit; moving in the deep things of God.

Supersonic Flight = Fast; powerful; soaring in the Spirit; fully empowered by the Spirit; deep in the Spirit; moving in the deep things of God; extreme acceleration into the new season and ministry. 2 Kings 2:9-11, Psalm 104:3-4.

Passenger Airplane = The Church.

Cargo Plane = Large ministry; bearer of large loads; apostolic ministry; releases international ministries. Acts 13:1-5, 13-14, & 46-51, Romans 15:19, 2 Corinthians 10:13, Colossians1:6, & 23-29.

Small Airplane = Small or personal ministry.

Helicopter = Ministry; individual; the Church; versatile, no forward movement; stationary; lack of progress. 2 Timothy 4:2a.

Military Helicopter = Powerful prayer life; challenging enemy attack.

Military Helicopter Fighting for One = Powerful intercession on one's behalf.

Attacking Military Helicopter = Enemy forces coming against oneself.

Fighter Jet = A call to intercessory ministry; spiritual warfare.

Genesis 41:43, 2 Kings 10:16, Zechariah 6:1-8, Isaiah 5:26-28.

Stealth Bomber = Strategic powerful ministry; effective; attacking; does not attract attention; very difficult to intercept ministry's assignment; effortless flow in the Spirit; a call to regional or national intercessory ministry; heavy spiritual warfare; great angelic protection. See Bomb, Nuclear Bomb.

Genesis 41:43, 2 Kings 10:16, Zechariah 6:1-8, Isaiah 5:26-28, Joshua 8:2-7, Daniel 10:12-13, & 20-21, Ephesians 6:12.

Planes Flying in Formation = Working together in unity; keeping the unity of the Spirit; every part doing its share; communicating effectively; skilled; trained up in the things of God; trained up in the gifts; alert to the will of God; faithful.

Psalm 133:1-3, Ephesians 4:1-16, 1 Corinthians 12:4-28, Romans 12:1-10.

Various Kinds of Aircraft = All the parts working together; no partiality; multi-generational; humble; in covenant.

1 Corinthians 3:6-10, 1 Corinthians 12:4-28, Romans 15:20, Romans 12:1-16, 2 Corinthians 10:13-16.

All the Same Type of Jet Aircraft = Specialized ministry (like the Snow Birds, or Dog-fighters); very agile and powerful ministry; highly skilled; specially trained; fiercely loyal; highly efficient communicators;

organized; completely unified; keeping one's position; Special Forces in spiritual warfare.

2 Samuel 23:8-39, 1 Chronicles 11:10-47.

All the Same Type of Domestic Aircraft = Associating only with ones' own kind ("Cliché"); excluding others different than ones' group; partiality; fear; pride; selfishness; not willing to move out of comfort zone; familiar spirit; could be a smaller unified and specialised ministry.

James 2:1-9, Romans 12:9-16.

Planes Flying out of Formation = Disunity; going AWOL; low or no communication; careless; concerned only with worldly cares; in collision course; in danger of catastrophic failure; in danger of church split.

2 Timothy 4:3-4, 1 John 2:19, Matthew 22:1-10, 1 John 2:15-16.

Various Kinds of Aircraft = Compromise for the sake of unity; false unity; fear of man; sold out to the world system.

Romans 12:2a, James 4:4, Romans 1:21-32.

All the Same Type of Aircraft = Disloyal; covenant breakers; betrayers; out of the will of God; never were a part of the ministry; have developed their own little group ("Cliché"); rejecting ones who are "different"; partiality; fear; pride; selfishness; not willing to move out of comfort zone; familiar spirit; offense; could be weaker members (newer believers) not properly equipped.

1 John 2:19, Acts 15:24, Acts 20:30, Matthew 26:21-25, 1 Timothy 1:19-20 Jude 1:19, Matthew 18:6.

Plane Mechanical Failure = Problem; sickness; spirit of poverty; demonic attack; hindrance to one's life, ministry, career, livelihood.

1 Thessalonians 2:18, Acts 16:6-7.

Plane Crash = Strife; contention; conflict; confrontation; calamity; offense; mistake or sin in ministry; failure; church split; apostasy; personal disaster (failed marriage, business venture, ministry, project etc.); end of one phase (for whatever reason unbeknownst to the dreamer).
Nahum 2:3-4, 2 Corinthians 11:25-27, 1 Timothy 1:19-20.

Play - Idolatry; covetousness; false worship; true worship; spiritual warfare; striving; competition. See Music, Dancing.
1 Corinthians 10:7, Exodus 32:19, Colossians 3:5, 1 Chronicles 15:29, Matthew 11:16-17.

Poisonous Snake (Fiery/Seraph) - High ranking evil spirit; deadly burning bite; poisonous words; "flying", a snake which springs like a dart from trees, on its prey, signifying the type of spiritual attack; high levels of spiritual warfare needed. See Snake.
Numbers 21:6-9, Isaiah 14:29, Isaiah 30:6, Ephesians 6:12, Psalm 58:3-5, Psalm 91:13, Psalm 140:3, Romans 3:13.
   Fangs = Evil intent or motive: poisonous; great danger.
   Psalm 57:4, Psalm 58:6, Proverbs 30:14, Daniel 7:5-7, Revelation 9:8.

Police - Authority; natural civil or spiritual authority (good or evil); protection; control; angels or demons; an enforcer of a curse of the law, judgment (because of transgression or an evil covenant).
Romans 13:1& 4, Luke 12:11, Psalm 94:20, Hebrews 1:7, &14.

Pomegranate - Fruitful; heart; beautiful thoughts and words; pleasant.
Song of Solomon 8:2, Exodus 28:33-35, Song of Solomon 4:3, & 13.

Pool - Spiritual place; church; home; family; God's blessings; time of refreshing; cleansing; the word of God; healing when water stirred. See Water.
Isaiah 41:18, Acts 3:19, Ephesians 5:26, John 5:2-9.
Dirty or Dry Pool = Corrupt or destitute spiritually; backslidden.
Jeremiah 50:38.

Porch, Front - Public; open to everyone; community; recreation; leisure; exposed; revealed.
Mark 14:68, Acts 5:12, Joel 2:17.

Porcupine - Destruction; confusion; desolation.
Isaiah 14:23, & Isaiah 34:11 (AMPC), Zephaniah 2:14 (ASV).

Postage Stamp - Seal; authority; authorisation; empowerment; small but powerful.
Esther 8:8, 2 Timothy 2:19.
Envelope = Important message from God; prophecy; personal instructions.
Job 33:14-16, Deuteronomy 29:29.
Sealed = Prophecy un-interpreted; message or instruction not revealed.
Daniel 8:26, Daniel 9:24, Daniel 12:4, & 9.
Opened = Prophecy interpreted; message or instruction revealed.
Revelation 22:10.
Letter = Important message from God; prophecy; personal instructions.
Job 33:14-16, Deuteronomy 29:29.

Port - A place of spiritual portals; distribution; exports the spiritual to the natural; spiritual gateway; family line; prophesy, speaks into existence.

Micah 5:2, Genesis 28:12, & 17, Genesis 32:1-2, Deuteronomy 28:12, Psalm 135:6-7, Revelation 11:3-6, & 19, Revelation 4:1, Revelation 8:3-5, Revelation 19:10b (testifying by the Spirit within), James 5:17-18.

Exportation or Shipping = Means of moving from the spiritual realm to the physical realm; releasing generational inheritances; distributing and speaking into existence what has been prayed for.

Genesis 28:12-17, Genesis 32:1-2, John 3:8, Ezekiel 37:9, Revelation 8:3-5.

Harbor = Safe place; divine protection; a place of God's refuge; a place of anchor; comfort zone; no progress; complacency, no growth; low expectations; hides weak faith; harbors anger, resentment, bitterness.

Psalm 91:1-2, John 10:10-13, Matthew 10:16, 1 Corinthians 16:9, Ezekiel 3:14.

> **Anchor** = Representation of security, safety and hope; Jesus the Anchor of our soul.
> Hebrews 6:19-20.
>
> > **Trying to Secure an Anchor** = Need to put things in order; need to make things more secure.
> > **Broken Anchor** = Lost firmness; lost security.
> > **Weak Shaking Anchor** = Need to strengthen existing security.
> > **Strong Firm Anchor** = Security in place.
> > Acts 27:29.
> > **Cutting off of an Anchor** = Letting go of security, in self or in God.
> > Acts 27:40.

Pot - Vessel; doctrine; tradition; a determination or resolve; form of the truth; a person.
Romans 2:20, Exodus 25:29, Isaiah 28:9-10, Jeremiah 1:13, 2 Kings 21:13, 1 Thessalonians 4:3-5.
God's wrath, judgement and plagues.
Revelation 15:7, Revelation 16:2-21, Revelation 17:1, Revelation 21:9.

Pot of Boiling Water - Spiritual condition; anger; war; judgment. See Water, and Hot Water subheading.
Isaiah 64:2, Jeremiah 1:13-16, Ezekiel 24:3-14.

Power - Holy Spirit anointing; authority; miraculous ability.
Acts 1:8, Luke 4:36, Luke 9:1, Revelation 13:2, Romans 15:19, Acts 10:38.

Power Lines - Power of God's Word; flow of the Holy Spirit; the presence of the kingdom.
Hebrews 1:3, Luke 4:14, & 32, Acts 10:37-38, Mark 9:1, 1 Corinthians 4:20, 1 Thessalonians 1:5.

Powerboat - Powerful ministry or fast progress; life; person; recreation; spare time.
Genesis 6:16, Luke 8:22-23, 1 Timothy 1:19.
Large Boat = The Church.
Small Boat = Small or personal ministry.

Preacher - Messenger; God's representative; Christ; spiritual authority, good or evil; deception; evangelism; proclaiming.
Jeremiah 3:15, Jeremiah 23:1, 2 Corinthians 11:13.

Preaching - Message of conviction from God.
Nehemiah 6:7, Luke 4:18.

Pregnancy - In process; preparatory stage; promise of God; word of God in seed form; prophetic word; expectancy. See Baby.
Isaiah 66:9, James 1:15, Luke 8:11.
>   **Labor Pains** = Trials; process of birthing something, good or bad.
>   Galatians 4:19, Revelation 12:2.

President - Christ Jesus; literal President; head of a company. See King.
Psalm 45:1-17, Romans 13:1-7, 1 Timothy 2:1-2, 1 Peter 2:13-17.

Prime Minister - Christ Jesus; a senior minister; literal Prime Minister. See King.
Hebrews 3:1-5, 1 Timothy 1:12, Acts 20:28, 1 Peter 5:1-4, 1 Timothy 2:1-2, Romans 13:1-7, 1 Peter 2:13-17.

Prison - Bondage; rebellion; strong emotion; addiction; sin; persecution. See Cage.
Luke 4:18, Hebrews 2:15, 2 Peter 2:14, 2 Timothy 2:25-26, Jeremiah 38:6, Zechariah 9:12a.
>   **Death Row** = Death sentence; cursed; judgement; certain death of something if unrepentant; in need of the Lord's intervention.
>   Genesis 20:3, Ezekiel 33:14-15, Luke 13:3-5.

Prisoners - Lost Souls; stubborn; sinners; persecuted saints.
Luke 4:18, Hebrews 2:15, 2 Peter 2:14, 2 Timothy 2:25-26, Jeremiah 38:6, Zechariah 9:12a.

Profanity - Curse; uncontrolled anger; hatred.
Psalm 109:17-18, Matthew 5:22, Colossians 3:8, Ephesians 4:29-31, Ephesians 5:4.

Prostitute - Seduction; the worldly church; adultery; fornication; temptation; snare; unclean person; stubborn. See Sex.
Revelation 17:5, Ecclesiastes 7:26, Jeremiah 3:3.

PTO (Power Take-off) - Empowerment through the Word of God; divine boldness; impartation of anointing from one to another; given miraculous ability to further the kingdom of God; manifest presence of God.
Acts 4:29-31, Acts 10:37-38, Romans 15:19, Acts 1:8, Luke 9:1, John 20:21-23, Mark 9:1, 1 Corinthians 4:20, 1 Thessalonians 1:5.

Public Toilet - Slander; gossip; church repeating a matter; public exposure of sin of any level, church, ministry, business, household. See Toilet.
Proverbs 6:16-19, Proverbs 17:9, Revelation 3:1, & 3, 3 John 1:10, 1 Corinthians 5:1-5.

Puffer Fish - Proud Christian; one who wants to appear more important than they are; Christian filled with head knowledge; Christian lacking love; religious spirit; vanity; inwardly poisonous.
1 Corinthians 4:18-19, 1 Corinthians 5:2, 1 Corinthians 8:1, 1 Corinthians 13:4, Colossians 2:18.

Pumpkin (Jack-O-Lantern) - Witchcraft; deception; snare; appeasement; trickery.
2 Kings 21: 7, 2 Chronicles 33: 7, Isaiah 8:19-20, Judges 18:17-20, Acts 8:9-11.
  A Normal Pumpkin = May just relate to thanksgiving or harvest.
  Halloween = A satanic holiday; a high offering day for witches, sorcerers, occultists and Satanists, to demonic spirits; a celebration of death.

Deuteronomy 18:10-12, 2 Kings 21:6-7, 2 Chronicles 33:6-7, Micah 5:12, Acts 8:9-11, Isaiah 8:19-20, Mark 12:26-27.

Puppy - Precious gift; helpless; must be attended to. See Dog. 1 Corinthians 12:4, 1 Timothy 4:14.

Purging - Cleanse; thrust away; wash. See Bathroom, Toilet. 2 Corinthians 7:1, Colossians 3:5-9, Isaiah 4:4, Psalm 51:7, 2 Timothy 2:20-21, Hebrews 9:14.

Purse - Treasure; heart; precious; valuable; identity. Mark 6:8, Luke 22:35-36, John 13:29.
> **Empty Purse** = Bankrupt.
> **Misplaced Purse** = Mistake in decision or investment; misplaced priorities.
> **Stolen Purse** = Risky or careless decision or bad investment that caused a loss; something valuable stolen. John 12:6.
> **Money** = Wealth; spiritual riches; provision; natural talents and skills; power; strength of man; greed; covetousness. Deuteronomy 8:18, Ecclesiastes 7:12, Matthew 17:27, Luke 16:11, Genesis 31:15, Ezekiel 22:12, 1 Timothy 6:10, James 5:1-4, 1 Timothy 6:10.
> > **Getting Money** = Literal financial increase; increase in favor.
> > Matthew 17:27.
> > **Bundle of Money** = Season of abundance of money or favor.
> > **International Currency** = Privilege or favor from that country.
> > **Short of Money** = Season of a lack of money or favor.

Puzzle - Riddle; parable; mystery; the body of Christ. Numbers 12:8, Ezekiel 17:2, Judges 14:12-19, 1 Corinthians 13:12, Hosea 12:10, 1 Corinthians 14:2, 1 Corinthians 12:12-28, Ephesians 4:16, Colossians 2:19.

Puzzle Pieces = Individual members of the body of Christ; individuals' purposes; innovation; a collective idea. 1 Corinthians 12:12-28, Psalm 139:15-16, Romans 12:4-11.

Puzzle Pieces Joined Together = Working together in unity; edifying one another. Ephesians 4:16, Colossians 2:19, Romans 12:4-11.

Putting Puzzle Pieces together = Alignment of the Body of Christ; problem solving; bringing together new solutions or ideas.

Scattered Puzzle Pieces = Disunity; working in one's own strength; independent spirit; one one's own; vulnerable; unprotected; unfruitful. Amos 3:3, Ecclesiastes 4:9-12, Psalm 119:176, Luke 10:1.

Breaking apart Puzzle Pieces = Destroying what God has put together.

Putting Back Together according to one's own Preference = Taking things into one's own hands; partiality; acting out in presumption.

Light or Colorful Puzzle = Heavenly realm; spiritual angelic atmosphere.

Shady or Dark Color Puzzle = Earthly realm; physical human atmosphere; demonic realm.

Two Puzzles, One Light and One Dark = Duality of the heavenly, angelic realm and the earthly physical human realm.

Python - Divination; familiar spirits; ancestral spirits; a regional spirit; a coiling spirit that squeezes out the breath of life (the Holy Spirit) and cut off a believer's lifeline to God (prayer); puts

believers in bondage; thwarts a believer's purpose; high level of spiritual warfare needed. See Snake.
Acts 16:16-18, Ephesians 6:12, Psalm 91:13, Daniel 10:13 & 20.

Quarter Horse - Strong; good times; fast; agility; success. See Horse.
Revelation 6:2.

Quick Sand - Sinking foundation; hidden trap of the enemy; pulled under.
Job 4:17-20, Luke 6:49, 1 Corinthians 3:11, Psalm 69:2, & 14-15, Acts 27:17.

> **Sand** = Improper foundation; weakness; weariness; drudgery; hindrance; fool's wrath; heaviness; grief; numerous.
> Matthew 7:26-27, Hebrews 12:1, Proverbs 27:3, Job 6:2-3, Genesis 32:12.

Quills - Defensive words; piercing words; accusation; slander; gossip. See Porcupine; Arrows.
Psalm 64:3, Psalm 11:2, Deuteronomy 32:42.

Quilt - Covering; warmth; covenant; protection; hidden.
Exodus 25:20-22, Ezekiel 16:8-10, Psalm 91:4-5, Proverbs 31:22, Proverbs 7:16, Job 31:20.

> **Patchwork Quilt** = Memories or influence of one's foremothers.
> **Comforter** = Holy Spirit; the Spirit of truth.
> John 14:16, & 26, John 16:7, John 15:26.

Blanket = Covering; warmth; covenant; protection; hidden.
Exodus 25:20-22, Ezekiel 16:8-10, Psalm 91:4-5, Proverbs 31:22, Proverbs 7:16, Job 31:20.

Quiver - Heart; children.
Psalm 127:3-5.

R

Rabbit - Increase; fast growth; multiplication, good or evil; pagan rituals; lust; fornication.
Proverbs 29:16, Job 27:14, Psalm 38:19.

Rabid Dog - Single-minded pursuit of evil; demonized; deliberately evil; contagious evil; persecution; great danger.
See Dog.
Galatians 5:15, Proverbs 26:17.
 Fangs = Evil intent or motive: poisonous; great danger.
 Psalm 57:4, Psalm 58:6, Proverbs 30:14, Daniel 7:5-7, Revelation 9:8.

Raccoon - Mischief; night raider; rascal; thief; bandit; deceitful; obsessive or excessive cleanliness.
Proverbs 4:16a, Proverbs 10:23a.

Radio - Continuous; unrelenting; chatter; nuisance; contention; tradition; news; preaching the Gospel; teaching; prophetic utterance.
Proverbs 9:13, Proverbs 27:15, Ecclesiastes 10:14, 1 Timothy 6:3-4, Proverbs 25:25, Revelation 14:6, Mark 16:15, Luke 24:47-48.
 Listening to a Radio = Impartation to the dreamer.
 Subject of the Broadcast = What is being imparted to the dreamer, good or bad.

Difficulty Tuning in the Right Frequency = Extraneous interference of one's ability to hear what is being said; a mindset unable to receive.

Radio Announcer - Preacher of truth or error.
Ecclesiastes 12:9-11.

Radio Tower - Broadcasts truth or error; Gospel; witness.
Matthew 24:24, Revelation 14:6.

Raft - Adrift; without direction; aimless; without purpose; powerless; makeshift.
Acts 27:44, Ephesians 4:14.

Rags - Useless; poor; humble; unrighteous; self righteous.
See Clothing.
Isaiah 64:6, Proverbs 23:21.

Railway Operator (Conductor) - Control; self; Christ; pastor; teacher; Satan; the emphasis is on the nature of the driver (Confident, kind, careful, frantic, careless, selfish, rude ...).
2 Kings 9:20.

Railroad Track - Tradition; unchanging habit; stubborn; caution; danger. See Train.
2 Thessalonians 2:15, 2 Thessalonians 3:6, Mark 7:9, & 13, Colossians 2:8, Jeremiah 18:15-16, Isaiah 62:10.

Rain - Blessing; life; refreshing; move of God; revival; Word of God; unclear time; depression; trial.
Deuteronomy 11:14, Joel 2:23-29, Zechariah 10:1, Isaiah 55:10-11, Matthew 7:27.
    Raining = Receiving from God; undergoing trials.
    Drought = Lack of blessing; absence of the presence of God.
    Jeremiah 3:3, Psalm 32:4.

Rainbow - Covenant; promise; good; protection; God's glory. Genesis 9:12-17, Ezekiel 1:28, Revelation 4:3.

Ram - Satanic or of the occult; evil rule. Daniel 8:3-4, & 20.
Fighting a Ram = Fighting an evil spirit with characteristics of a Ram.
Playing with a Ram = Character defect.

Rape - Violation of another's will and integrity; defile; abuse of authority; hatred. Genesis 34:1-2, 27, & 31, 2 Samuel 13:12-15, Deuteronomy 22:25-27.

Rapture - Revival; spiritual awakening; imminent. Hosea 6:2, Matthew 25:6, 1 Thessalonians 4:16-17, 1 Corinthians 15:51-52.
Left Behind = Warning; unpreparedness. Matthew 25:3, & 8-13.
Reveille = Beginning; wake-up, a call to assemble. Isaiah 58:1, 1 Corinthians 14:8, 1 Corinthians 15:52, Joel 2:15, Ephesians 5:14.

Rat - Unclean; wicked person; jerk; devourer; plague (curse because of sin); betrayer. See Mice. Leviticus 11:29, 1 Samuel 6:4-5, Proverbs 17:13, Psalm 37:12, Leviticus 26:21.

Rattlesnake - Words; threats; warning; alarm; fear. See Snake. Psalm 58:4 (MSG).

Raven - Unclean spirit; confusion; outspoken person; person operating under or out of a spirit of envy or strife, which causes confusion and disorder; hateful; depression; grief; death;

suicide; straight path or direct route; God's minister of justice or provision. See Bird.
James 3:16, Isaiah 13:20-22, Isaiah 34:11, Psalm 35:26, Proverbs 30:17.

Reap - Harvest; reward, good or bad.
Galatians 6:7-9, 2 Corinthians 9:6, Hosea 10:12, Job 4:8, Hosea 8:7.
Reaping = Reward of labor.
Sow = Plan ahead; plant seed; give; prayer.
Jeremiah 29:11-13, Galatians 6:7-9, 2 Corinthians 9:6.
Sowing = Planning for the future; creating by speaking the word of God.

Reed - Weakness; opposition through weak flesh; affliction.
Isaiah 42:3, Matthew 11:7-8, 2 Kings 18:21.

Rear-view Mirror - Looking back; focus on the past; warning to watch your back; warning to look ahead. See Vehicle.
Genesis 19:26.

Re-create - Regeneration; being born again; new life; new nature; renovation; Messianic restoration; new heavens and a new earth.
John 3:3-8, 1 Peter 1:3, Titus 3:5, Ephesians 4:23, Acts 3:19-21, Matthew 19:28.

Red Horse - Persecution; anger; danger; opposition; could have Apocalyptic meaning. See Horse, and Red in Part 2.
John 16:2, Revelation 6:4, Zechariah 1:8.

Refrigerator - Heart; motive; attitude; thoughts.
Matthew 12:35, Mark 7:21-22.
    Stored Food = Memories.
    Spoiled Food = Harboring a grudge; unclean thoughts.

Freezer = Stores spiritual food for the future; preservation of life.
Psalm 12:6-7, Genesis 45:5-7, Psalm 31:23, Psalm 37:28, Psalm 121:8, Psalm 145:20, Psalm 116:6, John 10:28-30, 2 Timothy 4:18, 1 Thessalonians 5:23.
Discover Food in the Freezer = Recovery of the reward of one's labor.
Spoiled Food in the Freezer = Must leave past hurts and losses behind.

Refuge - Protection; safety; security.
Psalm 91:1-2, Deuteronomy 33:27, Psalm 46:1, Psalm 142:4-5.

Harbor = Safe place; divine protection; a place of God's refuge; a place of anchor; comfort zone; no progress; complacency, no growth; low expectations; hides weak faith; harbors anger, resentment, bitterness.
Psalm 91:1-2, John 10:10-13, Matthew 10:16, 1 Corinthians 16:9, Ezekiel 3:14, Proverbs 10:1.
Anchor = Representation of security, safety and hope; Jesus the Anchor of our soul.
Hebrews 6:19-20.
Trying to Secure an Anchor = Need to put things in order; need to make things more secure.
Broken Anchor = Lost firmness; lost security.
Weak Shaking Anchor = Need to strengthen existing security.
Strong Firm Anchor = Security in place.
Acts 27:29.
Cutting off of an Anchor = Letting go of security, in self or in God.
Acts 27:40.

Reins - Means of control; restraint.
Psalm 32:9, James 3:3.

Rend - Sorrow; grief; disagreement; anger; repentance.
2 Chronicles 34:27, 2 Samuel 3:31, Psalm 7:2, Amos 1:11,
Hosea 13:8, Zechariah 11:16, Matthew 7:6, Joel 2:13.

Repairman - Minister; Christ; prophet; pastor; counsellor;
need for adjustment in theology, attitude, relationship.
Exodus 31:3-4, 2 Timothy 3:16.
   Repairman's Tools = Word of God: Gifts of the Spirit;
wisdom; knowledge.

Restaurant - A place of choice of spiritual food; a place where
the five-fold ministry is taught.
1 Peter 5:1-3, Acts 20:28, Isaiah 40:11, Jeremiah 3:15, Hebrews
5:12-14, John 21:12-17.

Reveille - Beginning; wake-up, a call to assemble.
Isaiah 58:1, 1 Corinthians 14:8, 1 Corinthians 15:52, Joel 2:15,
Ephesians 5:14.
   Rapture = Revival; spiritual awakening; imminent.
   Hosea 6:2, Matthew 25:6, 1 Thessalonians 4:16-17, 1
   Corinthians 15:51-52.
   Left Behind = Warning; unpreparedness.
   Matthew 25:3, & 8-13.

Rifle - Words; accusations; slander; gossip; power.
2 Samuel 11:24, Psalm 64:4, Luke 11:21-22.
   Being Shot by a Rifle = Powerful words coming against a
   person; curses; attacks.
   Holding a Rifle = Equipped with authority or ability; power;
   unhindered.
   Broken or Inoperative Rifle = Without authority or ability;
   without power; hindered.

Smaller Calibre = Weak or ineffective weapon; without power; lack of prayer and fasting.
Revelation 3:8.
Larger Calibre = Powerful; spiritual power through acceptable service; covenant; effective; the power of evil working through agreement (acquiescence) or conquest (our defeat).
2 Corinthians 10:4.

Right - Natural; authority; power; the strength of man; the power of God revealed through man, accepted.
Matthew 5:29-30a, Genesis 48:18, Exodus 15:6, Matthew 25:33. 1 Peter 3:22.

Right Turn - Natural change.

Ring - Covenant; authority; dignity; wealth; vanity. See Fingers, Hand.
Genesis 41:42, Luke 15:22, Esther 8:2, & 8, James 2:2.
    Engagement Ring = Promise; commitment.
    Wedding Ring = Covenant with God; actual marriage.
    Rings as Jewellery = Worldliness; vanity.

Ripping Clothes - Sorrow; grief; disagreement; anger; repentance.
2 Chronicles 34:27, 2 Samuel 3:31, Psalm 7:2, Amos 1:11, Hosea 13:8, Zechariah 11:16, Matthew 7:6, Joel 2:13.

River - Life; Spirit of God; righteousness; spirit of man; judgement. See Water.
John 7:38-39, Amos 5:24, Proverbs 21:1, Isaiah 43:2.
    Steady Flow = Passage of time.
    Long River = Time.
    Rapids = Danger; tossed about; judgement.
    Amos 5:24.

Deep River = Difficulty; obstacle; impassable; incomprehensible.
Ezekiel 47:5, Isaiah 43:2.
Muddy River = Traditions of man; spirit of the world; sin; wickedness.
Dry River Bed = Barren; religious traditions; backslidden.
Jeremiah 50:38.

Roaches - Unclean; infestation; crept in; defiled; hidden sin; in darkness; lies. See Insects.
Leviticus 5:2, Leviticus 11: 31, &43, 2 Corinthians 7:1; 2 Timothy 3:6, Jude 1:4, 1 Corinthians 4:5, 1 John 1:6.

Road - Way; Christ; the Christian faith; truth; life; way of error.
Isaiah 35:8, John 14:6, Matthew 7:13-14, Jeremiah 6:16, Nahum 2:4, Haggai 1:5-7, Luke 15:15-17, Psalm 69:2, Isaiah 57:20, Jeremiah 18:15-16.
Under Construction = In preparation; not ready; change; hindrance.
Crossroads = Decision; change of direction.
Jeremiah 6:16, Haggai 1:5-7.
Long Road = Time.
Country Road = Country ministry; wilderness training; alone; off track.
Acts 8:26, Matthew 3:1-3, 1 Kings 19:4, Deuteronomy 8:2-3, Luke 15:4.
Dead End = Change direction, stop and repent; certain failure.
Luke 15:15-17.
Narrow Road = Way to life; God's way.
Matthew 7:13-14.
Broad Road = Way of destruction; man's way.
Matthew 7:13-14.
Gravel or Stony Road = Difficult way, narrow way.
Psalm 17:5, Matthew 7:13-14.

Mud on Road = Flesh: man's way; difficulty (caused by weak flesh); not clear; uncertain; offense; lust; passion; strife; sin.
Psalm 69:2, Isaiah 57:20.
Ruts in Road = Habits or addiction; traditions of men.
Jeremiah 18:15-16, Isaiah 62:10.

Road Block - Delay, waiting for God's timing; sin stopping destiny; ambush; warning; personal agenda that needs to be changed; return back to God; inspection; alternate route required; hardened heart; potential heart or artery issue.
Acts 16:6-7 See with Acts 19:10 and 1 Peter 1:1, Psalm 105:19, and John 11:6, 14-17, & 39-45, Numbers 14:22-24, Proverbs 7:5-23, Numbers 22:22-35, Hosea 2:6-7, Genesis 42:16, Acts 16:6-10, Deuteronomy 2:30.

Road Grader - Restoration ministry; prophetic ministry. See Truck.
Galatians 6:1, Isaiah 40:3-4.

Road Work - Preparing one's ministry; removing a barrier in one's path; improving one's destiny; building a path for others; preparing hearts for God; warning to slow down; problems ahead; detour; delay.
Isaiah 40:3-4, Exodus 23:20, 2 Chronicles 27:6, Isaiah 57:14; Isaiah 62:10, Malachi 3:1, Matthew 3:3, Matthew 11:10, Numbers 22:22-35, Exodus 3:2-4, Genesis 11:31.

Robe - Covering of God; righteousness; salvation.
Isaiah 61:10, Job 29:14, Revelation 7:9.

Rock - Christ Jesus; solid foundation; apostles; prophets.
1 Corinthians 10:4, Deuteronomy 32:4, Ephesians 2:20, Revelation 21:14.

Rocket - Powerful ministry; launching into new territory; swift progress; spiritual warfare; swift destruction; sudden, unexpected attack.
Psalm 64:7, Proverbs 6:15, Proverbs 29:1.

Rocking Chair - Past; old age; long standing; memories; reflecting; meditation; rest; retirement.
Jeremiah 6:16.

Rod - Staff; scepter of authority; guard; discipline; Christ Jesus; rule; judgment. See Staff.
Psalm 110:2, Esther 5:1-2, Psalm 23:4, Micah 7:14, Proverbs 29:15, Proverbs 22:15, Isaiah 11:1, Revelation 2:6-7, Revelation 12:5, Psalm 2:8-9, Revelation 19:15.

Roller Blades - Fast; swift advancement or progress; skillful.
Romans 9:28, 2 Samuel 2:18, Habakkuk 3:19.

Roller Coaster - Emotional instability; unfaithfulness; wavering; manic-depressive, bi-polar; depression; trials; excitement.
James 1:6-8, Psalm 109:23 (KJV, ASV).

Roof - Covering; protection; mind; thought; vantage point, for good or bad; authority, good or bad; prayers; visions; proclamation; preaching; evil practices revealed. See House, Building.
Isaiah 30:1, Deuteronomy 22:8, Mark 2:4, Luke 5:18-19, 2 Samuel 11:2, Matthew 8:8-9, Genesis 19:8, Acts 10:9, Matthew 10:27, Zephaniah 1:5, Jeremiah 19:13, Luke 12:2-3.
    Roof with a Leak = A gap in authority structure or covering; lack of maintenance.
Mark 2:4, Luke 5:18-19, Ezekiel 13:5, Ezekiel 22:30.

Ceiling = Covering; authority, good or bad; limitation; hindered prayer (prayers that hit the ceiling).
Acts 10:1-9, 22-24, & 27, 1 Kings 6:12-15, Genesis 19:8, Job 42:8, 1 Peter 3:7, James 4:3, Romans 8:26-27.
Glass Ceiling = Fragile covering due to weakened relationship and opposition with godly authority; transparency with authority.
2 Timothy 3:8-9.

Rooster - Bragging; proud; boasting; arrogance; sexual pride.
John 18:27, Luke 22:33-34.
Hen = Gathering; protection; gossip.
Luke 13:34.
Chicken = Fear; cowardliness.
Deuteronomy 1:29, Luke 13:34.
Chick = Defenceless.

Root (Tree) - Origin; source; support; conviction; steadfastness; stable; unmovable; hidden sin; hidden motives; hidden or rotten attitude. See Trees.
Isaiah 11:1, Romans 11:16-18, Job 29:19, 2 Kings 19:30, 1 Timothy 6:10, Hebrews 12:15, Isaiah 5:24, Matthew 3:10.
See the Root = Discernment of the main cause of something.
Retain the Root or Stump = Ability to survive despite the situation.

Rope - Bondage; sin; covenant; vow; hindrances; rescue; salvation.
Proverbs 5:22, Psalm 118:27, Jeremiah 38:11.
Tied with Rope = Limitations; bondage; disabled.

Rose - Romance; Christ; love; courtship.
Song of Solomon 2:1.
Red Rose = Passion.

Yellow Rose Garden = Marriage counseling.

Rotten Egg - Bad company; bad idea; bad plan; schemes; no potential; unsure; without promise; promise breaker. Isaiah 59:5.

Rough & Unshaven Face - Spiritual neglect; uncleanness; coarse or harsh personality. See Beard. Leviticus 21:5, 2 Kings 1:8, Matthew 3:4, Genesis 25:25, Genesis 27:11.

Round - Spiritual; never-ending; mercy; compassion; grace; forgiveness; approximation (rounding off). See Circle. Leviticus 19:9-10.

Rowboat - Personal work or life; recreation; spare time; personal ministry; ministry that intervenes for others; intercessor. See Boat, Raft. Genesis 6:16, Luke 8:22-23, 1 Timothy 1:19.

Rowing - Working out life's problems personal or ministry; hard work; earnest prayer; spiritual labor. Mark 6:48, Philippians 2:30, Ezekiel 27:26.

Rug - Covering; covenant; Holy Spirit; deception or covering things up. Mark 4:22.

Run - Haste; race; to spread news (good or evil); execute works, good or evil; pursue; escape; transportation. See Legs. 1 Corinthians 9:24-27, Habakkuk 2:2, Psalm 19:5, Proverbs 1:16, Isaiah 59:7, Joel 2:7-9, 2 Samuel 2:18-19, &24 Daniel 12:4.

    Running = Striving; working out one's salvation; faith; trial. 1 Corinthians 9:24-27, Jeremiah 12:5.

Running Hunched Over = One like an animal, indicates a demonic attack and one is in need of deliverance, and to engage in spiritual warfare. Daniel 4:32-33.

Running from an Insane Person = Mental instability; irrational decision.

Running from a Dangerous Animal = Spiritual attack; weakness in spiritual issue represented by the specific animal.

Sailboat - Moved by the Spirit; person; recreation; spare time. Genesis 6:16, Luke 8:22-23, 1 Timothy 1:19.

Large Boat or Ship = The Church.

Genesis 6:16.

Small Boat or Ship = Small or personal ministry.

Salt - Seasoning; preservation; purifier; covenant; acceptable; rejected.
Colossians 4:6, Mark 9:50, 2 Chronicles 13:5, Genesis 19:26, Ezekiel 47:11.

Sand - Improper foundation; weakness; weariness; drudgery; hindrance; fool's wrath; heaviness; grief; numerous.
Matthew 7:26-27, Hebrews 12:1, Proverbs 27:3, Job 6:2-3, Genesis 32:12.

Quick Sand = Sinking foundation; hidden trap of the enemy; pulled under.
Job 4:17-20, Luke 6:49, 1 Corinthians 3:11, Psalm 69:2, & 14-15, Acts 27:17.

Sasquatch - Threatening authority; spirit of fear; intimidating threats; torment; demonic hoax; "wild man", based on a

Roman mythical deity; deception; antichrist spirit, evolution versus creation and the Creator.
Daniel 3:13-15, Acts 9:1, 1 Samuel 17:4-11, 16, 23-24, 32, & 44, 1 Chronicles 20:6-7, Galatians 1:7-9, 1 John 4:2-3.

Scales - Justice; judgement; business; falsehood; deceitful; divide; purchase; integrity; make judgement before hearing the matter; vanity. See Business, Merchant.
Proverbs 16:11, Ezekiel 45:10-12, Daniel 5:27, Proverbs 20:23, Proverbs 11:1, Deuteronomy 25:13-15, Leviticus 19:35-36, Hosea 12:7, Micah 6:10-11, Ezekiel 5:1, Jeremiah 32:9-10, Job 31:6, Job 6:2, Proverbs 18:13, John 7:51, Psalm 62:9.
Weighing of Oneself = Pondering truth; considering one's ways; looking at one's progress of ridding oneself of sins; natural concern for health; obsession of appearance.
2 Timothy 2:15, 1 Corinthians 14:29, 1 Thessalonians 5:21, Hebrews 12:1-3, 2 Corinthians 10:7, 12, & 17, 1 Corinthians 1:26-31, 1 John 2:16.

School - Teaching or learning; church; people or work; teaching ministry; training.
Acts 19:9, Acts 20:20, Matthew 9:35.
Elementary School = Infant stage; not yet mature.
Hebrews 5:12, Hebrews 6:1-3.
Middle School = Medium level of equipping; foundational level in Christianity; ready for discipleship; intermediate stage of situation.
Luke 2:46-52.
High School = Moving into higher level of walk with God; high level of training and equipping; capable of giving the same to others; need to be aware of false teaching (evolution, etc).
Hebrews 5:14, Ephesians 4:11-13, Matthew 28:19-20.
University = Moving to the highest levels of walk with God; specialized training and equipping; well able to apply

learned wisdom and knowledge; a place where if not prepared in the strength, wisdom and knowledge of God, can be caused to stumble (like teaching of evolution and persecution of those who stand on the truth).
2 Timothy 2:15, Philippians 3:4-5, Acts 22:3, Daniel 1:17-20, John 14:26, Acts 23:6-8, 1 Corinthians 2:1-6, & 12-16, 1 Corinthians 1:19-24, James 3:13-18.
School of the Prophets = Organization of true prophets who supervise the training of up-and-coming prophets.
1 Samuel 10:10, 1 Samuel 19:20, 1 Kings 18:4.
Eagle's Nest = Prophetic School; heavenly dwelling and rest.
Deuteronomy 32:11-12, Exodus 19:4b, Revelation 12:14, 2 Kings 4:38, Job 39:27, Proverbs 23:5b, Obadiah 1:4, Jeremiah 49:16.

School Bus - Teaching ministry; youth ministry; learning and working together. See School, Bus.
Stalled School Bus = Ministry on hold; operation in one's own strength; need to take authority; hindrance by Satan; opposition.
Isaiah 49:2, Exodus 14:13-16, Galatians 5:7-12, Nehemiah 4:1-18, 1 Thessalonians 2:18.

School Bus Breakdown - Problem; sickness; spirit of poverty; demonic attack; hindrance to one's life, ministry, career, livelihood.
1 Thessalonians 2:18, Acts 16:6-7.

School Bus Crash - Strife; contention; conflict; confrontation; calamity; offense; mistake or sin in ministry; failure; church split; apostasy; personal disaster (failed marriage, business venture, ministry, project etc.); end of one phase (for whatever reason unbeknownst to the dreamer).
Nahum 2:3-4, 2 Corinthians 11:25-27, 1 Timothy 1:19-20.

School Bus Driver - Self; if the school bus driver is a teacher in the dream, the passengers represent the driver's students.

Scorpion - Lust of the flesh; temptation; sin; deception; accusation; destruction; danger; demon.
Luke 10:19, 1 Corinthians 15:56, Romans 7:23.

Sea - Large groups, humanity, mission, or travel; anointing; covering large areas; numerous; large move of the Spirit.
Isaiah 60:5, Psalm 68:22, Isaiah 24:14-15, Psalm 98:7-9.
On the Sea = Influencing a nation; imparting large numbers of a multitude.
Acts 27:1-44, 2 Corinthians 11:25-28.
Undertow = Undercurrent; discontent; at wits end.
Psalm 107:25-27, Acts 27:17, 27-29, & 41.
Salt Water = Spirit of the world; source of evil.
James 3:11-12.
Ocean = Very large groups, humanity, mission, or travel to distant shores; great anointing; covering of the earth; innumerable; an awesome amount or expanse; very large move of the Spirit.
Isaiah 60:5, Psalm 68:22, Isaiah 24:14-15, Psalm 98:7-9, 2 Corinthians 11:25-28, Acts 27:1-44.
On the Ocean = Influencing the nations; imparting great numbers of multitudes.
Acts 27:1-44, 2 Corinthians 11:25-28.

Seacoast - Transition phase; boundary; limitation.
Jeremiah 5:22, Jeremiah 47:6-7, Proverbs 8:29, Genesis 1:9-10.

Sea Snake or Monster = Leviathan spirit; Satan; world power; extremely strategic level of spiritual warfare needed. See Snake.
Isaiah 27:1, Job 26:13, Psalm 74:13-14, Isaiah 51:9, Revelation 12:3-17, Ezekiel 29:3.

Sea Turtle - Specialized; graceful in water; awkward on land; rare.
1 Corinthians 7:20.
Out of Water = Out of its natural element.

Seat - Place of authority; position of power; throne of God; seat of Satan; rest; quietness.
Matthew 23:2-6, Matthew 20:21, Acts 2:32-33, 1 Peter 3:22, Ephesians 1:20, Hebrews 10:12, Isaiah 30:15.
Someone Else Sitting on a Seat = In place of authority; in position of power; throne of God; seat of Satan.
1 Peter 3:22, Ephesians 1:20, Hebrews 10:12, Hebrews 12:2, Matthew 23:1-2, Revelation 2:13.
Sitting on One's Seat = One's place of authority; one's position of power; rest.
1 Peter 3:22, Ephesians 1:20, Hebrews 10:12.
Difficulty Finding One's Seat = Hindrances to obtaining one's place of authority.
1 Samuel 18:8-29.
Stolen Seat = Warfare needed to maintain or recover one's authority, or designated place or position.
2 Samuel 15:1-36.

Seat Belt - Security; safety; preparedness; assurance.
Psalm 118:27.
Unfastened Seat Belt = Unprepared; careless.

Seed - Word of God; believers; unbelievers; faith; promise; lays down one's temporary earthly life to gain eternal spiritual life.
Luke 8:11, Matthew 13:38, Genesis 3:15, Luke 17:6, John 12:24-25, 1 Corinthians 15:36-38, & 42-58.

Semi-truck - Powerful ministry; large ministry; intimidating; deliverance ministry; leadership. See Truck.

1 Kings 10:2, 1 Samuel 14:6, Acts 4:33, Acts 6:8, 1 Samuel 17:4-11, Isaiah 37:10-11, Zechariah 3:9, Acts 13:43.
Freight truck = Business.
1 Kings 10:15.
Tractor Trailer = Large burden; ministry; powerful; large work; the size of the truck is often in proportion to the burden or size of the work); the Church. An 18-Wheeler, see 18 in Part 2.
2 Samuel 6:3, Acts 5:14.

Sewage - Corruption; filthiness of the flesh; sin; evil; corrupt authority; abuse of authority.
Isaiah 4:4, Deuteronomy 23:13-14, Galatians 6:8.

Sewing - Joining; union; reunion; counseling; reconciliation.
1 Samuel 18:1.
Sewing Notions = Inclination, to have a notion to do something.

Sex - Agreement; covenant; unity; love; allegory for unfaithfulness or deviation from spiritual truths; carnality; unbroken stronghold of the spirit of lust; fornication; abuse of authority; taken advantage of.
1 Corinthians 6:15-16, 1 Corinthians 7:9, Jeremiah 7:9-10, Exodus 22:16; 2 Timothy 3:2-4.
Sex with Old Lover = Desire for old life.
Masturbation = Self gratification; inordinate self love; selfish.
2 Timothy 3:2-4.
Genitals = Secret; private matter; shame.

Shadow - Spiritual cover; safety security; partial illumination; poor resemblance; imitation; delusion; lack of real substance.
Psalm 91:1, 2 Kings 20:9-11, Job 4:13-16.
Dark Shadows = Demons.

Shark - Worldly predator; evil spirit.
Psalm 17:9-14, Psalm 124:2-7, Judges 16:4-5, Proverbs 23:27-28, 1 Peter 5:8, Mark 9:20.

Sheep - Innocent; saints; unsaved persons.
Matthew 10:16, Psalm 44:11, 2 Samuel 24:17, Matthew 25:33, Isaiah 53:6, Matthew 10:6, Luke 15:3-7.

> **Lamb** = Humility; gentleness; traceableness; the Church; Christ; blamelessness; sacrifice; trusting; vulnerable.
> Revelation 5:12, John 1:29, 1 Corinthians 5:7, Genesis 22:7-8, Luke 10:3.
> **Sheepdog** = Brings together; one used by God for a good means of control.
> John 10:3.

Shepherd - Jesus; God; selfless; protector; leader, good or bad.
Hebrews 13:20, Psalm 23:1, Psalm 80:1, 1 Peter 2:25, John10:11-15, Jeremiah 23:1-6, Ezekiel 34:23, 1 Peter 5:1-4, Ezekiel 34:2-12.

Shield - Faith; protection; trust.
Genesis 15:1, Ephesians 6:16, Psalm 28:7, 2 Samuel 22:3, Proverbs 30:5.

Ship - Support; life; person; recreation; spare time.
Genesis 6:16, Luke 8:22-23, 1 Timothy 1:19.

> **Large Ship** = The Church; large ministry.
> **Small Ship**= Small or personal ministry.
> **Sailboat** = Moved by the Spirit.
> **Freight Ship** = Business, spiritual or natural. See Port.
> 1 Kings 10:15, Psalm 107:23, Acts 21:3.
> **Battleship** = Support; Spiritual warfare; powerful evangelistic ministry; rescue.
> Acts Chapter 27 (verses 22-25, & 31), 2 Corinthians 11:23-26, 1 Timothy 1:19.

Submarine = The Underground Church; persecuted; hidden ones; spies out new or enemy territory; flows with the Spirit of God; the Holy Spirit searching out the spirit of believers. See Water, Telescope, Torpedo.
John 8:59, John 12:36, Acts 8:1-4, John 14:22, Romans 16:25-26, Numbers 13:17-21, Numbers 14:6-8, Proverbs 20:27, Romans 8:27, Psalm 139:1-4, & 23-24.
On Dry Ground = Without the move of the Spirit; the work of the flesh; a miracle if moving on dry ground.

Shipping or Exportation - Means of moving from the spiritual realm to the physical realm; releasing generational inheritances; distributing and speaking into existence what has been prayed for. See Port.
Genesis 28:12-17, Genesis 32:1-2, John 3:8, Ezekiel 37:9, Revelation 8:3-5.
Freight truck = Business. See Truck.
1 Kings 10:15, 2 Chronicles 9:14.

Shipwreck - Strife; contention; conflict; confrontation; calamity; offense; mistake or sin in ministry; failure; church split; apostasy; personal disaster (failed marriage, business venture, ministry, project etc.); end of one phase (for whatever reason unbeknownst to the dreamer).
Nahum 2:3-4, 2 Corinthians 11:25-27, Acts 27:1-44, 1 Timothy 1:19-20.

Shirt - Covering; pertains to the heart, righteousness or sin. See Clothing.
2 Kings 2:14-15a, Psalm 109:17-19, & 29.

Shirtless - Self-righteousness; self-justification; legalism; shame; temptation. See Clothing.

Shittah or Acacia Tree - Symbolizes immortality, and the duality of life and death; thorny. See Trees.
Isaiah 41:19.

Shoes - Words; gospel; covenant; preparation. See Feet.
Ephesians 6:15, Ruth 4:7, Galatians 5:16.
New Shoes = New ministry; new understanding of the gospel; fresh mandate from God; new way of life.
Put on Shoes = Preparation for spiritual journey.
Taking off Shoes = Honoring God; ministering to the Lord.
Taking off Someone Else's Shoes = Showing respect.
Tennis Shoes = Spiritual giftedness.
Running Shoes/Sneakers = Running the race of life; strengthened by the Spirit of the Lord.
Hebrews 12:1, 1 Kings 18:46.
Snowshoes = Faith; walking in the Spirit; supported by faith in the Word of God; gospel of peace.
Matthew 14:29, Ephesians 6:15.
Boots = Equipped for spiritual warfare.
Deuteronomy 33:25, 1 Samuel 17:6, Ephesians 6:15.
Giving Away Shoes = Equipping others (depending on the context).
Shoes that Don't Fit = Walking in something you're not called to; walking in someone else's territory.
Romans 15:20, 1 Corinthians 3:6-10, 2 Corinthians 10:13-16.
High Heels = Seduction; discomfort.
In Need of Shoes = In need of comfort or protection; not dwelling on the Word of God.
Loafers = At ease; unconcern; hypocrisy; loafing.
Job 12:4-5, Amos 6:1-7.
Slippers = Too comfortable.

Shotgun - Words; accusations; slander; gossip; power.
2 Samuel 11:24. 2 Samuel 11:24, Psalm 64:4, Luke 11:21-22.

Being Shot by a Shotgun = Powerful words coming against a person; curses; attacks.

Holding a Shotgun = Equipped with authority or ability; power; unhindered.

Broken or Inoperative Shotgun = Without authority or ability; without power; hindered.

Smaller to Medium Calibre = Weak or ineffective weapon; without power; lack of prayer and fasting.
Revelation 3:8.

Larger Calibre = Powerful; spiritual power through acceptable service; covenant; effective; the power of evil working through agreement (acquiescence) or conquest (our defeat).
2 Corinthians 10:4.

Shoulder - Burden bearer; government; authority; responsibility; stubborn (see neck).
Psalm 81:6, Isaiah 9:6, Zechariah 7:11.

Broad Shoulders = Strength; consolation.
Drooped Shoulders = Tired; overburdened; discouraged; hopelessness.
Bare Female Shoulders = Seduction; temptation, witchcraft.

Shrine - A dedicated place for idol worship; where evil sacrifices are made.
2 Kings 10:21-27, Jeremiah 19:5.

Shut - To close up; keep silent; walled up.
Isaiah 29:10-12, Matthew 13:15.

Shovel - Dig; search; inquire; prayer; confession; gossip; slander.
2 Kings 3:16-17, Deuteronomy 23:13, Proverbs 16:27, Proverbs 26:27.

Shower - Cleansing; sanctification; repentance; temptation, outward appearance of righteousness. See Bathroom.
Psalm 51:2-3, Ephesians 5:25-26, 2 Samuel 11:2, Matthew 23:25-26.
Preparing for a Shower = Contemplating how to rid oneself of surrounding evil practices.
Having a Shower = Resisting the influence of vileness.
Running out of Warm Water for the Shower = Need for more prayer; need to move more in the Holy Spirit; an indulgence hindering the desire for holiness.
Cold Shower = Guilt or conviction of indulgence or unfaithfulness to God.
Showering in Public = Unashamed to disassociate from evil practices.

Sickness - Iniquity or sin; corrupted environment; corruption of world systems; actual sickness that needs prayer for healing; hopelessness.
John 5:14, Luke 5:18-25, & 31-32, James 5:14-16, Isaiah 1:5-6, Matthew 4:24, Matthew 8:16-17, Proverbs 13:12.

Sickle - Reap; the harvest; word of God.
Mark 4:29, Joel 3:13, Revelation 14:14-19.

Sidewalk - Way; Christ; the Christian faith; truth; life; way of error.
Isaiah 35:8, John 14:6, Matthew 7:13-14, Jeremiah 6:16, Nahum 2:4, Haggai 1:5-7, Luke 15:15-17, Psalm 69:2, Isaiah 57:20, Jeremiah 18:15-16.
Under Repair = In preparation; not ready; change; hindrance.
Long Sidewalk = Time.
End of Sidewalk = Change direction, stop and repent; certain failure.
Luke 15:15-17.

Narrow Sidewalk = Way to life; God's way.
Matthew 7:13-14.
Broad Sidewalk = Way of destruction; man's way.
Matthew 7:13-14.

Sieve - Separator of the pure from the impure; trial; testing.
Amos 9:9.

Sift - Separation by testing.
Luke 22:31.

Sign - Direction; information; warning.
Hosea 12:10, Joshua 4:6, Isaiah 66:19, John 19:19-20, Exodus 8:23.
    Detour Sign = Change of direction.
    Stop Sign = Stop and pray for guidance.
    Yield Sign = A sign of submission.
    Intersection = Decision or change.

Signature - Commitment; ownership; the seal of God; responsibility.
Exodus 28:11, 21, & 36, Haggai 2:23, Daniel 6:8-14, & 17.

Silver - Knowledge; redemption; refining; idolatry; spiritual adultery; betrayal (30 pieces of silver).
Proverbs 2:3-4, John 17:3, Acts 19:24, Matt 26:14-16.

Silver Cord - Connection to God; life; the spinal marrow.
Ecclesiastes 12:6-7.
    When the Silver Cord Breaks = The end of life.
    Ecclesiastes 12:6-7.
    Umbilical Cord = Soul tie, good or bad.
    Genesis 44:30, 1 Samuel 18:1-3.

Singing - Rejoicing; overflowing of thankfulness.
Isaiah 35:2, Psalm 98:1-9, Psalm 95:1-2.

Sink (Bathroom) - Prayer; repentance; petition to God; self-justification.
Isaiah 1:16, James 4:8, Psalm 26:6, Job 9:30, Matthew 27:24.
Soap = Cleansing; conviction; forgiveness; prayer; repentance.
Malachi 3:2, Jeremiah 2:22, Isaiah 1:16.
Washcloth = Truth; doctrine; understanding; enhances cleansing.
Psalm 51:7, John 15:3.
Dirty Washcloth = False doctrine; insincere apology; error.
Job 14:4.

Sister - Spiritual sister, sister in Christ; someone she reminds you of; self; the Church; she may represent herself in the natural.
Matthew 12:50.
Husband's Sister = The Church.

Sister-in-law - Representative; spiritual sister in another fellowship; someone she reminds you of or she may represent her family, herself, or the dreamer when the dreamer is female; adultery.
Leviticus 18:16.
Brother's Wife = The brother himself.
Wife's Sister = The wife herself.
Wife of a Recognized Minister = The Church.

Sitting - In place of authority; in position of power; throne of God; seat of Satan. See Seat.
1 Peter 3:22, Ephesians 1:20, Hebrews 10:12, Hebrews 12:2, Matthew 23:1-2, Revelation 2:13.

Skateboard - Balance; fast; skillful manoeuvring; skilled ministry; risky.
Romans 9:28, 2 Samuel 2:18, Habakkuk 3:19.

Skeleton - Death; without the Spirit; starvation or famine (skin and bones).
Ezekiel 37:1-14, Lamentations 4:8-9.

Skiing - Supported by God's power; stepping out in faith; swift; fast progress.
Matthew 14:29-31, John 6:19-21.

Skins - Covering; sacrifice.
Genesis 3:21, 2 Corinthians 5:2-4, Hebrews 9:13-14, & 22.

Skirt - Covering; Grace. See Clothing.
Jeremiah 2:34, Jeremiah 13:26.
No skirt = Uncovered; shame from sin; hypocrisy.

Sky - God's presence; heavenly places; up high in the Spirit.
Ephesians 2:6, Ephesians 1:3, Acts 26:19, Ezekiel 8:1-3, Ezekiel 11:1, & 22-25, Revelation 4:2.

Skyscraper - Multilevel ministry; built up in the Spirit; prophetic giftedness; high level of spiritual experience; revelation.
2 Corinthians 12:1-4, Ezekiel 11:1, & 22-25, Revelation 1:10, Revelation 4:2.

Sleep - Unconscious; unaware; ignorant; danger; death; laziness; rest.
Romans 13:11, Isaiah 29:10, John 11:11-14, Proverbs 20:13, Ecclesiastes 5:12,
Jeremiah 31:26. See Bed.
Lack of sleep = Overworked.
Psalm 127:2, Ecclesiastes 5:12b.

Sleeping = Being overtaken; out of control; something being hidden from one's consciousness; in danger.
Proverbs 20:13, Jonah 1:5-6.
Oversleep = Late.
Romans 13:11.

Slug or Snail - Slowly eats away the truth of the word of God; corruption of injustices; unclean issues; lawlessness. See Insects.
2 Timothy 2:17, Nahum 3:15, James 5:3, Leviticus 11:29-30, & 41-45, Leviticus 22:5-6, Habakkuk 1:14.

Sloth - Lazy; Lethargic; lifeless; slow.
1Timothy 5:8, Proverbs 18:9, Ecclesiastes 10:18.

Smile - friendly; benevolent; good will; act of kindness; without offense; agreement; seduction.
Psalm 34:5, Proverbs 15:13, Proverbs18:24.
　　Smiling = Sign of friendship; seducing.
　　Numbers 6:26, Proverbs 16:15.

Smoke - Manifest glory of God; prayers of the saints; a sign; hindrance.
Isaiah 6:3-4, Revelation 8:4, Acts 10:4, Genesis 19:28, Proverbs 10:26.
　　Toxic Smoke = Demonic strongholds.
　　Revelation 9:2-3.

Smoking - Pride; bitterness; bitter memories; offense; unforgiving; envy; jealousy; self-righteousness.
Isaiah 65:5, Proverbs 21:24, 1 Corinthians 8:1, Deuteronomy 29:19-20.

Smoking Furnace - Offense; anger; trouble. Isaiah 65:5, Proverbs 21:24, 1 Corinthians 8:1, Deuteronomy 29:19-20.

Snake - Satan; curse; demon; creeper; subtle; deception; threat; danger; hatred; slander; critical spirit; drunkenness; witchcraft; sorcery; deliberate spiritual warfare needed. Genesis 3:14a, Revelation 12:9, Revelation 20:2, 2 Corinthians 11:3, & 13-15, Isaiah 27:1, Psalm 58:3-5, Psalm 91:13, Job 26:13b, Exodus 7:9-12, Amos 5:19, Psalm 140:3, Romans 3:13, Proverbs 23:32, Isaiah 59:5.

Fangs = Evil intent or motive: poisonous; great danger. Psalm 57:4, Psalm 58:6, Proverbs 30:14, Daniel 7:5-7, Revelation 9:8.

Bit by a Snake = Attack of the enemy; retribution of an injurious or oppressive act against another; consequence of sin; doubting the providence and goodness of God; injured by venomous words. Acts 28:3-5, Ecclesiastes 10:8, Numbers 21:5-9, 1 Corinthians 10:9, Revelation 9:19.

Rattlesnake = Words; threats; warning; alarm; fear. Psalm 58:4 (MSG).

Cobra = Power to rule; authority; under the grip of Satan; spiritual warfare. Exodus 7:9-12, Psalm 91:13.

King Cobra = Satan. Revelation 12:9, Genesis 3:1, 2 Corinthians 11:3, & 14, Ephesians 6:12, & 16.

Python, Anaconda or Boa Constrictor = Divination; familiar spirits; ancestral spirits; a regional spirit; a coiling spirit that squeezes out the breath of life (the Holy Spirit) and cut off a believer's lifeline to God (prayer); puts believers in bondage; thwarts a believer's purpose; high level of spiritual warfare needed.

Acts 16:16-18, Ephesians 6:12, Psalm 91:13, Daniel 10:13 & 20.

Viper or Cockatrice = Demon; curse; deception; threat; danger; hatred; slander; critical spirit; fiery; deadly glance (evil eye); envy; malignant; fierce spiritual warfare needed. Isaiah 59:5, Isaiah 11:8, Isaiah 14:29, Amos 5:19, Psalm 140:3, Proverbs 23:32, Matthew 3:7, Matthew 12:34, Ephesians 6:12, Psalm 91:13.

Fiery (Seraph) or Poisonous Snake = High ranking evil spirit; deadly burning bite; poisonous words; "flying", a snake which springs like a dart from trees, on its prey, signifying the type of spiritual attack; high levels of spiritual warfare needed. Numbers 21:6-9, Isaiah 14:29, Isaiah 30:6, Ephesians 6:12, Psalm 58:3-5, Psalm 91:13, Psalm 140:3, Romans 3:13.

Sea Snake or Monster = Leviathan spirit; Satan; world power; extremely strategic level of spiritual warfare needed. Isaiah 27:1, Job 26:13, Psalm 74:13-14, Isaiah 51:9, Revelation 12:3-17, Ezekiel 29:3.

Leviathan = Satan; high level demonic spirit against the Government of God; global level of wickedness; division; confusion; twists the Word of God, and the words of spiritual leaders; causes miscommunications between believers; instigator of overwhelming situations or tribulation; extremely strategic level of spiritual warfare needed. Isaiah 27:1-3, Psalm 74:13-14, Ezekiel 29:3, Ezekiel 32:2, Job Chapter 41, Ephesians 6:12, & 16, Genesis 3:1, Matthew 4:6, Romans 8:35-39, Matthew 24:6-13, Revelation 20:2.

Dragon = Satan; high level demonic spirit; global level of wickedness; the nation of China (the Dragon being China's national symbol); antichrist, extremely strategic level of spiritual warfare needed.

Revelation 12:3-17, Ephesians 6:12, & 16, Isaiah 27:1, Isaiah 51:9, Revelation 13:2-4, Psalm 74:13, Ezekiel 29:3, Revelation 20:2.

Snow - Pure; word; grace; favor; yet to be fulfilled.
Psalm 147:16, Isaiah 55:10-11, Job 38:22-23.
> **Dirty Snow** = Impure.
> **Snowdrift** = Barrier; hindrance; opposition; snare.
> Job 6:16.

Snowshoes - Faith; walking in the Spirit; supported by faith in the Word of God, gospel of peace.
Matthew 14:29, Ephesians 6:15.

Soap - Cleansing; conviction; forgiveness; prayer; repentance.
See Bathroom.
Malachi 3:2, Jeremiah 2:22, Isaiah 1:16.

Socks - Covering; partial protection; partially prepared; heart and walk in the word of God. See Feet, Shoes.
Ephesians 6:15,
> **Clean White Socks** = Pure heart; pure walk before God.
> See White in Part 2.
> **Black or Dirty Socks** = Impure heart; impure walk before God. See Black in Part 2.

Soaring or Flying - Moved by the Spirit; ministering in the gifts of the Spirit. See Airplane, Pilot.

Soldier - Spiritual warfare; Christ; angel, protection; demon, accuser or opponent; persecution.
Daniel 10:13, Joshua 5:13-15, Revelation 12:7, & 10, 2 Timothy 2:3-4; Psalm 55:21.

A Team = A powerful specialized deliverance ministry; Special Forces unit; falsely accused by the accuser of the brethren; AWOL from corrupt systems; spiritual mercenaries; a diversified tight-knit group working in unity; secret weapon; strong leadership; consistent accurate communication; strategic operations of God; spiritual warfare; a force to be reckoned with.
Revelation 12:6-10, 2 Timothy 3:3, Luke 22:31-32, Colossians 2:13-15, 1 Peter 5:7-8, 2 Corinthians 10:3-6, Ephesians 6:10-18.

Son - Similar characteristics or behavior of oneself; someone the son reminds the dreamer of; innocence; purity; humble; trusting; new believer; immaturity; undisciplined; disobedient.
Isaiah 3:4, & 12a, Matthew 18:3-6, 1 John 2:12-14, 1 Corinthians 13:11, Hebrews 12:8, Ephesians 5:6, Colossians 3:6.
Many Sons = Future children of God; the church.
Jeremiah 31:17, John 1:12.

South - Natural; world; sin; temptation; trial; flesh; corruption; deception.
Joshua 10:40, Job 37:9.

Sow (Plant Seed) - Plan ahead; plant seed; give; prayer.
Jeremiah 29:11-13, Galatians 6:7-9, 2 Corinthians 9:6.
Sowing = Planning for the future; creating by speaking the word of God.
Reap = Harvest; reward, good or bad.
Galatians 6:7-9, 2 Corinthians 9:6, Hosea 10:12, Job 4:8, Hosea 8:7.
Reaping = Reward of labor.

Speaking Out or Crying Out - Communication in prayer; message from God; conversation with God; counsel; gossip; the enemy's voice.

Psalm 4:1, Psalm 20:9, 2 Samuel 22:7, Psalm 18:6, Jeremiah 33:3, Psalm 32:1-11, 1 Timothy 5:13, Genesis3:3-4, Jeremiah 29:8-9, 1 John 4:1.

Spear - Words; accusations; slander; gossip; attacks of the enemy; children; prayers; deliverance. See Knife, Sword.
Psalm 64:3, Psalm 11:2, Ephesians 6:17-18, Isaiah 49:2, Deuteronomy 32:42, 2 Kings 13:17.

Spider - Evil; sin; false doctrine; temptation; deceiver; difficult escape from entanglement; conflict; stronghold; threatening issue with danger of entanglement or possibly death; false trust; tenacious; clever; evil spirit; religious spirit; predatory person.
Proverbs 30:24, & 28, Proverbs 7:22-23, Isaiah 59:5-6, Genesis 31:27, 2 Corinthians 10:4-5, Acts 4:17, 21, & 29, 1 Peter 2:23, Job 8:13-15, 1 Timothy 6:9, 2 Timothy 2:26, Matthew 23:27-28; Psalm 91:3, Psalm 124:7, Hosea 9:8.

Black Widow = Great danger; deadly; life-threatening; evil; slander.
James 3:8.

Fangs = Evil intent or motive: poisonous; great danger.
Psalm 57:4, Psalm 58:6, Proverbs 30:14, Daniel 7:5-7, Revelation 9:8.

Spider Web = Snare; lies and deception; scheme; trap; ruin; internet.
Ecclesiastes 7:26, Isaiah 59:5-7; Psalm 91:3, Psalm 124:7, Ecclesiastes 9:12; Psalm 140:5, Psalm 119:110, Psalm 141:9.

Sports Games or Competitions - Teamwork; contest; competition; recreation; sportsmanship; unsportsmanlike conduct.
2 Timothy 2:5, 1 Corinthians 9:24-27.

Stepping out of Bounds = Disqualified; conduct out of order.
Galatians 5:7.

Spot - Unrighteousness; sin; iniquity; self-righteousness; uncleanness. See Clothing.
Psalm 109:18, Isaiah 64:6, Zechariah 3:3-4.
Wrinkled = Still issues that need to be dealt with.
Without Spot or Wrinkle = Glorious church.
Ephesians 5:26-27.

Spring Time - New beginning; fresh start; revival; renewal; regeneration; salvation; refreshing.
Song of Solomon 2:11-12, Isaiah 43:19, Acts 3:19.

Square - Legalistic; religious tradition; cold; heartless; no mercy; harsh; worldly.
Leviticus 19:9.

Squid - Mind control; fleshly control or influence (tentacles "tongue") by words; fast; sneaky; changes its behaviour and appearance to stay hidden; controlling spirit; soul-tie stronghold (on head); in need of deliverance; need spiritual warfare and prayer coverage. See Eight in Part 2.
Exodus 2:14, Proverbs 6:5, Galatians 2:4, 1 Kings 21:7-10, 2 Corinthians 10:4-5.

Stadium - Tremendous impact; great influence.
Acts 17:18-23.

Staff - Support; strength; authority; support of life; discipline; abuse; judgement.
Zechariah 8:4, Exodus 14:16, 1 Samuel 17:40, 43, & 45, 2 Samuel 23:21, Mark 6:8, Hebrews 11:21, Numbers 13:23, Numbers 17:6-9, Isaiah 14:5, Psalm 105:16 (KJV), Leviticus

26:26, Ezekiel 5:16 (KJV), Ezekiel 14:13 (KJV), Psalm 23:4, Exodus 21:19-20, Numbers 22:27, Isaiah 10:5.

Stage - Public platform, success; facade.
Luke 1:80, Genesis 37:9 See with Genesis 42:6, Matthew 2:3-8.

Stairs - Progress; promotion; procedure; ambition.
Exodus 20:26, 2 Kings 9:13.
Stair Rail = Safety; precaution.
Climbing the Stairs = Going higher in the Spirit; taking steps to a promotion.
Psalm 24:3.
Finding it Hard to Climb the Stairs = Struggles in the spirit realm.
Going down the Stairs = Demotion; failure; backslide.

Stalled Vehicle - Ministry on hold; operation in one's own strength; need to take authority; hindrance by Satan; opposition.
Isaiah 49:2, Exodus 14:13-16, Galatians 5:7-12, Nehemiah 4:1-18, 1 Thessalonians 2:18.

Stamp - Seal; authority; authorisation; small but powerful.
Esther 8:8, 2 Timothy 2:19.
Envelope = Important message from God; prophecy; personal instructions.
Job 33:14-16, Deuteronomy 29:29.
Sealed = Prophecy un-interpreted; message or instruction not revealed.
Daniel 8:26, Daniel 9:24, Daniel 12:4, & 9.
Opened = Prophecy interpreted; message or instruction revealed.
Revelation 22:10.

Letter = Important message from God; prophecy; personal instructions.
Job 33:14-16, Deuteronomy 29:29.

Standing - Firm in the faith; steadfast; committed; not finished.
Ephesians 6:13-14, Exodus 14:13, Psalm 122:2, Proverbs 22:29, Zechariah 4:14.
   Standing Straight = Not crooked; correct direction.
   Luke 13:13.

Star(s) - Multitudes; Christian; apostle; preacher; pastor; angel; soul winner; minister; leader; priest; role model, good or bad; hero; movie star.
Genesis 22:17, Genesis 37:9-10, Philippians 2:15, Revelation 1:20, Daniel 12:3, Revelation 12:4, Jude 1:13.
   Falling Star = Fallen angel; Satan; apostate church.
   Daniel 8:10, Revelation 12:4, Luke 10:18.

Station Wagon - Natural or spiritual family; family ministry; fellowship. See Vehicle.
Ephesians 3:14-15, 1 John 1:7.

Stealth Bomber - Strategic powerful ministry; effective; attacking; does not attract attention; very difficult to intercept ministry's assignment; effortless flow in the Spirit; a call to regional or national intercessory ministry; heavy spiritual warfare; great angelic protection. See Airplane, Bomb, Nuclear Bomb.
Genesis 41:43, 2 Kings 10:16, Zechariah 6:1-8, Isaiah 5:26-28, Joshua 8:2-7, Daniel 10:12-13, & 20-21, Ephesians 6:12.

Steering Wheel - The controlling or leading part; the means by which leadership is affected. See Vehicle.

Steel - Weight; wickedness; sin; burden, the cares of the world; judgment; fool or foolishness.
Zechariah 5:8, Exodus 15:10, Proverbs 27:3, Hebrews 12:1.

Sticker Thorns or Cocklebur (Xanthium) - Irritant; irritated; minor afflictions.
Hebrews 6:8, Exodus 22:6, Matthew 13:22.
Thorns = Hindrance; poverty; gossip, evil circumstance; curse; defense; persecution; vexation; attack on understanding (if in eyes); cares of this life.
Hebrews 6:8, Exodus 22:6, Numbers 33:55, 2 Corinthians 12:7-9, 1 Corinthians 11:23-28, Ephesians 1:18, Matthew 13:22.
Thorn in ones' Flesh = Vexation; persecution.
Numbers 33:55, 2 Corinthians 12:7-9 See with 2 Corinthians 11:23-28.

Stone - Christ Jesus, our Chief Cornerstone; solid foundation; word of God; witness; precious; chosen; offense; defiance.
Ephesians 2:20-22, Isaiah 28:16, Psalm 118:22, Matthew 21:42, Acts 4:11, Romans 9:33, Joshua 24:27, 1 Peter 2:4-8, Isaiah 8:14.

Stoning Someone – Involved in malicious accusation of others; unforgiveness; wicked action.
Acts 7:58, Ezekiel 23:47, 1 Kings 21:10-14.

Stork - Expectant; new birth; pregnancy; new baby; new experiences; forthcoming. See Bird, Baby.
Jeremiah 8:7.

Storm - Disturbance; spiritual warfare; witchcraft; sudden calamity or destruction; judgement; trial; persecution; opposition; outpouring of revival; powerful move of the Spirit. See Tornado, Whirlwind.

Isaiah 25:4, Acts 27:14-15, & 18-25, 1 Thessalonians 5:3, Nahum 1:3, 2 Samuel 22:10-15, Psalm 18:9-14, Psalm 104:3, Psalm 58:9, Hosea 13:3, Zechariah 7:14.

Straight - Fixed in attitude; going in the right direction.
Isaiah 40:3-4, John 1:23, Isaiah 45:2, Luke 3:5.

Straight Jacket - Bound by the enemy; helpless situation; spirit of control; weakness of the flesh; out of control; demonic strength and influence.
Judges 15:12-13, Lamentations 1:14, Daniel 3:21-24, Ephesians 6:10-11, Mark 5:3-5.

Strange Man - Angel, oneself, or a demon: God's messenger, person with evil intent; danger. See Kind Stranger, White-headed Stranger.
Matthew 2:13, Hebrews 13:2, Luke 10:33.

Strange Woman - Seducing spirit; temptation; deception; witchcraft; messenger from God; angel; messenger from Satan; demonic spirit. See Harlot.
Proverbs 2:16, Proverbs 23:27, Proverbs 22:14.

Straw – Worthless; unprofitable works that are burned up.
1 Corinthians 3:12-15, Jeremiah 23:28, Isaiah 5:24, Psalm 1:4, Matthew 3:12.

Street - Way; Christ; the Christian faith; truth; life; way of error.
Isaiah 35:8, John 14:6, Matthew 7:13-14, Jeremiah 6:16, Nahum 2:4, Haggai 1:5-7, Luke 15:15-17, Psalm 69:2, Isaiah 57:20, Jeremiah 18:15-16.
   Under Construction = In preparation; not ready; change; hindrance.
   Crossroads = Decision; change of direction.
   Jeremiah 6:16, Haggai 1:5-7.

Long Street = Time.
Dead End = Change direction, stop and repent; certain failure.
Luke 15:15-17.
Narrow Street = Way to life; God's way.
Matthew 7:13-14.
Broad Street = Way of destruction; man's way.
Matthew 7:13-14.

Stripper - Seduction; base carnality; lust; the worldly church; adultery; fornication; temptation; snare; unclean person; stubborn. See Sex.
Revelation 17:5, Ecclesiastes 7:26, Jeremiah 3:3.

Stumble - Fail; sin; mistake; overcome; obstacle; ignorance; deceived; backslide.
Psalm 27:2, John 11:10, 1 Samuel 2:4.

Submarine - The Underground Church; persecuted; hidden ones; spies out new or enemy territory; flows with the Spirit of God; the Holy Spirit searching out the spirit of believers. See Water, Telescope, Torpedo.
John 8:59, John 12:36, Acts 8:1-4, John 14:22, Romans 16:25-26, Numbers 13:17-21, Numbers 14:6-8, Proverbs 20:27, Romans 8:27, Psalm 139:1-4, & 23-24.

Suicide - Self destruction; self hatred; grief; hopeless; remorse; foolish action.
Ecclesiastes 7:16, Matthew 27:5.

Suitcase - Private walk; transition; move; temporary; travel.
Ezekiel 12:3-4.

Summer - Harvest; opportunity; time to prepare for the second coming of Christ; trial; fruit of one's labor; drought; heat of affliction.
Proverbs 6:8, Proverbs 10:5, Proverbs 30:25, Matthew 24:32-33, Daniel 2:35, 2 Samuel 16:1-2, Micah 7:1-2, Psalm 32:4.

Super Hero - Christ; Holy Spirit; Christian empowered by the Holy Spirit; powerful man or woman of God; demonic spirit.
Luke 24:19, & 51, Acts 10:38, Acts 7:22, 2 Corinthians 12:12, Luke 4:6, Luke 10:19.
Superman can be an antichrist.
2 Thessalonians 2:9.

Supersonic Flight - Fast; powerful; soaring in the Spirit; fully empowered by the Spirit; deep in the Spirit; moving in the deep things of God; extreme acceleration into the new season and ministry. See Airplane, Flying.
2 Kings 2:9-11, Psalm 104:3-4.

Surf - Wave of the Holy Spirit; flow of the Holy Spirit.
1 Kings 18:12, Isaiah 44:3, Isaiah 59:19, Mark 1:8, Acts 2:17.

Surfer - Prophet; worship leader; moving in the gifts of the Spirit.
Isaiah 40:31, Habakkuk 2:1-2, Matthew 14:29-30, 1 Samuel 10:5-6, Romans 5:15 (NIV, HCSB, AMP/AMPC).

Surfing - Flowing in the Holy Spirit.
Acts 11:28, Revelation 11:11.

Swamp - Stagnant in the flow of the Holy Spirit; illness; blocked flow due to neglect or perversion of the gospel; rejection of the gospel; bitter; spiritually dead.
Ezekiel 47:11, Exodus 15:23, Mark 12:1-12, Isaiah 42:15, Isaiah 50:2, Psalm 107:33-35.

Swimming - Move in the spirit, recreation, spiritual life. See Water.
Ezekiel 47:5, Ephesians 3:8.

Swimming in clear water = Time of refreshing; cleansing; the word of God; healing when water stirred.
Acts 3:19, Ephesians 5:26, John 5:2-9.

Swimming in dirty water = Corrupted spiritually; causing strife; bitter words; unstable hypocrite; sin; false doctrine; unattractive or too common to the proud.
Ezekiel 32:2, Ezekiel 34:18-19, Isaiah 57:20, Exodus 15:23-24, Job 8:11, 2 Kings 5:12, Ezekiel 47:11.

Swimming in fast-flowing water = Get ready for things to accelerate and get exciting.

Swimming in stagnant water = Stale in the things of God.
Ezekiel 47:11.

Swimming in shallow water = You might be too comfortable and need a challenge.
Ezekiel 47:4.

Swimming in deep water = You are maturing spiritually, possibly taking more risks.
Ezekiel 47:5.

Swimming Pool - Spiritual place; church; home; family; God's blessings; time of refreshing; cleansing; the word of God; healing when water stirred. See Water.
Isaiah 41:18, Acts 3:19, Ephesians 5:26, John 5:2-9.

Dirty or Dry Pool = Corrupt or destitute spiritually; backslidden.
Jeremiah 50:38.

Swine - Unclean; selfish; backslider; unbeliever; glutton; fornicator; hypocrite; destroyer; devourer; idolater.
2 Peter 2:22, Matthew 7:6.

Boar = Persecutor; hostile to virtue; vicious; vengeful; danger.
Psalm 80:13, 2 Timothy 3:2-3.

Swing - Peaceful; quietness; fellowship; romance; ups and downs in life.
Isaiah 30:15, Isaiah 55:12.
Swinging = Full flow of peace.
Swinging High = Overindulgence; unnecessary risks; danger.

Sword - Words; word of God; critical words; evil intent; threaten; strife; war; persecution. See Knife, Arrows.
Hebrews 4:12, Psalm 64:3, Ephesians 6:17, Isaiah 49:2, Deuteronomy 32:42, Proverbs 12:18, Revelation 6:4.
Double Edged Sword = Rhema word, a specific Scripture from the Lord as a deadly weapon to speak against the enemy for a specific situation; prophetic utterance.
Matthew 4:3-10, Luke 4:4-12.

Synagogue - Jewish place of worship; Jewish people gathering together; a Jewish place of teaching the Torah.
Luke 4:16-20, John 12:42, John 18:20, Acts 14:1, Acts 17:1-2, & 10-11.

T

Taekwondo - Spiritual warfare; deliverance ministry; self-defence.
Ephesians 6:12, 1 Timothy 6:12.

Table – Communion; agreement; conference; provision.
Psalm 23:5, 1 Corinthians 10:20-21.

Under the Table = Deceitful dealings; hidden motives; evil intent.
Daniel 11:27, Psalm 78:19.

Tail - End of something; last time; the least; subservient; disobedient; beneath; cursed; trouble maker; powerful sting; support; powerful weapon; false prophet; influence; allegiance.
Exodus 4:4, Deuteronomy 28:13, & 44, Isaiah 7:4, Revelation 9:10, & 19, Job 40:17, Judges 15:4, Isaiah 9:14-15, Revelation 12:3-4.
Wagging Dog Tail = Friend or acceptance.
Large Animal Tail = Powerful support or weapon.
Job 40:17.
Dog Tail Tucked In = Betrayal; guilt; shame; cowardly.

Tape Measure - Measure for service; boundaries of one's service; fitting preparation; preparation for expansion; change of heart to enter in.
Ephesians 4:13-16, 2 Corinthians 10:12-16, 1 Samuel 2:19, Isaiah 54:2, Mark 12:34.
Measuring = Determining one's faith and growth; time; distance; decision; precision; reciprocity; judgement; the heart receiving by hearing.
Romans 12:3, Ephesians 4:13, Psalm 39:4, Joshua 3:4, Deuteronomy 21:2, Job 28:25, Isaiah 40:12, Luke 6:38, Matthew 7:1-2, Isaiah 65:7, Daniel 5:27, Mark 4:24.
Precise Measurement = Diligent study of the Word; possible confirmation of a future event.
2 Timothy 2:15, Zechariah 2:1-5, Ezekiel 40:2-4.
Measuring Oneself = Pondering truth; considering one's ways; looking at one's progress of ridding oneself of sins; natural concern for health; obsession of appearance.
2 Timothy 2:15, 1 Corinthians 14:29, 1 Thessalonians 5:21, Hebrews 12:1-3, 2 Corinthians 10:7, 12, & 17, 1 Corinthians 1:26-31, 1 John 2:16.

Balances = Justice; judgement; business; falsehood; deceitful; divide; purchase; integrity; make judgement before hearing the matter; vanity. See Business, Merchant. Proverbs 16:11, Ezekiel 45:10-12, Daniel 5:27, Proverbs 20:23, Proverbs 11:1, Deuteronomy 25:13-15, Leviticus 19:35-36, Hosea 12:7, Micah 6:10-11, Ezekiel 5:1, Jeremiah 32:9-10, Job 31:6, Job 6:2, Proverbs 18:13, John 7:51, Psalm 62:9.

Taps (Bugle Call) - End; finished; announcement.
John 19:28-30, 1 Corinthians 15:52, Numbers 10:2-3, Joel 2:1, & 15, Revelation 10:7.

Tar - Covering; repair; patch; bitterness; offense; hatred; grudge.
Genesis 6:14, Genesis 11:3, Exodus 2:3, Isaiah 34:8-9.

Tares - Children of darkness; evil ones; dangerous; deceptive.
Matthew 13:36-43.

Tasting – Experience; discern; try; test; judge.
Psalm 34:8, Job 6:30, Hebrews 2:9.

Tattoo - Identity; message; mark of God; God's protection; fugitive; tough; in some cultures, may reflect a mark of an idol, but rarely so.
If the tattoo has a recognizable image or number, see the corresponding listing.
Genesis 4:14-15, Song of Solomon 8:6, Isaiah 49:16, Revelation 14:1, Psalm 22:16, Leviticus 19:28.

Tea (Iced Tea) - Refreshing; grace; good news; salvation; soothing; time of refreshing (Tea time).
Proverbs 25:25, Isaiah 28:12, Acts 3:19.

Tea Bag = Healing.
Revelation 22:2, Ezekiel 47:12.
Hot Tea = Warmth; social gathering.

Team - Church; ministries; business; spiritual opposition.
Ephesians 4:16, John 10:16, Nehemiah 4:6 - the whole
Chapter, Romans 8:31, & 35-39, Ephesians 6:12.
Teams Working Together = Fighting for a common cause;
specialized ministries working together in unity; fully
committed; united to fight against the plots of the enemy;
a heart that completes the assigned work of the Lord.
Nehemiah Chapters 4 and 6, John 10:16, 1 Corinthians
15:58.
The A Team = A powerful specialized deliverance ministry;
Special Forces unit; falsely accused by the accuser of
the brethren; goes AWOL from corrupt systems; spiritual
mercenaries; a diversified tight-knit group working in unity;
secret weapon; strong leadership; consistent accurate
communication; strategic operations of God; spiritual
warfare; a force to be reckoned with.
Revelation 12:6-10, 2 Timothy 3:3, Luke 22:31-32,
Colossians 2:13-15, 1 Peter 5:7-8, 2 Corinthians 10:3-6,
Ephesians 6:10-18.

Tearing Clothes - Sorrow; grief; disagreement; anger;
repentance.
2 Chronicles 34:27, 2 Samuel 3:31, Psalm 7:2, Amos 1:11,
Hosea 13:8, Zechariah 11:16, Matthew 7:6, Joel 2:13.

Tears - Sorrow; grief; trouble; affliction; pain; repentance; joy.
Psalm 56:8, Psalm 6:6-7, Psalm 31:9, Psalm 88:9, 2 Kings 20:5,
Jeremiah 31:16, Hebrews 12:17, Ecclesiastes 4:1, John 16:20,
Isaiah 25:8, Revelation 21:4, 2 Timothy 1:4, Psalm 126:5-6.

Teeth - Wisdom; consuming power; experience; work out one's own salvation; devours; narrow escape. Jeremiah 15:16, Hebrews 5:12-14, Isaiah 41:15, Zechariah 9:7-8, Song of Solomon 4:2, Song of Solomon 6:6, Proverbs 30:14, Micah 3:2-6, Job 19:20.

> **Wisdom Teeth** = Great wisdom and understanding; maturity.
> Hebrews 5:14, 1 Kings 3:9-12.
>
>> **Impacted Wisdom Teeth** = Not given enough room for growth; painful experience; damaging doctrine; corrupting situation.
>
> **Toothache** = Trial; trouble; pain.
> Proverbs 25:19.
>
> **Dull Teeth** = Worn down from bad experiences; weakened by consequences of bad influence.
> Ezekiel 18:2, Jeremiah 31:29-30.
>
> **Loose Teeth** = Loss of power; uncertain.
>
> **False Teeth** = Worldly reasoning; philosophical reasoning; wisdom and knowledge through natural experience or failures; replacement; tradition; error.
> Colossians 2:8,1 Timothy 6:20, 2 Timothy 2:16-17.
>
> **Broken Tooth** = Bad experience; problem; suffering; damaged.
> Ezekiel 18:2, Jeremiah 31:29-30, Proverbs 25:19, Hebrews 5:8, Psalm 3:7.
>
> **Grinding Teeth** = Anger; indignation; complaining; grievance; anxiousness; nervousness.
> Matthew 24:51, Matthew 25:30, Luke 13:28, Psalm 37:12, Psalm 112:10.
>
> **Animal Teeth** = Danger.
> Psalm 58:6, Job 4:10, Proverbs 30:14, Daniel 7:5-7, Revelation 9:8.
>
>> **Fangs** = Evil intent or motive; poisonous; great danger.
>> Psalm 57:4, Psalm 58:6, Proverbs 30:14, Daniel 7:5-7, Revelation 9:8.

Brushing Teeth = Cleaning one's thoughts and words; meditation.
Psalm 119:9.
Baby Teeth = Immaturity; no experience; without wisdom and knowledge; innocent.
Isaiah 7:16, see with Hebrews 5:12-14.

Telephone - Communication; prayer; message from God; conversation with God; counsel; gossip; the enemy's voice.
Psalm 4:1, Psalm 20:9, 2 Samuel 22:7, Psalm 18:6, Jeremiah 33:3, Genesis 3:9-11, Psalm 32:1-11, 1 Timothy 5:13, Jeremiah 29:8-9, 1 John 4:1, Jeremiah 22:5, John 8:43.
Busy or bad signal = Barrier or hindrance to prayer.
Jeremiah 22:5, John 8:43.

Telescope - Future; prophetic vision; at a distance; far away in time; make a problem appear larger or closer. See binoculars.
Revelation 4:1, John 16:13.

Television - Vision; message; prophetic dreams and visions; news; warning; idolatry; entertainment; distraction; spirit of stupor; laziness; deception.
Numbers 24:4, & 16, Daniel 2:19, Psalm 89:19, Numbers 12:6, Jeremiah 23:28, Daniel 7:1, 2 Samuel 18:26, 1 Corinthians 10:11-13, Daniel 3:5b, Revelation 16:2b; 1 Thessalonians 5:6-7.

Temple - God's habitation; refuge; human body; place to meet with God.
Isaiah 4:5-6, Revelation 7:15, John 2:21, 1 Corinthians 3:16-17, 1 Corinthians 6:19-20, Ephesians 2:21.

Tent - Temporary covering; flexible; leisure.
2 Corinthians 5:1-4, 2 Peter 1:13-14, Isaiah 54:2.

Termites - Corruption; hidden destruction; secret sin; deception; demons; unclean spirits. See Insects.
Psalm 11:3, Haggai 1:6.

Test - Being tested.
Genesis 22:1-14, Hebrews 11:17, Proverbs 17:3, 1 Peter 1:6-7.
Prepared = Ready for promotion or advancement.
Unprepared = Need to get more training or help.

The A Team - A powerful specialized deliverance ministry; Special Forces unit; falsely accused by the accuser of the brethren; goes AWOL from corrupt systems; spiritual mercenaries; a diversified tight-knit group working in unity; secret weapon; strong leadership; consistent accurate communication; strategic operations of God; spiritual warfare; a force to be reckoned with. See Team.
Revelation 12:6-10, 2 Timothy 3:3, Luke 22:31-32, Colossians 2:13-15, 1 Peter 5:7-8, 2 Corinthians 10:3-6, Ephesians 6:10-18.

Thickets - Snare; obstacles; hindrances; trial; wicked person; rejected; cursed. See Thorns.
Isaiah 32:13a, Micah 7:4a, Hebrews 6:8.

Thief - Hidden; deceiver; deception; fraud; destruction; Satan; evil intent; works of the flesh; unexpected loss.
John 10:10a, Colossians 2:8, Proverbs 29:24, 1 Thessalonians 5:2 & 4.

Thief's Victim - Victim of false doctrine; truth lost through tradition or philosophy; loss of liberty; temptation; unaware; secret; covert operation; God's judgment on the wicked.
1 Thessalonians 5:2-4, verse 3, Luke 11:22, Luke 10:30.

Thigh - Works of the flesh; the natural man; strength; oath; seduction; lust.
Genesis 32:31-32, Numbers 5:21, Isaiah 47:2.

Thorns - Hindrance; poverty; gossip, evil circumstance; curse; defence; persecution; vexation; attack on understanding (if in eyes); cares of this life.
Hebrews 6:8, Exodus 22:6, Joshua 23:12-13, Ezekiel 2:6, Numbers 33:55, 2 Corinthians 12:7-9, 1 Corinthians 11:23-28, Ephesians 1:18, Matthew 13:22.

> **Thorn in ones' Flesh** = Vexation; persecution.
> Numbers 33:55, 2 Corinthians 12:7-9 See with 2 Corinthians 11:23-28.
> **Sticker Thorns or Cocklebur (Xanthium)** = Irritant; Irritated; minor afflictions.
> Hebrews 6:8, Exodus 22:6, Matthew 13:22.
> **Briers (Thickets)** = Snare; obstacles; hindrances; trial; wicked person; rejected; cursed.
> Ezekiel 2:6, Isaiah 32:13a, Micah 7:4a, Hebrews 6:8.

Throne - Place of authority; position of power; throne of God; seat of Satan.
Revelation 4:2-3, Matthew 23:2-6, Matthew 20:21, Acts 2:32-33, 1 Peter 3:22, Ephesians 1:20, Hebrews 10:12.

> **Someone Sitting on the Throne** = One in place of authority; in position of power; throne of God; seat of Satan.
> 1 Peter 3:22, Ephesians 1:20, Hebrews 10:12, Hebrews 12:2, Matthew 23:1-2, Revelation 2:13.
> **Sitting on a Throne** = One's place of authority; one's position of power.
> 1 Peter 3:22, Ephesians 1:20, Hebrews 10:12.
> **Difficulty Finding the Throne** = Hindrances to obtaining the place of authority.
> 1 Samuel 18:8-29.

Stolen Throne = Warfare needed to maintain or recover one's authority, or designated place or position.
2 Samuel 15:1-36.

Thunder - Loud signal from God; warning; voice of God; dispensational change.
John 12:28-30, 2 Samuel 22:14, Psalm 18:13.

Tick - Hidden unclean spirit; oblivious to one's true self, self-justification and self-righteousness; parasite; life-stealing; draining; pest. See Insects.
Leviticus 5:2, Jeremiah 17:9.

Tide - Influence of God; flow of the Holy Spirit; breakthrough; pull of the world.
Proverbs 8:27-29, Job 12:5, Isaiah 59:19, Psalm 93:3-4, 2 Samuel 5:20, Isaiah 28:17-21, Psalm 33:7, Job 38:8-11, 2 Samuel 22:5-6, Psalm 18:4, Matthew 16:13-19.
   High Tide = Surrounded by sin; engulfed in sin.
   2 Samuel 22:5-6, Psalm 18:4.
   Tide Out = Impending judgement; imminent revival.
   Job 30:14, Isaiah 35:1-6.

Tidal Wave - Surrounded by sin; engulfed in sin; the standard of the Lord rising up; judgement; revival. See Tsunami, Water, Waves.
2 Samuel 22:5-6, Psalm 18:4, Isaiah 17:12-13, Ezekiel 26:19, Isaiah 59:19, Isaiah 35:1-6.

Tiger - Danger; powerful minister (danger for the devil); evil; dangerous person (good or evil).
Leviticus 26:22, Mark 1:13, Micah 3:1-3.
   Fangs = Evil intent or motive; poisonous; great danger.
   Psalm 57:4, Psalm 58:6, Proverbs 30:14, Daniel 7:5-7, Revelation 9:8.

Tin - Dross; waste; worthless; impurity; cheap; purification. Isaiah 1:25.

Tin Roof - Covering; protection; mind; thought. Matthew 10:27, Isaiah 30:1, 2 Samuel 11:2.

Tires - Spirit; life; relates the spiritual condition. Exodus 14:25, Ezekiel 1:16-21.
  Fully Inflated Tires = Encouraged in the Lord; enabled in ministry; prayerful; going in the power of the Lord.
  Deflated Tires = Discouragement; dismay; hindrance; lack of prayer; lack of covering; lack of power.
  Tires with no Tread = Worn out; unsafe ministry; careless ministry.
  Exodus 18:18, 1 Timothy 1:19-20, Psalm 73:2.

Titanic - Pride; large plan with wrong motives; disaster. Genesis 11:4-9.

Tithe - One tenth (tenth part); God's portion and economy. Malachi 3:10-11, Genesis 14:20, Hebrews Chapter 7.

Title Deed - Ownership; seal; potential to possess. Genesis 23:20.

TNT - Power; miracle; potential; danger; destruction. Acts 10:38, Matthew 9:8, Mark 9:1, Luke 10:19, Luke 22:53.
  Having Explosives in a vehicle = Powerful ministry.

Toes - Walk; smallest division of a kingdom or church; smallest members of a church. See Feet. Daniel 2:41-42, 1 Corinthians 12:21-26.
  Big Toe = Power; dominion; king; leader; leverage. Exodus 29:20, Leviticus 8:23, Leviticus 14:14, Judges 1:6-7.

Six Toes = Ultimate means of dominion; excess.
2 Samuel 21:20.
On Tip-toes = Straining to see, or reach.
Luke 19:3.
Tip-toeing = Sneaking in; secrecy; walking quietly; careful.
2 Timothy 3:6, Jude 1:4.

Toilet - Place of repentance. See Bathroom, Purging, Feces, Urinating.
Revelation 2:21, 1 Kings 8:47, Ezekiel 14:6, Ezekiel 18:30-32, Acts 8:22-24, 2 Timothy 2:25, 1 Corinthians 15:33, 2 Peter 2:14-22.
To Pass Feces = Rid oneself of sins; unforgiveness; anger; bitterness; any ungodly thing or habit.
Constipated = Difficulty or hindrance to repentance.
Having Diarrhea = Things are out of control and in need of help (counselling or deliverance).
Not able to use the Toilet being Dirty, Plugged, or Damaged = Not fully ready, or able to repent.
Overflowing toilet = Spreading contamination or corruption; out of control.
Difficulty in Finding a Toilet = Hindrances to repentance within the dreamer or circumstance.
Public Toilet = Slander; gossip; church repeating a matter; public exposure of sin of any level, church, ministry, business, household.
Proverbs 6:16-19, Proverbs 17:9, Revelation 3:1, 3 John 1:10, 1 Corinthians 5:1-5.

Tongue - Words; powerful; accusations; slander; gossip; attacks of the enemy; children; prayers; deliverance; untameable.
Psalm 64:3, Psalm 11:2, Ephesians 6:17, Isaiah 49:2, Deuteronomy 32:42, 2 Kings 13:17, James 3:2-10.

Torch Light - Intense light; examine; word of God; great wisdom and understanding; manifest; revealed; highly illuminated; advanced knowledge of the word; exposed.
Psalm 27:1, Psalm 119:105, John 8:12, John 3:19-21, 1 Kings 3:9-12, 2 Corinthians 12:1, Ephesians 5:13.

Tornado - Destruction; great danger; strong demonic force; calamity; death.
Amos 1:14, Psalm 55:8, Acts 27:4, John 10:10, Matthew 8:24-27, Jonah 1:4, Psalm 11:6, Isaiah 28:2, Amos 1:14-15.
Tornado Sighted, but not Alarmed = God's protection in day of calamity.
Isaiah 30:30, Matthew 8:24, Acts 27:18-25.
White Tornado = God's power; revival.
Storm = Disturbance; spiritual warfare; witchcraft; sudden calamity or destruction; judgement; trial; persecution; opposition; outpouring of revival; powerful move of the Spirit.
Isaiah 25:4, Acts 27:14-15, & 18-25, 1 Thessalonians 5:3, Nahum 1:3, 2 Samuel 22:10-15, Psalm 18:9-14, Psalm 104:3, Psalm 58:9, Hosea 13:3, Zechariah 7:14.

Torpedo - Powerful underground ministry; all-powerful Word of God; swift progress; spiritual warfare; powerful words of destruction; swift destruction; sudden, unexpected attack, judgement. See Submarine.
Psalm 64:7, Hebrews 4:12, Isaiah 55:11, Proverbs 6:15, Proverbs 29:1, Isaiah 54:17, Ezekiel 39:3, 2 Samuel 22:14-15, Psalm 18:13-14.

Tow Truck - Five-fold ministry gift; helps ministry; strength in Christ. See Truck.
Ephesians 4:11-12, Acts 18:26, Acts 5:12, 2 Corinthians 12:12, 1 Corinthians 12:28, Acts 27:17.

Being Towed = One without strength; along for the ride; being brought into line.
Acts 16:9.

Towing Another = One with strength; powerhouse; helping a broken ministry; leading the way.
1 Kings 19:19, Galatians 6:2, Psalm 23:1-2, Isaiah 40:11.

Towel - Service; covering; surrender.
John 13:4-5.

Tower - High spiritual experience; supernatural experience; pride; large plan with wrong motives; disaster.
2 Corinthians 12:1-7, Genesis 11:4-9.

Toxic Smoke - Demonic strongholds.
Revelation 9:2-3.

Tractor Trailer - Large burden; ministry; powerful; large work; the size of the truck is often in proportion to the burden or size of the work); the Church. See Truck.
2 Samuel 6:3, Acts 5:14.

> **Semi-truck** = Powerful ministry; large ministry; intimidating; deliverance ministry; leadership.
> 1 Kings 10:2, 1 Samuel 14:6, Acts 4:33, Acts 6:8, 2 Chronicles 11:28, 1 Samuel 17:4-11, Isaiah 37:10-11, Zechariah 3:9, Acts 13:43.
> **Freight truck** = Business.
> 1 Kings 10:15.

Tractor, Farm - Powerful work; slow but powerful ministry; if ploughing, may represent preaching or teaching. See Truck.
Acts 1:8, Acts 4:33.

Traffic - Looking for one's purpose in life; searching out the knowledge of God; ministries fulfilling the purposes of God.

Matthew 7:13-14, Proverbs 14:12-16, Deuteronomy 30:15-19, Daniel 12:4, 1 Corinthians 12:28, Ephesians 4:11-12, Romans 12:6-8.

Traffic Jam - Too many ministries in one territory; in another ministries' territory; competition.
Romans 15:20-25, 2 Corinthians 10:13-16.

Traffic Lights - Guidance; timing of God; waiting for the right time; go, warning to slow down, or warning to stop. See associated Colors in Part 2.
John 8:12, Psalm 43:3, Exodus 13:21-22, Nehemiah 9:12, & 19, Isaiah 25:9, Psalm 27:14.

Traffic Signs - Direction; information; warning.
Hosea 12:10, Joshua 4:6, Isaiah 66:19, John 19:19-20, Exodus 8:23.
   Detour Sign = Change of direction.
   Stop Sign = Stop and pray for guidance.
   Yield Sign = A sign of submission.
   Intersection = Decision or change.

Trail - Way; Christ; the Christian faith; truth; life; way of error.
Isaiah 35:8, John 14:6, Matthew 7:13-14, Jeremiah 6:16, Nahum 2:4, Haggai 1:5-7, Luke 15:15-17, Psalm 69:2, Isaiah 57:20, Jeremiah 18:15-16.
   Under Restoration or Repair = In preparation; not ready; change; hindrance.
   Adjoining Trail = Decision; change of direction.
   Jeremiah 6:16, Haggai 1:5-7.
   Long Trail = Time.
   Dead End Trail = Change direction, stop and repent; certain failure.
   Luke 15:15-17.

Narrow Trail = Way to life; God's way.
Matthew 7:13-14.
Broad Trail = Way of destruction; man's way.
Matthew 7:13-14.
Crooked Trail = Trouble; difficulties; lack of clarity.
Isaiah 42:16, Isaiah 45:2.
Make the Trail Straight = Bring correction; clarified; the right way.
Matthew 3:1-3, Luke 3:4-5, Isaiah 40:3.
Gravel or Stony Trail = Difficult way, narrow way.
Psalm 17:5, Matthew 7:13-14.
Muddy Trail = Flesh: man's way; difficulty (caused by weak flesh); not clear; uncertain; offense; lust; passion; strife; sin.
Psalm 69:2, Isaiah 57:20.
Ruts in Trail = Habits or addiction; traditions of men.
Jeremiah 18:15-16, Isaiah 62:10.

Trail Motor Bike - Independent ministry; pioneering spirit; trail blazer. See Vehicle.
2 Samuel 22:34, Psalm 18:33, Habakkuk 3:19.

Train - Continuous; unceasing work; the Church; connected; fast.
Acts 2:42.
Train Tracks = Tradition; unchanging; habit; stubborn; caution; danger.
2 Thessalonians 2:15, 2 Thessalonians 3:6, Mark 7:9, & 13, Colossians 2:8.

Train Breakdown - Problem; sickness; spirit of poverty; demonic attack; hindrance to one's life, ministry, career, livelihood.
1 Thessalonians 2:18, Acts 16:6-7.

Train Operator (Conductor) - Control; self; Christ; pastor; teacher; Satan; the emphasis is on the nature of the driver (careless, careful, frantic, confident, selfish, rude, kind, etc.). 2 Kings 9:20.

Train Station - Wait; prepare; be made ready (for ministry, travel, change); the Church. 1 Peter 3:20, Jeremiah 23:22.

Train Derailment - Strife; contention; conflict; confrontation; calamity; offense; mistake or sin in ministry; failure; church split; apostasy; personal disaster (failed marriage, business venture, ministry, project etc.); end of one phase (for whatever reason unbeknownst to the dreamer). Nahum 2:3-4, 2 Corinthians 11:25-27, 1 Timothy 1:19-20.

Transmission - Change of direction; change of purpose or intensity of ministry; transformation. Romans 12:2.

Trap - Warning of danger; deceit; sudden destruction; stronghold; backslide; sin of iniquity. 2 Kings 6:9, 2 Corinthians 2:11, 2 Timothy 2:26, Isaiah 5:26-27, Ecclesiastes 9:12, Proverbs 11:6, Proverbs 12:13, Joshua 23:12-13, Proverbs 5:22.

Trapeze Act - Supernatural ministry; moving in the gifts of the Spirit; complete trust in God, our Catcher. Psalm 63:8.

Trees - Humanity; person; covering; leader; shelter; false worship; evil influence. Ezekiel 17:24, 1 Chronicles 16:33, Psalm 96:12, Isaiah 55:12-13, Judges 9:8-15, 2 Kings 17:10, Matthew 7:17-19, Jeremiah 17:7-8, Isaiah 60:13, Isaiah 61:3, Isaiah 41:19.

Christmas Tree = Celebration; spiritual gifts.
Luke 2:10-11, 1 Corinthians 2:12, Ephesians 4:7-8, 1 Corinthians 12:1, 4, & 7-11.
Evergreen Tree (Pine, Spruce, & Fir Trees etc.) = Long-lasting life; everlasting life.
Isaiah 55:13, Isaiah 60:13.
Oak Tree = Great strength; durable; righteousness; elder; unmovable; shelter.
Amos 2:9, Joshua 24:26, Isaiah 6:13, Ezekiel 6:13, Hosea 4:13.
Olive Tree = Anointing oil; anointing of God; Israel; church; peace.
Psalm 52:8, Genesis 8:11, Isaiah 41:19.
Fig Tree = Israel; prosperity.
Hosea 9:10, Luke 13:6-9, 1 Kings 4:25, Micah 4:4, Zechariah 3:10.
Apple Tree = Young man; lover, Jesus; grace; mercy; bears fruit, good or bad.
Song of Solomon 2:3, Song of Solomon 8:5, Matthew 7:17.
Palm Tree = Fruit producing leader; righteous flourishing.
Judges 4:5, Psalm 92:12.
Willow Tree = Sadness; weeping.
Psalm 137:1-2.
Almond Tree = Symbol of Gods' early execution of His purpose (this tree buds earlier than the other trees).
Jeremiah 1:11-12.
Cedar Tree = Rooted and grounded in the things of God; firm in the faith; persistent; determined.
1 Kings 5:8, & 10, Ezekiel 17:22-23, Psalm 92:12, Isaiah 41:19.
Fir or Cypress Tree = One who is a provider of shade, or rest from the desert experience; grateful for the one who provides relief; godly; durable (the White Cedar).
1 Kings 5:8, & 10, Isaiah 55:12-13, Isaiah 60:13, Isaiah 41:19.

Broom or Juniper Tree = One who provides just enough shade, or rest from the desert experience.
1 Kings 19:4-5.

Acacia or Shittah Tree = Symbolizes immortality, and the duality of life and death; thorny.
Isaiah 41:19.

Pine Tree = Enduring; faithful; has staying power; does not bend to circumstances.
Isaiah 60:13, Isaiah 41:19.

Myrtle Tree = The Hebrew name *Hedassah,* is the original name of Esther, therefore, a type of the Christian church or person, lowly, though beautiful, fragrant.
Isaiah 55:12-13, Isaiah 41:19.

Tree Stump - Stubborn; unbelief; roots; tenacious; obstacle; unmovable; hope of restoration; regeneration; Christ.
Daniel 4:15, Job 14:7-9, Isaiah 11:1.

Tribe - Division.
1 Kings 12:16-20, Ezekiel 37:16-22, Matthew 12:25, Luke 12:51-53.

Tribalism = Political spirit; controlling spirit; opposition; organized activism; destructive; unlawful; violent; demanding conformity; out for one's own interest; unjust cause.
1 Kings 12:16-20.

Trophy - Victory; award; competition; memorial.
1 Samuel 17:57, 1 Corinthians 9:24-27, 2 Timothy 4:7-8, Philippians 3:14.

Troubled Water - Troubled mind; healing when water stirred. See Water.
John 5:2-9.

Truck - Small, medium, or large ministry or work in the natural; dependable; humble.
1 Chronicles 13:7, Genesis 45:27, Galatians 6:5.
Air Conditioning = If in good condition, adequate comfort; if not working, faulty provision for comfort.
Brakes = Slowing down; compelled to stop; stopping; hindrance.
1 Thessalonians 2:18, Acts 16:6-7, 2 Peter 2:14.
Driver's Seat = Indicates leadership; taking control.
Engine = Holy Spirit power; supernatural empowerment.
Catalytic Converter (Smaller Trucks) = New anointing of fire; transformative power; yoke-destroying power; gains territory; destroys strongholds; bringer of change; pioneer of new beginnings.
Acts 3:19, James 5:19-20, Ezekiel 18:30-32, Lamentations 5:21, Jeremiah 31:18-20, Isaiah 1:16-20, Psalm 51:13, Acts 15:3, Acts 26:16-18.
Rear-view Mirror = Looking back; focus on the past; warning to watch your back; warning to look ahead.
Genesis 19:7, & 26, Luke 17:31-32.
Seatbelts = Security; safety; preparedness when fastened; assurance; careless when unfastened.
Steering Wheel = The controlling or leading part; the means by which leadership is affected.
Tires = Spirit; life; relates to the spiritual condition.
Exodus 14:25, Ezekiel 1:16-21.
    Fully Inflated Tires = Encouraged in the Lord; enabled in ministry; prayerful; going in the power of the Lord.
    Deflated Tires = Discouragement; dismay; hindrance; lack of prayer; lack of covering; lack of power.
    Tires with no Tread = Worn out; unsafe ministry; careless ministry.
Exodus 18:18, 1 Timothy 1:19-20, Psalm 73:2.

Keys = Authority; power to bind or loose; lock or unlock; wisdom; knowledge; important.
Matthew 16:19, Isaiah 22:22, Revelation 3:7, Luke 11:52, Proverbs 4:7.
To be Given Keys = Given power and authority.
Isaiah 22:22.
To Lose One's Keys = Lose the power and authority one was given.
Truck Box or Canopy = Heart; baggage.
Proverbs 14:14, Hebrews 13:9 (KJV), Luke 11:46, Matthew 23:4, Acts 15:28.
Being Given a Replacement Truck for One's Current Truck = New work assignment or ministry is being given to one, possible change of ministry.
Difficulty or Inability to Find One's Truck = Hindrance; subversion or distraction; interference; opposition; being hidden from the truck owner; losing one's way.
Vandalized Truck = Ministry or work being destroyed, could be from all sorts of wrong motives.
John 10:10, Matthew 23:14.
Stolen Truck = Ministry or work being taken away through opposition; attack of the enemy to destroy one's purpose; trip up one from an assignment; over-reaching of boundaries; restraint from living out one's heritage.
John 10:10, Genesis 27:35-36, Matthew 16:22-23, Jeremiah 9:4, 2 Corinthians 10:13-16, Micah 2:2.
Junkyard = Abandoned ministries; ministries need repair.
PTO (Power Take-off) = Empowerment through the Word of God; divine boldness; impartation of anointing from one to another; given miraculous ability to further the kingdom of God; manifest presence of God.
Acts 4:29-31, Acts 10:37-38, Romans 15:19, Acts 1:8, Luke 9:1, John 20:21-23, Mark 9:1, 1 Corinthians 4:20, 1 Thessalonians 1:5.

Large Truck = Large ministry or church; influence large people groups; clunky and burdensome; costly to power; prideful.

1 Chronicles 13:7, Genesis 45:27, Galatians 6:5.

Pick-up Truck = Personal ministry or work in the natural; dependable; humble.

1 Chronicles 13:7, Genesis 45:27, Galatians 6:5.

Moving Van = Geographical move, natural or spiritual, (house, area, church, including change of affiliations, denominations); relocation.

Ezekiel 12:2-3.

Semi-truck = Powerful ministry; large ministry; intimidating; deliverance ministry; leadership.

1 Kings 10:2, 1 Samuel 14:6, Acts 4:33, Acts 6:8, 1 Samuel 17:4-11, Isaiah 37:10-11, Zechariah 3:9, Acts 13:43.

Freight Truck = Business. See Shipping.

1 Kings 10:15, 2 Chronicles 9:14.

Tractor Trailer = Large burden; ministry; powerful; large work; the size of the truck is often in proportion to the burden or size of the work); the Church. An 18-Wheeler, see 18 in Part 2.

2 Samuel 6:3, Acts 5:14.

Farm Tractor = Powerful work; slow but powerful ministry; if ploughing, may represent preaching or teaching.

Acts 1:8, Acts 4:33.

Earthmover = Leadership working in the flesh; the dead raised up.

1 Corinthians 15:47-49.

> **Excavate** = Prepares foundation; opens one's heart; searching one's heart; uncovering secrets of the heart; clearing one's heart; enlarging one's heart.
>
> Matthew 7:25, Song of Solomon 5:2, Acts 16:14, Psalm 139:1, & 23, 1 Chronicles 28:9, Jeremiah 17:10, Romans 8:27, Psalm 44:21, Genesis 26:18 See with 2 Corinthians 4:7.

Road Grader = Restoration ministry; prophetic ministry. Galatians 6:1, Isaiah 40:3-4.

Bulldozer = Very powerful ministry, good or evil; evangelist; apostle; prophet; preparation ministry; powerful pioneering ministry; heavy-handed leader. Acts 8:5-10, Isaiah 40:3-4, Matthew 3:1-3, 1 Samuel 22:11-18.

Garbage Truck = Large deliverance ministry; removes sin; unclean ministry; unclean church; corrupt business. Matthew 8:16, Job 8:4, Isaiah 31:7, John 2:14-16, Revelation 19:2-3, Isaiah 1:4.

Fire Truck = Emergency assistance; quick response to an urgent need; help on its way.

Car-carrier Transport Truck = Riding on another's ministry; large ministry about to release new ministries. 2 Kings 5:20, Matthew 28:19-20, Luke 9:1-2.

Tow Truck = Five-fold ministry gift; helps ministry; strength in Christ. Ephesians 4:11-12, Acts 18:26, Acts 5:12, 2 Corinthians 12:12, 1 Corinthians 12:28, Acts 27:17.

> **Being Towed** = One without strength; along for the ride; being brought into line. Acts 16:9.

> **Towing Another** = One with strength; powerhouse; helping a broken ministry; leading the way. 1 Kings 19:19, Galatians 6:2, Psalm 23:1-2, Isaiah 40:11.

Forklift Truck = Organizer; burden lifter; lying spirit, falsely raising hopes. Nehemiah 12:44, Matthew 11:28, 1 Kings 22:22, Micah 2:11.

Crane Truck = Burden lifter; load made easy; powerful salvation ministry; burden. Matthew 11:30, Matthew 27:32, Isaiah 49:22, Isaiah 59:19b, Psalm 3:3, James 4:10, Psalm 113:7, Psalm 27:6a, Matthew 23:4, Luke 11:46.

Army Tank = Powerful deliverance ministry; impacting ministry; spiritual warfare; weighty words.
Nahum 2:3, 1 Samuel 2:10, Deuteronomy 20:1, Joel 2:5, Matthew 17:18, Ephesians 6:11, Ecclesiastes 8:4, Luke 4:32.
Dune Buggy = Powerful itinerate ministry
Luke 1:80, 1 Samuel 3:19-20, Judges 13:24-25, Luke 1:15.
Stalled Truck = Ministry on hold; operation in one's own strength; need to take authority; hindrance by Satan; opposition.
Isaiah 49:2, Exodus 14:13-16, Galatians 5:7-12, Nehemiah 4:1-18, 1 Thessalonians 2:18.

Truck Breakdown - Problem; sickness; spirit of poverty; demonic attack; hindrance to one's life, ministry, career, livelihood.
1 Thessalonians 2:18, Acts 16:6-7.

Truck Crash - Strife; contention; conflict; confrontation; calamity; offense; mistake or sin in ministry; failure; church split; apostasy; personal disaster (failed marriage, business venture, ministry, project etc.); end of one phase (for whatever reason unbeknownst to the dreamer).
Nahum 2:3-4, 2 Corinthians 11:25-27, 1 Timothy 1:19-20.

Truck Driver - Control; self; Christ; pastor; teacher; Satan; the emphasis is on the nature of the driver (Confident, kind, careful, frantic, careless, selfish, rude ...).
2 Kings 9:20.
Keys = Authority; power to bind or loose; lock or unlock; wisdom; knowledge; important.
Matthew 16:19, Isaiah 22:22, Revelation 3:7, Luke 11:52, Proverbs 4:7.
To be Given Keys = Given power and authority.
Isaiah 22:22.

Trumpet - Voice; announcement; preaching; prophesying; warning; call to assemble; worship; tongues; the rapture; if sounding reveille, then beginning, wake-up, call to assemble; finished.
Isaiah 58:1, 1 Corinthians 14:8, 1 Corinthians 15:52, Joel 2:15, Ephesians 5:14.
> **Sounding Reveille** - Beginning; wake-up, a call to assemble.
> Isaiah 58:1, 1 Corinthians 14:8, 1 Corinthians 15:52, Joel 2:15, Ephesians 5:14.
> **Rapture** = Revival; spiritual awakening; imminent.
> Hosea 6:2, Matthew 25:6, 1 Thessalonians 4:16-17, 1 Corinthians 15:51-52.
> **Left Behind** = Warning; unpreparedness.
> Matthew 25:3, & 8-13.
Taps (Bugle Call) = End; finished; announcement.
John 19:28-30, 1 Corinthians 15:52, Numbers 10:2-3, Joel 2:1, & 15, Revelation 10:7.

Trunk - Heart; baggage.
Proverbs 14:14, Hebrews 13:9 (KJV), Luke 11:46, Matthew 23:4, Acts 15:28.

Tsunami - Irresistible force; upheaval; overwhelm; disaster; destruction; calamity; judgement; Holy Spirit outpouring. See Earthquake, Water, Waves.
Isaiah 28:2-3, & 17-19, Acts 27:14, & 41, Isaiah 59:19, Acts 2:17.

Tumor - Judgement; corruption; literal tumor.
1 Samuel 5:6, 2 Corinthians 10:5, 2 Timothy 2:16-17.
> **Brain Tumor** = Self-destructive thoughts and words.
> 2 Corinthians 10:5, 2 Timothy 2:16-17.

Cancer = Sin within the church; offence; sinfulness; heresy; consuming destructive words; bitterness; unforgiveness; stress; literal cancer disease.
Genesis 13:7, 2 Timothy 2:16-17, Hosea 9:9, Job 21:25, Job 2:4-5.

Tunnel - Passage; transition; dark season; troubling experience; way of escape; trial.
Job 28:10, 2 Kings 20:20.
Light at the End of the Tunnel = Hope.

Turkey - Thanksgiving; provision, Christmas; contemptuously rich; forgetting God; foolish, dumb; clumsy, in word or deed.
Psalm 107:22, Psalm 116:17, Esther 5:4, Proverbs 30:8-9, Luke 12:19-20, Ecclesiastes 9:12, Proverbs 7:22-23.

Turtle - Slow; withdrawn; spirit of stupor; cautious; protected; safe; steady.
James 1:19, Proverbs 16:32.

Two or Three-Story House - Multi level giftedness; multi talented church.
Acts 20:7-11.

Typhoon - Great disturbance; intense spiritual warfare; witchcraft; sudden calamity or destruction; judgement; trial; persecution; opposition; outpouring of revival; powerful move of the Spirit. See Tornado, Whirlwind.
Isaiah 25:4, Acts 27:14-15, & 18-25, 1 Thessalonians 5:3, Nahum 1:3, 2 Samuel 22:10-15, Psalm 18:9-14, Psalm 104:3, Psalm 58:9, Hosea 13:3, Zechariah 7:14.

UFO - Demonic principalities; demonic powers; wicked demonic spirits in celestial places; the second heaven where demonic spirits dwell; demonic portals; demonic encounter (being abducted); deception. See Aliens.
Ephesians 6:12, 2 Corinthians 11:13-15, Revelation 13:2, & 13-15, Matthew 4:5, & 8, Romans 8:38-39, Galatians 1:8.

Umbilical Cord - Soul tie, good or bad.
Genesis 44:30, 1 Samuel 18:1-3.
> **Silver Cord** = Connection to God; life; the spinal marrow.
> Ecclesiastes 12:6-7.
>> **When the Silver Cord Breaks** = The end of life.
>> Ecclesiastes 12:6-7.

Uncle - Married brother in Christ; similar characteristics or behaviour; literal uncle; could be a relative that takes advantage of the dreamer.
Genesis 28:2, Genesis 29:16-25.

Undertow - Undercurrent; discontent; at wits end. See Water.
Psalm 107:25-27, Acts 27:17, 27-29, & 41.

University - Moving to the highest levels of walk with God; specialized training and equipping; well able to apply learned wisdom and knowledge; a place where if not prepared in the strength, wisdom and knowledge of God, can be caused to stumble (like teaching of evolution and persecution of those who stand on the truth). See School.
2 Timothy 2:15, Philippians 3:4-5, Acts 22:3, Daniel 1:17-20, John 14:26, Acts 23:6-8, 1 Corinthians 2:1-6, & 12-16, 1 Corinthians 1:19-24, James 3:13-18.

Unknown Man - Angel, oneself, or a demon: God's messenger, person with evil intent; danger. See Kind Stranger, White-headed Stranger.
Matthew 2:13, Hebrews 13:2, Luke 10:33.

Unknown Woman - Seducing spirit; temptation; deception; witchcraft; messenger from God; angel; messenger from Satan; demonic spirit. See Harlot.
Proverbs 2:16, Proverbs 23:27, Proverbs 22:14.

Unshaven, Rough Face - Spiritual Neglect; uncleanness; coarse or harsh personality. See Beard.
Leviticus 21:5.

Up - Above; help; advancement; promotion, difficulty (uphill battle); salvation.
2 Samuel 22:17, Psalm 18:16, Psalm 27:10, Matthew 17:27, Mark 8:34, Mark 10:21.

Upper Room - Spiritual; thought; prayer; spiritual service.
Acts 1:13-14, Acts 20:7-8.

Upstairs - Spiritual; thought; prayer; spiritual service. See Attic.
Acts 1:13-14, Acts 20:7-8.

Urinating - Cleansing; an urge for relief; repenting; desire; strife; temptation; lust. See Bathroom, Toilet.
1 Kings 16:11-13, 1 Kings 8:47, Ezekiel 18:31, Acts 8:22-24, Proverbs 17:14, 1 Samuel 25:22, 1 Kings 21:21, Genesis 49:4.
> **Urinating Blood** = Hatred; anger; revenge.
> **Bladder** = An urge to release something; strife; temptation; lust.
> Proverbs 17:14, 1 Samuel 25:22, 1 Kings 21:21, Genesis 49:4.

Full Bladder = Pressure; compelling urge.
Bladder Infection or Cancer = Offense; enmity.
Acts 8:22-24.

V

Van - Natural or spiritual family; family ministry; fellowship.
See Vehicle.
Ephesians 3:14-15, 1 John 1:7.

Vapour - Temporary; presence of God; evidence of something.
James 4:14, Job 36:27-33, Psalm 148:8.

Vehicle - Life; person; ministry; if new, then new ministry or new way of life; if fast may mean a reckless, self-righteous, or unsaved person (living life in the fast lane).
Genesis 41:43, 2 Kings 10:16, 1 Chronicles 13:7, Acts 16:6-7, Genesis 45:27, Nahum 2:3-4, Isaiah 37:24.
   Air Conditioning = If in good condition, adequate comfort; if not working, faulty provision for comfort.
   Brakes = Slowing down; compelled to stop; stopping; hindrance.
   1 Thessalonians 2:18, Acts 16:6-7, 2 Peter 2:14.
   Driver's Seat = Indicates leadership; taking control.
   Engine = Holy Spirit power; supernatural empowerment.
   Catalytic Converter = New anointing of fire; transformative power; yoke-destroying power; gains territory; destroys strongholds; bringer of change; pioneer of new beginnings.
   Acts 3:19, James 5:19-20, Ezekiel 18:30-32, Lamentations 5:21, Jeremiah 31:18-20, Isaiah 1:16-20, Psalm 51:13, Acts 15:3, Acts 26:16-18.
   Rear-view Mirror = Looking back; focus on the past; warning to watch your back; warning to look ahead.
   Genesis 19:7, & 26, Luke 17:31-32.

Seatbelts = Security; safety; preparedness when fastened; assurance; careless when unfastened.

Steering Wheel = The controlling or leading part; the means by which leadership is affected.

Tires = Spirit; life; relates to the spiritual condition. Exodus 14:25, Ezekiel 1:16-21.

> **Fully Inflated Tires** = Encouraged in the Lord; enabled in ministry; prayerful; going in the power of the Lord.

> **Deflated Tires** = Discouragement; dismay; hindrance; lack of prayer; lack of covering; lack of power.

> **Tires with no Tread** = Worn out; unsafe ministry; careless ministry.
>
> Exodus 18:18, 1 Timothy 1:19-20, Psalm 73:2.

Keys = Authority; power to bind or loose; lock or unlock; wisdom; knowledge; important.
Matthew 16:19, Isaiah 22:22, Revelation 3:7, Luke 11:52, Proverbs 4:7.

> **To be Given Keys** = Given power and authority. Isaiah 22:22.

> **To Lose One's Keys** = Lose the power and authority one was given.

Trunk = Heart; baggage.
Proverbs 14:14, Hebrews 13:9 (KJV), Luke 11:46, Matthew 23:4, Acts 15:28.

Being Given a Replacement Vehicle for One's Current Vehicle = New assignment or ministry is being given to one, possible change of ministry.

Difficulty or Inability to Find One's Vehicle = Hindrance; subversion or distraction; interference; opposition; being hidden from the vehicle owner; losing one's way.

Vandalized Vehicle = Ministry being destroyed, could be from all sorts of wrong motives.
John 10:10, Matthew 23:14.

Stolen Vehicle = Ministry being taken away through opposition; attack of the enemy to destroy one's purpose;

trip up one from an assignment; over-reaching of boundaries; restraint from living out one's heritage. John 10:10, Genesis 27:35-36, Matthew 16:22-23, Jeremiah 9:4, 2 Corinthians 10:13-16, Micah 2:2.

Junkyard = Abandoned ministries; ministries need repair.

PTO (Power Take-off, Larger Trucks) = Empowerment through the Word of God; divine boldness; impartation of anointing from one to another; given miraculous ability to further the kingdom of God; manifest presence of God. Acts 4:29-31, Acts 10:37-38, Romans 15:19, Acts 1:8, Luke 9:1, John 20:21-23, Mark 9:1, 1 Corinthians 4:20, 1 Thessalonians 1:5.

Convertible = Capable of open heaven administration; indicative of revelatory ministry.

With the Top Up = Covered; protected; closed heaven; closed to revelation.

With the Top Down = Uncovered; exposed; vulnerable; open heaven; open to receive revelation.

Motorcycle = Personal ministry; independence; rebellion; selfish; pride; swift progress. Acts 8:4-7, & 26-39, 1 Corinthians 3:4-5, 1 Corinthians 12:14-16, & 20-21, 1 Samuel 15:23a.

Trail Motor Bike = Independent ministry; pioneering spirit; trail blazer. 2 Samuel 22:34, Psalm 18:33, Habakkuk 3:19.

Indy Race Car = Acceleration into the new season and ministry.

Four-wheel Drive or All Wheel Drive = Powerful ministry; ground breaking; capable of global influence; personal ministry or work in the natural; dependable; hard work; rescue; solid biblical and gospel foundation. Nahum 2:4, Isaiah 37:24.

Car-carrier Transport Truck = Riding on another's ministry; large ministry about to release new ministries. 2 Kings 5:20, Matthew 28:19-20, Luke 9:1-2.

Tow Truck = Five-fold ministry gift; helps ministry; strength in Christ.
Ephesians 4:11-12, Acts 18:26, Acts 5:12, 2 Corinthians 12:12, 1 Corinthians 12:28, Acts 27:17.
Being Towed = One without strength; along for the ride; being brought into line.
Acts 16:9.
Towing Another = One with strength; powerhouse; helping a broken ministry; leading the way.
1 Kings 19:19, Galatians 6:2, Psalm 23:1-2, Isaiah 40:11.
Army Tank = Powerful deliverance ministry; impacting ministry; spiritual warfare; weighty words.
Nahum 2:3, 1 Samuel 2:10, Deuteronomy 20:1, Joel 2:5, Matthew 17:18, Ephesians 6:11, Ecclesiastes 8:4, Luke 4:32.
Dune Buggy = Powerful itinerate ministry
Luke 1:80, 1 Samuel 3:19-20, Judges 13:24-25, Luke 1:15.
Pick-up Truck = Personal ministry or work in the natural; dependable; humble.
1 Chronicles 13:7, Genesis 45:27, Galatians 6:5.
Large Vehicle = Large ministry or church; influence large people groups; clunky and burdensome; costly to power; prideful.
Fire Truck = Emergency assistance; quick response to an urgent need; help on its way.
Semi-truck = Powerful ministry; large ministry; intimidating; deliverance ministry; leadership.
1 Kings 10:2, 1 Samuel 14:6, Acts 4:33, Acts 6:8, 1 Samuel 17:4-11, Isaiah 37:10-11, Zechariah 3:9, Acts 13:43.
Freight truck = Business.
1 Kings 10:15, 2 Chronicles 9:14.
Tractor Trailer = Large Burden; ministry; powerful; large work, the size of the truck is often in proportion to the burden or size of the work; the Church.
2 Samuel 6:3, Acts 5:14.

Station Wagon = Natural or spiritual family; family ministry; fellowship.
Ephesians 3:14-15, 1 John 1:7.
Van = Natural or spiritual family; family ministry; fellowship.
Ephesians 3:14-15, 1 John 1:7.
Moving Van = Geographical move, natural or spiritual, (house, area, church, including change of affiliations, denominations); relocation.
Ezekiel 12:2-3.
Stalled Vehicle = Ministry on hold; operation in one's own strength; need to take authority; hindrance by Satan; opposition.
Isaiah 49:2, Exodus 14:13-16, Galatians 5:7-12, Nehemiah 4:1-18, 1 Thessalonians 2:18.
Vehicle Breakdown = Problem; sickness; spirit of poverty; demonic attack; hindrance to one's life, ministry, career, livelihood.
1 Thessalonians 2:18, Acts 16:6-7.
Vehicle Crash = Strife; contention; conflict; confrontation; calamity; offense; mistake or sin in ministry; failure; church split; apostasy; personal disaster (failed marriage, business venture, ministry, project etc.); end of one phase (for whatever reason unbeknownst to the dreamer).
Nahum 2:3-4, 2 Corinthians 11:25-27, 1 Timothy 1:19-20.
Vehicle Driver = Control; self; Christ; pastor; teacher; Satan; the emphasis is on the nature of the driver (Confident, kind, careful, frantic, careless, selfish, rude ...).
2 Kings 9:20.

Keys = Authority; power to bind or loose; lock or unlock; wisdom; knowledge; important.
Matthew 16:19, Isaiah 22:22, Revelation 3:7, Luke 11:52, Proverbs 4:7.

To be Given Keys = Given power and authority.
Isaiah 22:22.

Veil - Concealment; hidden; covering; deception; without understanding; law versus liberty; flesh versus the Spirit.
2 Corinthians 3:13-18; Isaiah 25:7-8, Hebrews 9:3, & 8.
   Separated by a Veil = Unrevealed; not exposed.
   2 Corinthians 3:13-16.
   Torn Veil = Revealed; exposed; barrier removed.
   Mark 15:37-38, Luke 23:45, Isaiah 25:7-8.

Vessel - Container; doctrine; tradition; a determination or resolve; form of the truth; a person; a believer.
Romans 2:20, Exodus 25:29, Isaiah 28:9-10, Jeremiah 1:13, 2 Kings 21:13, 1 Thessalonians 4:3-5, Acts 9:15.
God's wrath, judgement and plagues.
Revelation 15:7, Revelation 16:2-21, Revelation 17:1, Revelation 21:9.

Vials - God's vials of wrath, judgement and plagues.
Revelation 15:7, Revelation 16:2-21, Revelation 17:1, Revelation 21:9.

Victim of Theft - Victim of false doctrine; truth lost through tradition or philosophy; loss of liberty; temptation; unaware; secret; covert operation; God's judgment on the wicked. See Thief.
1 Thessalonians 5:2-4, verse 3, Luke 11:22, Luke 10:30.

Video Camera - Focusing; recording; memories; publishing; fame; reliving memories; seeing the promises of God. See Movie.
Hebrews12:1-2, Mark 5:20, Mark 7:36, Matthew 26:13, John 21:25, 1 Corinthians 2:9-10.
   Video Camera Operator = Seer; prophet; one with clear focus.
   Numbers 24:4, & 16, 2 Samuel 18:24, Acts 10:10-20.

Vine - Source; Jesus; people; family; city; nation; flesh; entanglement; snare.
John 15:1, & 5, Jeremiah 2:21, Judges 9:13.

Vineyard - Heavenly kingdom; place of planting; harvest.
Isaiah 5:7, Matthew 21:33-44, Proverbs 31:16, Matthew 20:1-16, 1 Corinthians 9:7.

Viper or Cockatrice - Demon; curse; deception; threat; danger; hatred; slander; critical spirit; fiery; deadly glance (evil eye); envy; malignant; fierce spiritual warfare needed. See Snake.
Isaiah 59:5, Isaiah 11:8, Isaiah 14:29, Amos 5:19, Psalm 140:3, Proverbs 23:32, Matthew 3:7, Matthew 12:34, Ephesians 6:12, Psalm 91:13.

Voice - Message from God, the word of God; godly instructions; message from the devil.
John 12:28-30, Matthew 17:5, Matthew 3:3, Mark 5:7, John 10:3-5.

Volcano - Sudden; explosive; violent reaction to pressure; emotionally unstable; unpredictable; trouble erupting; judgement.
Deuteronomy 32:22, Psalm 11:6.

Vomit - Offensive; deep disgust; loathing; unhealthy; poisoned; nauseated; ill; rejected; purging.
Revelation 3:16.

Vulture - Scavenger; unclean; impure; an evil person; all seeing and waiting; evil spirit; preys on human weakness; opportunistic. See Bird.
Deuteronomy 14:12-13, Proverbs 30:17.

W

Wall - Barrier; obstacle; hindrance; limitation; unbelief; defense.
2 Samuel 22:30, Psalm 18:29, 1 Samuel 25:16, Numbers 22:24-26, Proverbs 18:11.

Wallet - Treasure; heart; precious; valuable; identity.
Mark 6:8, Luke 22:35-36, John 13:29.
    Empty Wallet = Bankrupt.
    Misplaced Wallet = Mistake in decision or investment; misplaced priorities.
    Stolen Wallet = Risky or careless decision or bad investment that caused a loss; something valuable stolen.
    John 12:6.
    Money = Wealth; spiritual riches; provision; natural talents and skills; power; strength of man; greed; covetousness.
    Deuteronomy 8:18, Ecclesiastes 7:12, Matthew 17:27, Luke 16:11, Genesis 31:15, Ezekiel 22:12, 1 Timothy 6:10, James 5:1-4, 1 Timothy 6:10.
        Getting Money = Literal financial increase; increase in favor.
        Matthew 17:27.
        Bundle of Money = Season of abundance of money or favor.
        International Currency = Privilege or favor from that country.
        Short of Money = Season of a lack of money.

Walking - Progress; led by the Spirit; living in sin.
Galatians 5:16, & 25, Ephesians 4:17.
    Difficulty in Walking = Trials; evil opposition to destiny.
    Unable to Walk = Hindrance to do what one's called to do.

Warehouse - Production; getting things done; the Kingdom of God; the Church; the world; the motions of sin. See Machines, Forklift Truck.
Luke 2:49, Romans 12:11.
Working in a Warehouse = Being useful in the corporate plan.
Warehouse Not Working Well = Set-up not in order.
Flooding or Flooded Warehouse Building = Overwhelming situation; challenge.
Warehouse Building on Fire = End of one phase; significant change. See Fire.
Abandoned Warehouse = Non- Productive: Is not reaching full potential, lazy, sloth, or actual workplace.
Basement = Soul; carnal nature; lust; discouragement; depression; refuge; retreat; hidden; beneath the surface; foundational issues; forgotten; secret sin; bloodline issue; demonic realm. See Foundation.
Jeremiah 38:6, Isaiah 24:22.
Supplies in the Basement = Inherited giftedness; great potential yet to be revealed or manifested.
Fault in the Basement = Broken foundation; spiritual forefathers' issues needing repentance.

Warlock - Witchcraft; control, evil influence; evil intent; seduction; non-submissive person; rebellion; slander; gossip; worldly 'church;' evil, unclean spirit; demonic.
1 Samuel 15:23a, 1 Kings 21:25, Revelation 2:20.

Warrior - Spiritual warfare; Christ; angel of protection; demon (accuser or opponent); persecution.
Revelation 12:7, & 10, 2 Timothy 2:3-4, Psalm 55:21.

Washbasin - Prayer; repentance; petition to God; self-justification. See Bathroom.
Isaiah 1:16, James 4:8, Psalm 26:6, job 9:30, Matthew 27:24.

Soap = Cleansing; conviction; forgiveness; prayer; repentance.
Malachi 3:2, Jeremiah 2:22, Isaiah 1:16.
Washcloth = Truth; doctrine; understanding; enhances cleansing.
Psalm 51:7, John 15:3.
Dirty Washcloth = False doctrine; insincere apology; error.
Job 14:4.

Wasps - Affliction; stinging; biting words; slander; strife; curse, because of sin; persecution; trouble; offense; demon spirits. See Bees.
Deuteronomy 7:20, Exodus 23:28, Joshua 24:12.

Watch - Timing; late; early; delay. See Calendar.
John 11:9-10, Ephesians 5:16, Colossians 4:5.
Watch Hands or Numbers Moving Faster than Normal = There is an acceleration coming in one's life.
John 4:35.
Watch Hands or Numbers Nearing Midnight = The end of something is near; opportunity nearing an end.
John 9:4-5, John 11:9-10, John 12:35, Colossians 4:5, Ephesians 5:15-17.
Watch Hands or Numbers Slow or Stopped = Hindrance to one's assignment.
1 Thessalonians 2:18, Romans 15:22, Luke 11:52, Ezra 4:21-24, Ezra 6:7-8.
Old Wrist Watch - Past.

Watchdog - Watchman elder; minister; alert; beware; warning; wake up. See Dog.
Isaiah 56:10-11, Psalm 68:23, Ezekiel 33:1-9.

Water - Spiritual life; Holy Spirit; the spiritual realm; healing; everlasting life; the word of God; the gospel preached; the outpouring of the Holy Spirit; cleansing; yearning heart for God; refreshment.

John 7:37-39, Isaiah 12:3, Revelation 7:17, John 5:2-4, John 4:10 -14, John 13:5-10, Revelation 22:1, Ezekiel 47: 1-12, Psalm 46:4, 1 Corinthians 10:4, Ephesians 5:26, Psalm 23:2, Psalm 42:1-2, Psalm 63:1, Psalm 107:35, Isaiah 41:18, Psalm 78:15-16, Matthew 10:42, Jeremiah 17:8, Isaiah 58:11.

Hot Water = A heart on fire for God; anger; war; judgment. Isaiah 64:2, Jeremiah 1:13-16, Ezekiel 24:3-14, Psalm 58:9.

Waters = Nations of the earth; agitation; under-currents; cross-currents.

Revelation 17:15, Isaiah 17:13, 2 Samuel 22:5, Psalm 18:4, Psalm 93:3-4, Revelation 12:15, Revelation 17:15, Isaiah 59:19.

Ocean = Very large groups, humanity, mission, or travel to distant shores; great anointing; covering of the earth; innumerable; an awesome amount or expanse; very large move of the Spirit.

Isaiah 60:5, Psalm 68:22, Isaiah 24:14-15, Psalm 98:7-9, 2 Corinthians 11:25-28, Acts 27:1-44.

On the Ocean = Influencing the nations; imparting great numbers of multitudes.

Acts 27:1-44, 2 Corinthians 11:25-28.

Sea = Large groups, humanity, mission, or travel; anointing; covering large areas; numerous; large move of the Spirit.

Isaiah 60:5, Psalm 68:22, Isaiah 24:14-15, Psalm 98:7-9.

On the Sea = Influencing a nation; imparting large numbers of a multitude.

Acts 27:1-44, 2 Corinthians 11:25-28.

Undertow = Undercurrent; discontent; at wits end.

Psalm 107:25-27, Acts 27:17, 27-29, & 41.

Salt Water = Spirit of the world; source of evil.
James 3:11-12.

Seacoast = Transition phase; boundary; limitation.
Jeremiah 5:22, Psalm 33:7, Proverbs 8:29, Genesis 1:9-10.

Dirty Waters = Corrupted spiritually; causing strife; bitter words; unstable hypocrite; sin; false doctrine; unattractive or too common to the proud.
Ezekiel 32:2, Ezekiel 34:18-19, Isaiah 57:20, Exodus 15:23-24, Job 8:11, 2 Kings 5:12, Ezekiel 47:11.

Stagnant Waters = Stale in the things of God.
Ezekiel 47:11.

Troubled Waters = Troubled mind; healing when water stirred.
John 5:2-9.

Waves = Raging voices of the peoples; multitude rising up against another; storms of life; inner turmoil; restless; chastisement; overwhelming calamities; the voices false teachers; pride; double mindedness.
Psalm 65:7, Psalm 93:3-4, Jeremiah 51:42, Luke 21:25, Mark 4:37-41, Acts 27:41, Matthew 14:24, & 30, Psalm 88:7, Psalm 42:7, Jonah 2:3, Jude 1:13, Isaiah 57:20-21, 2 Peter 2:17-18, Job 38:11, James 1:6-8.

River = Life; Spirit of God; righteousness; spirit of man; judgement.
John 7:38-39, Amos 5:24, Proverbs 21:1, Isaiah 43:2.

Steady Flow = Passage of time.

Long River = Time.

Rapids = Danger; tossed about; judgement.
Amos 5:24.

Deep River = Difficulty; obstacle; impassable; incomprehensible.
Ezekiel 47:5, Isaiah 43:2.

Muddy River = Traditions of man; spirit of the world; sin; wickedness.

Dry River Bed = Barren; religious traditions; backslidden.
Jeremiah 50:38.

Waterfall - Outpouring of the Holy Spirit; baptizing of the Holy Spirit.
Isaiah 44:3-4, Isaiah 32:15, Joel 2:28-29, Acts 2: 17-18, John 7:37-39, 1 Corinthians 12:13, Acts 10:44-45.

Water Fountain - Spirit; source; words of life; spirit of man; Holy Spirit; salvation.
Revelation 21:6, James 3:11-12, Jeremiah 2:13.

Water Melon - Spirit-ruled soul; fruitfulness; refreshing; picnic.
Numbers 11:5, Proverbs 18:21, Isaiah 3:10.

Water Well - Source of livelihood; heart; spirit of man; Holy Spirit; salvation; replenishing; renewal.
John 4:6-14, Proverbs 4:23, 2 Peter 2:17.

Water Skiing - Supported by God's power; stepping out in faith; swift; fast progress.
Matthew 14:29-31, John 6:19-21.

Waves - Raging voices of the peoples; multitude rising up against another; storms of life; inner turmoil; restless; chastisement; overwhelming calamities; the voices false teachers; pride; double mindedness.
Psalm 65:7, Psalm 93:3-4, Jeremiah 51:42, Luke 21:25, Mark 4:37-41, Acts 27:41, Matthew 14:24, & 30, Psalm 88:7, Psalm 42:7, Jonah 2:3, Jude 1:13, Isaiah 57:20-21, 2 Peter 2:17-18, Job 38:11, James 1:6-8.

Wax - Seal; melts away.
1 Kings 21:8, Esther 8:8, Psalm 97:5, Psalm 22:14, Psalm 68:2, Micah 1:4.

Weasel - Wicked; renege on a promise (weasel out of a deal); informant; a betrayer; traitor.
Mark 14:10.

Web - Snare; lies and deception; scheme; trap; ruin; internet; search tool; research. See Net, Spider, and Trap.
Ecclesiastes 7:26, Isaiah 59:5-7; Psalm 91:3, Psalm 124:7, Ecclesiastes 9:12; Psalm 140:5,
Psalm 119:110, Psalm 141:9, Ecclesiastes 7:25, John 1:38, Luke 19:10.

Wedding - Covenant; the Church as the Bride of Christ; agreement; joined; natural marriage.
Ephesians 5:31-32, see Nehemiah 13:27 with Exodus 23:32 and 2 Corinthians 6:14.
Getting Married = Going higher with Jesus.
Issues Arising during Marriage = Hindrances coming against one's effort to go higher with Jesus.
Soiled Marriage Clothes = Life issues hindering the ability of intimacy with Jesus.
Sexual Intimacy = One in agreement.
Interruption of Intimacy = Interference or trouble in the marriage or covenant relationship.

Weeds - Unkempt; works of the flesh; sin; neglect; laziness; worry.
Genesis 3:17-18, Proverbs 24:30-31, Jonah 2:5.
Weeds Gone to Seed = Fullness of iniquity.
1 Thessalonians 2:16, 2 Thessalonians 2:7-8.

Weight - Great responsibility; heavy load; large burden; encumbrance.
Hebrews 12:1.

Weight Lifter or Weightlifting - Burden bearer; building one's faith; overburdened; bearing the weight of sin.
Galatians 6:5, Jude 1:20, Matthew 11:28-30, Psalm 55:22, Isaiah 10:27, Hebrews 12:1.

Welding - Joining; strong bond; manufacturing; repairing.
1 Chronicles 22:3 (KJV), Exodus 28:7, Nehemiah 3:6.

Well - Source of livelihood; heart; spirit of man; Holy Spirit; salvation; replenishing; renewal.
John 4:6-14, Proverbs 4:23, 2 Peter 2:17.

West - End; grace; death; last; conformed.
Exodus 10:19, Psalm 103:12, Luke 12:54.

Western - Frontier; pioneering spirit; spiritual warfare; boldness; challenge.
Joshua 3:4, Deuteronomy 20:10.

Whale - Danger, destruction, evil spirit; large mouthed enemy; verbal attack.
Ezekiel 32:2, Job 7:12, Matthew 12:40, Jonah 1:17.

Wheat Field - Harvest field; economy; believers.
Hosea 6:11, John 4:35, Revelation 6:6, Matthew 13:24-30.
  Wheat Seed = Believers, who lay down their lives to live for Christ.
  John 12:24-25, 1 Corinthians 15:36-38, Matthew 10:38-39.

Wheel - Life cycle; continuous; long-lasting.
Ecclesiastes 1:9-10, Ecclesiastes 3:1-8, 11, & 15, Acts 17:28.

Fully Inflated Wheels = Encouraged in the Lord; enabled in ministry; prayerful; going in the power of the Lord.
Deflated Wheels = Discouragement; dismay; hindrance; lack of prayer; lack of covering; lack of power.

Wheel in the Middle of a Wheel - Representation of the omnipresence of God; the wheels representing the flexibility and mobility as the reflection of the attributes of God and the moving of His angels and of the Holy Spirit.
Ezekiel 1:15-21, Ezekiel 10:9-17.

Whirlwind - God's manifest power; opening of heaven; destruction; great danger; calamity; death.
Nahum 1:3, 2 Kings 2:1, & 11, Job 38:1, Job 40:6, Psalm 50:3, Ezekiel 1:4, Jeremiah 23:19, Proverbs 1:26-27, Amos 1:14, Jonah 1:4, Zechariah 7:14, Jeremiah 30:23, Isaiah 66:15, Psalm 58:9, Isaiah 40:24, Amos 1:14-15.
Whirlwind Sighted, but not Alarmed = God's protection and manifestation in day of calamity.
Acts 27:18-25, Psalm 58:9-11, Isaiah 41:16, Zechariah 9:14-16.
White Whirlwind = God's power; open heaven; revival; rapture.
2 Kings 2:1, & 11, Ezekiel 1:4, Genesis 5:24.
Storm = Disturbance; spiritual warfare; witchcraft; sudden calamity or destruction; judgement; trial; persecution; opposition; outpouring of revival; powerful move of the Spirit.
Isaiah 25:4, Acts 27:14-15, & 18-25, 1 Thessalonians 5:3, Nahum 1:3, 2 Samuel 22:10-15, Psalm 18:9-14, Psalm 104:3, Psalm 58:9, Hosea 13:3, Zechariah 7:14.

White Clouds - Good change; glory; rest; manifest presence of God; covering; government and protection of God; revival.
See Clouds.
Exodus 13:21, Leviticus 16:2, Zechariah 10:1.

White Elephant - Unusable item; unwanted.

White Hair - Wisdom; glory; status; victory; grace.
Daniel 7:9, Revelation 1:14.

White Horse - Righteous; true; pure; peace; conquer. See Horse.
Revelation 19:11, Revelation 6:2.

Whore - Seduction; the worldly church; lust; adultery; fornication; temptation; snare; unclean person; stubborn. See Sex.
Revelation 17:5, Ecclesiastes 7:26, Jeremiah 3:3.

Wife - Covenant; joined; job; business; hobby; passion; Church; dedicated involvement in any activity; help; her husband's own person; may represent herself in the natural. See Marriage.
Galatians 4:24a, Ephesians 5:23, & 32, 1Corinthians 7:33.

Wife of a Recognized Minister - The Church.

Wife's Sister - The wife herself.

Wild Game - Work: Seeking and doing God's Word and work; sorcery. See Hunting, Food.
Proverbs 12:27.

Wilderness - Hard times; trial; testing; distant from God; training; provision.
2 Corinthians 11:26, Acts 13:18, Hebrews 3:8-11, Matthew 3:1-3, Matthew 4:1-2, Matthew 11:7-10, John 6:49, Revelation 12:14.

Willow Tree - Sadness; weeping. See Trees.
Psalm 137:1-2.

Wind - The spirit of a doctrine; Holy Spirit; move of the Spirit; disappears quickly; difficult to understand; idle words. See storm.
Ephesians 4:14, John 3:8, Acts 2:2, & 4.
> **Strong Wind** = Demonic or strong opposition.
> Job 1:12, & 19, Job 8:2, Jeremiah 4:11-12.

Window - Vision; insight revealed; truth; prophetic gifting; revelation; understanding; avenue of blessing; unguarded opening for an intruder or thief.
Genesis 26:8, 2 Kings 7:19, Malachi 3:10, Joel 2:9.
> **Curtains** = Concealment; hidden; covering; deception; without understanding; law versus liberty; flesh versus the Spirit.
> 2 Corinthians 3:13-18; Isaiah 25:7-8, Hebrews 9:3, & 8.
>> **Separated by Curtains** = Unrevealed; not exposed.
>> 2 Corinthians 3:13-16.
>> **Open Curtains** = Revealed; exposed; barrier removed.
>> Mark 15:37-38, Luke 24:45, Isaiah 25:7-8.

Wine or Strong Drink - Intoxicated emotions; spiritual dissipation; toxic; spirit of man; counterfeit spirit; witchcraft; delusion; mocker; spirit of joy; Spirit of God; revelation; teaching truth; blessing.
Ephesians 5:18, Proverbs 31:6, Deuteronomy 32:32, Proverbs 4:17, Acts 2:13-17, Proverbs 20:1, Luke 5:37-38, 1 Corinthians 10:16, Titus 2:3, Deuteronomy 11:14.
> **Wineskins** = Human body as a vessel; the church; believers.
> Luke 5:37-38.
> **Winepress** = True doctrine; spiritual birthplace.
> Matthew 21:33, Isaiah 5:1-2, Mark 12:1.

Drink Wine in Moderation = Representative of healing in certain circumstances; giving into temptation if one had a previous bondage.
1 Timothy 5:23, Proverbs 23:29-32.
Drinking Wine with Another = Representative of communion; spiritual fellowship.
1 Corinthians 10:16.

Wings - Prophet; Holy Spirit; under protection of God; shelter; covering; demon.
Exodus 19:4, Psalm 91:4, Psalm 57:1, Luke 13:34, Isaiah 40:31, Isaiah 8:8, Malachi 4:2, Revelation 4:8, Revelation 9:9.

Winter - Barron; unfruitful season; death; dormant; waiting; cold hearted. See Snow.
Matthew 24:20, 2 Timothy 4:21, Acts 27:12, Acts 28:11.

Witch - Control, evil influence; evil intent; seduction; non-submissive person; spirit of rebellion; manipulative person; slander; gossip; worldly church; evil, unclean spirit; spirit of control; Jezebel spirit; demonic.
1 Samuel 15:23a, 1 Kings 21:25, Revelation 2:20.

Wolf - Predator; devourer; false prophet; evil minister or governor; person seeking their own gain; opportunistic; womanizer; loner; God's minister of justice.
Matthew 7:15, Acts 20:29-30, Matthew 10:16, Zephaniah 3:3, John 10:12.

Woman - Church; virgin or harlot, mature fruit, good or bad.
1 Corinthians 7:34, Luke 1:27-36, Matthew 1:18-25, Acts 9:36, Matthew 26:7, & 10, Judges 4:4-5, Luke 2:36-37.
    Younger Woman = Newness; strength; fertility.
Luke 1:27-36, Matthew 1:18-25.

Older Woman = Wisdom; maturity; seasoning; stability.
Acts 9:36, Luke 2:36-37.

Woman (Unknown) - Seducing spirit; temptation; deception; witchcraft; messenger from God; angel; messenger from Satan; demonic spirit. See Harlot.
Proverbs 2:16, Proverbs 23:27, Proverbs 22:14.

Wood - Life; humanity; spiritual building material; temporary; flesh; carnal. See Trees.
Jeremiah 5:14, Proverbs 26:20-21, 1 Corinthians 3:12.

Woodpecker - One who seeks out areas of disturbance; nests where one's spirituality or life has been affected by the fires of trial; births new life out of chaos. See Bird.
Isaiah 61:1-4, Luke 4:18, Acts 10:38.

Worm - Corruption; weak; insignificant; filthiness of the flesh; evil; eats from the inside; pride; transgressor; death; rotten motives; bitter; temptation leading to sin; fearful; reproached; despised. See Insects.
Job 17:14, Job 25:6, Job 7:5, Isaiah 14:11, Isaiah 66:24, Proverbs 5:4, Mark 9:43-50, Isaiah 41:14, Psalm 22:6.

Worn Out Clothing - Useless; poor; humble; unrighteous; self righteous. See Clothing.
Isaiah 64:6, Proverbs 23:21.

Worship – Sacrificed life; service; release of the kingdom of heaven; divine warfare.
Genesis 22:5, &10, Matthew 4:10, 2 Chronicles 20:21-22, Psalm 22:3, 2 Corinthians 10:4.

Wreck or Crash, Vehicle, Ship, Train, Airplane etc. - Strife; contention; conflict; confrontation; calamity; offense; mistake

or sin in ministry; failure; church split; personal disaster (failed marriage, business venture, ministry, project etc.); end of one phase (for whatever reason unbeknownst to the dreamer). See Driver, Captain, Conductor, or Pilot, and associated means of transportation.
Nahum 2:3-4, 2 Corinthians 11:25-27, 1 Timothy 1:19-20.

Wrecking Ball - Demolishes strongholds; heavy-handed oppressor.
2 Corinthians 10:4-5, 1 Kings 12:13-14.

Wrestling - Striving; struggle; deliverance; resistance; persistence; trial; tribulation; controlling spirit in a person.
Genesis 32:24-28, Ephesians 6:12, 2 Timothy 2:24.

Wrist Watch - Timing; late; early; delay. See Calendar.
John 11:9-10, Ephesians 5:16, Colossians 4:5.
    Watch Hands or Numbers Moving Faster than Normal = There is an acceleration coming in one's life.
John 4:35.
    Watch Hands or Numbers Nearing Midnight = The end of something is near; opportunity nearing an end.
John 9:4-5, John 11:9-10, John 12:35, Colossians 4:5, Ephesians 5:15-17.
    Watch Hands or Numbers Slow or Stopped = Hindrance to one's assignment.
1 Thessalonians 2:18, Romans 15:22, Luke 11:52, Ezra 4:21-24, Ezra 6:7-8.
    Old Wrist Watch - Past.

Xanthium = Irritant; irritated; minor afflictions. See Thorns.
Hebrews 6:8, Exodus 22:6, Matthew 13:22.

X-Box - Playing games, entertaining self, taking no thought of God; wasting time.
1 Corinthians 10:7 (Strong's G3815: to *sport* (as a boy): - play.), Luke 7:31-35, Ephesians 5:14-17.

X-Ray - Spiritual insight; could be revelation that an actual x-ray is needed.
John 2:24, Matthew 16:16-17, John 6:68-71, John 16:13, Acts 2:17-18.

Yard - Past, present, or future depending on whether it is back, or front yard.
Philippians 3:13.
> **Back** = Past, as in back yard or back door; previous event or experience, good or evil; that which is behind (in time, past sins or the sins of the forefathers); unaware; unsuspecting; hidden; memory.
> Genesis 22:13, Joshua 8:4.
> **Front** = Future or now, as in front yard or front door; prophecy; in presence of; immediate; current.
> Genesis 6:11-13, Revelation 1:19.

Yeast - Religious doctrine; imposed legalism; hypocrisy; pride; sin; corruption; the kingdom of heaven.
Matthew 16:12 (See with Matthew 23:13-28), Luke 12:1, Mark 8:15, 1 Corinthians 5:6-8, Galatians 5:9, Matthew 13:33, Luke 13:20-21.

Yellow Clouds - Angelic presence; blessings from heaven; enlightenment and glory. See Clouds.

Yeti - Cold-hearted abuser; abomination of the Lord; demonic deception.
Exodus 7:14, Exodus 1:22, Acts 7:19, Proverbs 11:20, Proverbs 6:16-19.

Yoyo - Vacillates; unstable; indecisive; wavers between two opinions; continual changing of mind; recurring issues or illness.
James 1:6-8, 1 Kings 18:21, Ephesians 4:14, Matthew 12:43-45, Matthew 4:23-24.

Yoke - Bondage; enslaved; oppression; burden.
1 Kings 12:10-11, Jeremiah 28:10-14, Isaiah 9:4, Matthew 11:29-30.

Z

Zion - God's kingdom; strength; protection.
Isaiah 8:18, Joel 3:21, Obadiah 1:17.
The Mountain of the LORD = The Chief of the Mountains; Mount Zion; the governing mountain above all other mountains and hills; kingdom cultural influence (equity and justice) over the 7 mountains of society.
Micah 4:1-2, Isaiah 2:2-3, Zechariah 8:3, Amos 4:13, Psalm 2:6.

Zipper - Admonition to silence (zip your lip); revealed.
Psalm 141:3, Isaiah 6:5.
Unzipped fly = Fornication; exhibitionism, embarrassing exposure.
1 Corinthians 6:13-18, 2 Samuel 10:4-5, 1 Chronicles 19:3-5.

Zoo - Strange; commotion; confusion; chaos; disarray; very busy place; tumultuous; noisy; strife; caged in; put on display; diversity of nationalities and types.
Luke 5:26, James 3:16, Judges 16:25.

PART 2

COLORS

Amber - God's glory; purity; holy; God is ministering; anointing of fire.
Ezekiel 1:4, & 27, Ezekiel 8:2.

Black - Lack; sin; ignorance; grief; mourning; gloomy; evil; ominous; famine; burned.
Proverbs 7:6-9, Jeremiah 4:28, Jeremiah 8:21-22, Job 30:30, Lamentations 5:10, Song of Solomon 5:11.

Blue - Spiritual gifts; divine revelation; heavenly visitation; depressed; a male infant.
Numbers 4:7, & 9, Ezekiel 23:6, Proverbs 20:30a, Luke 2:13-14.
The Fear of the LORD. See Candlestick.
Isaiah 11:2 with Exodus 37:17-24, Revelation 4:5, Revelation 5:6, Zechariah 3:8-9, Zechariah 4:2,6, & 10.
Light or Very Light Blue = Spirit of man; evil spirit; corrupt; immature.
Navy Blue = Military authority, strength, and assignments.
Ezekiel 23:6.
Indigo = Power; ruler ship; unimpeded growth; unlimited potential; unstoppable opportunity; God's appearance; God's government.
Numbers 4:12, Numbers 15:38, Esther 8:15, Ezekiel 10:1.
The Spirit of Might. See Candlestick.
See Ezekiel 23:6.
Also see Isaiah 11:2 with Exodus 37:17-24, Revelation 4:5, Revelation 5:6, Zechariah 3:8-9, Zechariah 4:2,6, & 10.

Brass Color - Word of God; word of man; judgment; hypocrisy; self-justification; fake; man's tradition.
Revelation 1:15, Daniel 10:6, Ezekiel 1:7, 1 Corinthians 13:1, Ezekiel 40:3, Isaiah 48:4, 1 Samuel 17:5-6.

Bright-Fire Orange - Power; force; energy; energetic; the emotion of God; danger.
Matthew 5:22, Proverbs 6:27, Deuteronomy 4:36 with Ezekiel 1:26-28, Ephesians 6:14, John 17:17.
The Spirit of Counsel. See Candlestick.
See Deuteronomy 4:36 See with Ezekiel 1:26-28, Ephesians 6:14, and John 17:17.
Also see Isaiah 11:2 with Exodus 37:17-24, Revelation 4:5, Revelation 5:6, Zechariah 3:8-9, Zechariah 4:2,6, & 10.

Bronze Color - Demotion; primitive; unrefined; displacement of gold and silver with bronze a consequence of sin; lewdness; harlotry.
1 Kings 14:25-27.

Brown - Dead (as in plant life); repented; born again; without spirit.
1 Peter 1:24.

Crimson - Blood atonement; forgiveness; Jesus; passion; strong emotion; washing white as snow; wine; sacrifice. See Red.
Isaiah 1:18, Numbers 19:2-10.

Dark or Medium Blue - God's Spirit or Word; blessing; healing; good will.
Proverbs 20:30.

Emerald Green - Christian faith and the Godhead; divine revelation; covenant of mercy.
Revelation 4:3, Isaiah 54:9-10.
The Spirit of the LORD. See Candlestick.
See Revelation 4:3, Revelation 21:19.
Also see Isaiah 11:2 with Exodus 37:17-24, Revelation 4:5, Revelation 5:6, Zechariah 3:8-9, Zechariah 4:2,6, & 10.

Evergreen - Eternal life; immortal. See Trees.
Psalm 92:12.

Fire Orange - Power; force; energy; energetic; emotion of God; danger.
Matthew 5:22, Proverbs 6:27, Deuteronomy 4:36 with Ezekiel 1:26-28, Ephesians 6:14, John 17:17.
The Spirit of Counsel. See Candlestick.
Deuteronomy 4:36 See with Ezekiel 1:26-28, Ephesians 6:14, and John 17:17.
Also see Isaiah 11:2 with Exodus 37:17-24, Revelation 4:5, Revelation 5:6, Zechariah 3:8-9, Zechariah 4:2,6, & 10.

Gold Color - Glory; wisdom; truth; something precious; refining; righteousness; glory of God; kingship; royalty; purity; wealth; favor; prosperity; self-glorification; idolatry; greed; defilement.
2 Chronicles 16:2a, 1 Peter 1:7, Revelation 3:18, Revelation 4:4, Colossians 2:3,
James 2:2-4, Revelation 17:4.

Gray - Not defined; unclear, gray area; vague; not specific; hazy; deceived; ambiguous; deception; hidden; crafty; false doctrine.
Hosea 7:9.

Green - Life; Mortal; renewal; signal to go (green light); wealth; prosperity; prophetic operation.
Genesis 9:3, 1 Peter 1:24, Psalm 37:35, Luke 23:31.
  Emerald Green = Christian faith & the Godhead; divine revelation; covenant of mercy.
  Revelation 4:3, Isaiah 54:9-10.
  The Spirit of the LORD. See Candlestick.
  See Revelation 4:3, Revelation 21:19.

Also see Isaiah 11:2 with Exodus 37:17-24, Revelation 4:5, Revelation 5:6, Zechariah 3:8-9, Zechariah 4:2, 6, & 10.
Evergreen = Eternal life; immortality. See Trees.
Psalm 92:12.
Light Green = Illness; envy; inexperience; carnal; flesh; immature.
Genesis 9:3, 1 Peter 1:24, Job 8:12, Revelation 6:8.

Indigo - Power; ruler ship; unimpeded growth; unlimited potential; unstoppable opportunity; God's appearance; God's government.
Numbers 4:12, Numbers 15:38, Esther 8:15, Ezekiel 10:1.
The Spirit of Might. See Candlestick.
See Ezekiel 23:6.
Also see Isaiah 11:2 with Exodus 37:17-24, Revelation 4:5, Revelation 5:6, Zechariah 3:8-9, Zechariah 4:2,6, & 10.

Iron Color - Strength; powerful; invincible; stronghold; stubborn; judgement from sin.
Daniel 2:40a, Isaiah 48:4, Deuteronomy 28:48, Daniel 4:15.

Lead Color - Weight; wickedness; sin; burden (the cares of the world); judgment; fool, foolishness.
Zechariah 5:8, Exodus 15:10, Proverbs 27:3, Hebrews 12:1.

Light Green - Illness; envy; inexperience; carnal; flesh; immature.
Genesis 9:3, 1 Peter 1:24, Job 8:12, Revelation 6:8.

Light or Very Light Blue - Spirit of man; evil spirit; corrupt; immature.

Navy Blue - Military authority, strength, and assignments.
Ezekiel 23:6.

Orange - Danger; great jeopardy; harm; warning; stubbornness; strong willed; rebellion; witchcraft; Buddhism.
A common color combination is orange and black, which together usually signifies great evil or great danger.
Fire Orange = power; force; energy. Persecution; perseverance; purification.
The Spirit of Counsel. See Candlestick.
Matthew 5:22, Proverbs 6:27.
See Deut 4:36 with Ezekiel 1:26-28, Ephesians 6:14, John 17:17.
Also see Isaiah 11:2 with Exodus 37:17-24, Revelation 4:5, Revelation 5:6, Zechariah 3:8-9, Zechariah 4: 2,6, & 10.

Pink - Flesh; sensual; sensuous; immoral; female rebellion; moral, a heart of flesh; chaste; innocence; feminine; a female infant.
Ezekiel 36:26, 2 Corinthians 3:3, 2 Corinthians 11:2, 1 Samuel 17:42.

Purple - Royalty; rule (good or evil); majestic; noble.
Judges 8:26b, Revelation 17:4, Acts 16:14.
The Spirit of Understanding. See Candlestick.
See Isaiah 11:2 with Exodus 37:17-24, Revelation 4:5, Revelation 5:6, Zechariah 3:8-9, Zechariah 4: 2,6, & 10.

Red - Passion; emotion; enthusiasm; zeal; royalty in warfare; anger; rage; hatred; lust; sin; suffering. See Crimson.
Revelation 6:4, James 4:1, Isaiah 1:18.
The Spirit of Wisdom. See Candlestick.
See Isaiah 11:2 with Exodus 37:17-24, Revelation 4:5, Revelation 5:6, Zechariah 3:8-9, Zechariah 4: 2,6, & 10.

Silver - Knowledge; redemption; refining; idolatry; spiritual adultery; betrayal (30 pieces of silver).
Proverbs 2:3-4, John 17:3, Acts 19:24, Matt 26:14-16.

Steel Color - Weight; wickedness; sin; burden, the cares of the world; judgment; fool or foolishness.
Zechariah 5:8, Exodus 15:10, Proverbs 27:3, Hebrews 12:1.

Tan - Dead (as in plant life); repented; born again; without spirit.
1 Peter 1:24.

Tin - Dross; waste; worthless; impurity; cheap; purification.
Isaiah 1:25.

Very Light Blue - Spirit of man: evil spirit; corrupt; immature.

Violet - Spiritual; modesty; moderation; sobriety; shift from the harsh and brutal to the calm and serene. Amethyst, the twelfth foundational stone of the New Jerusalem.
Revelation 21:20.

White - Pure; without mixture or compromise; unblemished; spotless; triumph; victory in conflict; righteousness; blameless; truth; innocence; illness; judgement.
Revelation 7:9-10, & 13-14, Revelation 19:8, &14, Matthew 8:2-3, Luke 17:12-19, 2 Kings 5:27, Numbers 12:10.

Yellow - Enlightenment; revelation; spiritual insight; gift of God; marriage; family; honour; deceitful gift; timidity; fear; cowardliness.
Psalm 68:13, Proverbs 19:14, 2 Timothy 1:7.
The Spirit of Knowledge. See Candlestick.
See Psalm 68:13, Habakkuk 2:14, 1 Corinthians 2:2, & 9-12.
Also see Isaiah 11:2 with Exodus 37:17-24, Revelation 4:5, Revelation 5:6, Zechariah 3:8-9, Zechariah 4: 2,6, & 10.

PART 3

NUMBERS

One - Beginning; first in time, rank, order, or importance; new; wholeness; unity.
Genesis 1:1, & 5b, Genesis 8:13.

Two - Divide; judge; separate; discern; witness; covenant; marriage.
Genesis 1:6, & 8b, 1 Kings 3:25-28, Genesis 15:10, & 17-18, Jeremiah 34:18-19, Matthew 18:16, Revelation 11:3, Genesis 7:2-3, 9, & 15-16, Matthew 10:6-9.

Three - Conform; obey; copy; imitate; likeness; tradition; indivisible power (the number of the Godhead); invincible.
Genesis 1:9-13, Romans 8:38-39, Ecclesiastes 4:12, 1 John 5:7-8.

Four - Reign; rule, over the world; kingdom; creation, including things in heaven and earth; world impact (world-wide impact – four ends of the earth).
Genesis 1:16-19, Genesis 2:10, Jeremiah 49:36, Ezekiel 1:8, Daniel 7:6, Zechariah 6:5.

Five - Serve; works; service; God's grace to man; responsibility of man; five-fold ministry; bondage (including debt, sickness, phobias, etc.); taxes; prison; sin; motion.
Genesis 1:20, & 23, Genesis 41:34, Leviticus 27:31, Ephesians 4:11, 1 Corinthians 15:10, John 8:34, Revelation 9:5.

Six - Image of man; flesh; carnal; idol; form.
Genesis 1:26a, & 31b, Revelation 13:18.

Seven - Complete; all; finished; rest; perfection.
Genesis 2:1-3, Genesis 7:10.

Eight - New beginning; put off the old man, the works of the flesh; sanctify; manifest; reveal; die; death.

Genesis 17:12a, 2 Chronicles 29:17, 1 Peter 3:18-21, Colossians 3:9, 2 Peter 1:14.

Nine - Harvest of the fruit of your labor; fruit of the Spirit; nine gifts of the Spirit; fruitfulness; gestation, reproduction, fully formed.
Isaiah 65:21, Proverbs 31:16, & 31, Galatians 5:22-23, 1 Corinthians 12:8-10, Romans 6:22, Psalm 139:13-16.

Ten - Measure; try or trial; test or to be tested; temptation; law.
Revelation 2:10a, Daniel 5:27, Genesis 31:7; Exodus 34:28.

Eleven - End; finish; last; stop; incomplete; disorder and chaos.
Matthew 20: 9, & 12.

Twelve - Joined; united; govern; government; oversight.
Luke 9:1-2, Luke 22:30, 1 Corinthians 1:10, Hebrews 13:17.

Thirteen - Rebellion; revolution; rejection.
Genesis 14:4.

Fourteen - Double; recreate; reproduce; generations, lineage of Jesus; disciple; servant; employee or bond slave.
1 Kings 8:65, Matthew 1:17.

Fifteen - Free; grace; liberty; sin covered; honor.
2 Kings 20:6a, Hosea 3:2a, Genesis 7:20.

Sixteen - Spirit; free spirited; without boundaries; without limitations; without law and therefore, without sin, see Romans 4:15; salvation.
Acts 27:34, & 37-38.

Seventeen - Victory (adding all numbers from 1 to 17=153, the number of fish the disciples caught in John 21:11); breakthrough.
Jeremiah 32:17-25 (prayer of victory), & 37-40, 2 Samuel 5:7, & 20.

Eighteen – Justice for losses; repayment; restoration of what the enemy has stolen; put on the Spirit of Christ; judgment; destruction; captivity; overcome.
Judges 10:7-8a, Luke 13:4, 11, & 16.

Nineteen - Barren; ashamed; repentant; selflessness; without self-righteousness.
2 Samuel 2:30, Romans 6:21.

Twenty - Holy; tried and approved or tried and found wanting.
Genesis 37:28, Genesis 45:4-5, Psalm 105:17-20, Acts 7:9-10.

Twenty-One - Conformed into complete perfection (3x7); exceeding sinfulness of sin (complete imperfection).
Exodus 12:18.

Twenty-Two - Light (22 letters in the Hebrew alphabet used to compose the Word of God, is called a lamp). Jesus, the Word is also referred as the Light. Also double 11 therefore double disorder and chaos.
Psalm 119:105, John 1:1-14, John 8:12, John 12:46, Revelation 21:23, Proverbs 6:23, 1 Kings 14:20, 1 Kings 16:29.

Twenty-Three - Death and resurrection life.
Genesis Chapter 23, 1 Corinthians 10:8 (times 1000), Romans Chapter 6.

Twenty-Four - Symbol of Priesthood courses and order; God's perfect government.
1 Chronicles 24:1-19, Revelation 4:4.

Twenty-Five - The forgiveness of sins; grace upon grace (5x5). John 1:14, & 16-17.

Twenty-Six - The gospel of Christ; power of God to salvation. The Hebrew values of God, YHWH adds up to 26 (10+5+6+5). Romans 1:16, 1 Thessalonians 1:5, Hebrews 4:12, Jeremiah 23:29, John 16:7-11.

Twenty-Seven - Preach/minister the gospel in victory (17+10 =27).
1 Timothy 3:1-7 (17 qualifications for ministering the <u>word</u> in <u>victory</u>), Romans 3:19-31.

Twenty-Eight - Eternal life. Also see 4, & 7 (4x7).

Twenty-Nine - Departure.

Thirty - Conformed to the world; maturity for ministry; blood of Jesus (30 pieces of silver); salvation; beginning of service; dedication.
Matthew 26: 14-15, Numbers 4:3-4, Genesis 41:46, 2 Samuel 5:4, Luke 3:21-23.

Thirty-Two - Covenant. Also see 2, & 16 (2x16).

Thirty-Three - Promise.
Luke 3:23 (Jesus at 30 + 3 to 31/2 years of ministry equalling 33 years), 1 Kings 2:11b-12, 1 Chronicles 29:26-28, Acts 13:22-23.

Thirty-Four - Naming of a son. Also see 2, & 17 (2x17).

Thirty-Five - Hope.

Thirty-Six - Enemy. Also see 2, & 18 (2x18).

Thirty-Seven - The Word of God.

Thirty-Eight – Slavery; wandering. 2x19 Also see 2, & 19.
Deuteronomy 2:14.

Thirty-Nine - Disease (39 stripes for 39 root sources to all diseases).
Isaiah 53:5, 1 Peter 2:24, 2 Corinthians 11:24.

Forty - Testing; trial; closing in victory or defeat; probation; full measure of judgement.
Deuteronomy 8:2-5, Luke 4:1-2, 1 Kings 19:8, Jonah 3:4, Genesis 7:12, Numbers 14:33-34.

Forty-Two - Israel's oppression; purging through tests for all wrongdoing; the Lord's advent to the earth; the generations of the lineage of Jesus (14x3).
Revelation 11:2, Revelation 13:5, Matthew 1:17.

Forty-Five - Preservation.
Joshua 14:10-11.

Fifty - Pentecost; Holy Spirit; jubilee; liberty; consecrated ones.
Acts Chapter 2 (Verse 33 particularly), Leviticus 25:10, Psalm 50 = Consecrated ones.

Sixty - Pride; carnal leadership.
Daniel 3:1.

Sixty-Six - Idol worship.
Daniel 3:1-7(sixty cubits... six cubits) AMPC.

Seventy - Number of increase, perfected ministry; restoration; impartation of the Holy Spirit; a generation.
Daniel 9:2, Numbers 11:16-17, Psalm 90:10.

Seventy-Five - Purification and separation.
Genesis 12:4.

Eighty - Beginning of high calling.
Exodus 7:7.

Ninety - Completely tested and approved; complete fruitfulness.
Ezekiel 41:12, John 15:16, Hebrews 11:4.

Ninety-nine – Realization of covenant promise through faith; quickened by the Spirit for spiritual reproduction
Genesis 17:1-8, Romans 4:16-17.

One Hundred - Fullness; full measure; full recompense; full reward; full increase; complete; God's election of grace; children of promise.
Matthew 13:8, &23, Mark 4:8, & 20, Genesis 26:12.

One Hundred Nineteen - The resurrection day; the Lord's Day.
Psalm 119 is an alphabetical Psalm. It consists of twenty-two parts, answering to the number of the Hebrew letters, used to compose the Word of God; every part being divided into eight verses, and each verse beginning with that letter which forms the title of the part.
Psalm 119:119 (See with Malachi 3:2-3, and Matthew 3:12).

One Hundred Twenty - End of all flesh; beginning of life in the Spirit; divine period of probation; dedication.
Genesis 6:3, Deuteronomy 34:7, Acts 1:15, 2 Chronicles 5:12.

One Hundred Forty-Four - God's ultimate in creation; God's ultimate government (12 x12).
Note: The 144,000 (12,000 x12,000 from the 12 tribes of Israel) in Revelation 7:4 and Revelation 14:1-3, marked with God's seal and redeemed, eternally, by God. See One Thousand below.

One Hundred Fifty-Three - Salvation; redemption.
John 21:6-11 See with Matthew 4:18-19, & Ezekiel 47:10.

Three Hundred - Faithful remnant (Gideon's army).
Judges Chapter 7.

Four Hundred - Fullness of kingdom rule (4x100). See 4, & 100.

Four Hundred Ninety - Perfect forgiveness; liberally forgiving.
Matthew 18:21-22 See with Luke 17:3-4.

Five Hundred - Fullness of grace (5 x 100); witness.
1 Corinthians 15:6.

Six Hundred - Warfare.
Exodus 14:7, Judges 3:31, Judges 18:11, & 16.

Six Hundred Sixty-Six (666) - Sign of the number of the beast; antichrist; unholy triad - the dragon, the beast, & the false prophet.
Revelation 13:18, Revelation 16:13.

Seven Thousand - Perfected remnant; 100% faithfulness to God; complete protection.
Romans 11:4-5, 1 Kings 19:18, Romans 9:27.

Seven Hundred Seventy-Seven (777) - Threefold perfection of the Trinity: 7 horns, (Perfect power of God /Jesus - omnipotence), 7 eyes (Infinite knowledge and wisdom of Jesus - omniscience), 7 lamps which are the seven Spirits of God (Holy Spirit - omnipresence), "Holy, holy, holy" See Revelation 4:8, and Isaiah 6:3.
Note, the symbol of the seven horns (perfect power), attributes to the Lamb complete power (See the words of Jesus in Matthew 28:18, "All power is given to me in heaven and in earth").
Revelation 5:6, Zechariah 3:8-9, Zechariah 4:10, Revelation 4:5.

Eight Hundred Eighty-Eight (888) - The first resurrection saints.
Numerical value of the name of Jesus (10+8+200+70+400+200 = 888).
1 Corinthians15:20.

One Thousand - Maturity; full stature; mature service; mature judgement; divine 100 % completeness and the glory of God; millennial rule of Jesus (See Revelation 20:1-6); multiplication; increase. See One Hundred Forty Four's Note on the 144, 000 above.
Daniel 7:9-10, Revelation 5:11-12, Deuteronomy 1:10-11.

PART 4

DIRECTIONS

Back - Past, as in back yard or back door; previous event or experience, good or evil; that which is behind (in time, past sins or the sins of the forefathers); unaware; unsuspecting; hidden; memory.
Genesis 22:13, Joshua 8:4.

Down - Beneath; humbled; demotion; worldly.
Psalm 75:7, Psalm 113:5-6, 2 Samuel 22:28, Psalm 18:27, James 1:9-10, James 2:3.

East - Beginning; God's glory; Law of Moses (therefore, blessed or cursed); birth; first; anticipate; false religion; judgement (east wind).
Genesis 11:2, Job 38:24, Genesis 41:23, & 27, Exodus 10:13, Psalm 103:12, Hosea 12:1, Job 15:2.

Front - Future or Now, as in front yard or front door; prophecy; in presence of; immediate; current.
Genesis 6:11-13, Revelation 1:19.

Left - Spiritual; weakness (of man), and therefore God's strength or ability demonstrated through man's weakness; rejection.
2 Corinthians 12:9a, & 10b, Judges 3:20-21, Judges 20:16, Matthew 24:32-33.
Left Turn = spiritual change.

North - Spiritual; judgment; heaven or heavenly; spiritual warfare (taking your inheritance).
Proverbs 25:23, Jeremiah 1:13-14, Deuteronomy 2:3.

Right - Natural; authority; power; the strength of man or the power of God revealed through man; accepted.
Matthew 5:29a, & 30a, 1 Peter 3:22.
Right Turn = natural change.

South - Natural; sin; world; temptation; trial; flesh; corruption; deception.
Joshua 10:40, Job 37:9.

Up - Above; help; advancement; promotion, difficulty (uphill battle); salvation.
2 Samuel 22:17, Psalm 18:16, Psalm 27:10, Matthew 17:27, Mark 8:34, Mark 10:21.

West - End; grace; death; last; conformed.
Exodus 10:19, Luke 12:54.

ABOUT THE AUTHOR

SANDRA L. DAWSON IS A MEMBER OF VICTORY CHURCH ON THE ROCK Church, in Grande Prairie, Alberta, Canada. She has attended and served as a part of the Tech Team, as well as with a Prayer Team, for 10 years. . She also makes music videos with the current prophetic season in mind. As she is led, specific songs come to mind, along with a visual that she sees, of what the song portrays. She has a YouTube channel where she shares all the music videos she has created.

She received this gift of prophetic dreams and interpretations not long after her salvation, which she has continuously grown in.

Scripture has been a big part of Sandra's maturing in the Lord. Once saved, immediately, she started devouring the Scriptures, memorizing many passages and even certain chapters. This came so naturally to her as a gift from God. This gifting has helped Sandra immensely with knowing and having the ability to search out the Scriptures for many things, coupled with the ability of declaring all the memorized Scriptures to specific situations as well as in intersession. It also, of course, helped with being transformed by the Lord.

Sandra started her Christian walk later in life; it was just a few months before her 40th birthday that she accepted Jesus as her Lord and Saviour.

Before conversion, Sandra did not know anything about the Bible. Not even about it having an Old Testament and a New Testament. All the Scripture she has, has been supernaturally imparted and accelerated. It just goes to show; it is never too late.

Previously, Sandra L. Dawson served at Victory Church of the Peace (originally called Cornerstone Worship Centre), the Church where she first found Salvation. A few years later she moved to Grande Prairie, as she was directed by the Lord, through a dream, of which she received confirmation.

BIBLIOGRAPHY

Doug Addison at https://dougaddison.com "is the founder and president of InLight Connection. Doug is a prophetic speaker, author and coach...
Over the past twenty years, Doug Addison has been a cutting-edge prophetic leader, dream interpreter, entrepreneur, life coach, consultant and trainer...
As a leading expert, Doug has studied, interpreted and instructed many on dreams, visions and the supernatural, bringing deep insight to countless people worldwide."
Quoted from: https://dougaddison.com/about-us
He has many resources on his website. Doug Addison is a very accurate and trustworthy prophetic voice and very knowledgeable in various prophetic interpretations.

Adrian Beale and Adam F. Thompson, DREAMS the Divinity Code, The Keys to Decoding your Dreams and Visions. Updated and Expanded. April 2008, Revised November 2009. This is a very complete and detailed interpretation guide, very informative.

Paul Keith Davis
https://whitedoveministries.org/
Paul Keith Davis

Founder & Leader of WhiteDove Ministries
Paul Keith Davis has written numerous articles appearing in various Christian publications, including the MorningStar Journal, Charisma and Church Growth International. ..." Quote from: https://whitedoveministries.org/about/
The 7 Spirits of God
https://vod.whitedoveministries.org/webinar-56-the-seven-spirits-of-god/
Notes and Chart PDF links below the Video.
https://vod.whitedoveministries.org/wp-content/uploads/Webinar-56-The-Seven-Spirits-of-God.pdf
https://vod.whitedoveministries.org/wp-content/uploads/Webinar-56-Menorah.pdf

James W. and Michal Ann Goll, Dream Language, the prophetic power of dreams, revelations, and the spirit of wisdom. 2006.
This book has a lot of wisdom on dreams, many kinds of dreams, and gives understanding on how to recognize what is from God. Good clear interpretations.
James W. Goll
https://www.godencounters.com/
"JAMES W. GOLL is the president of God Encounters Ministries and has traveled around the world sharing the love of Jesus, imparting the power of intercession, prophetic ministry and life in the Spirit. He has recorded numerous classes with corresponding study guides and is the author of more than forty books, including *The Seer, The Lost Art of Intercession*, *The Coming Israel Awakening* and *The Lifestyle of a Prophet*..." Quote from: https://www.godencounters.com/james-w-goll-bio/
Do You Know the 7 Spirits of God? James W. Goll Article
https://www.godencounters.com/7-spirits-of-god/
"This material is taken in part from the **God Encounters Today book** by James W. with Michal Ann Goll". Quoted from above link. 2017.

Dr. Joe Ibojie, BIBLE-BASED DICTIONARY OF PROPHETIC SYMBOLS FOR EVERY CHRISTIAN Bridging the Gap Between Revelation and Application. PLUS THE EXPANDED VERSION OF THE ILLUSTRATED BIBLE-BASED DICTIONARY OF DREAMS AND VISIONS. 2009.

Ira Milligan, UNDERSTANDING THE DREAMS YOU DREAM, Biblical Keys for Hearing God's Voice in the Night. Revised and Expanded. 2010.
This book has Scripture, with Greek and Hebrew word definitions, included with the references, very handy for the reader.

Dr. Paula A. Price, PH.D., The PROPHET'S DICTIONARY The Ultimate Guide to Supernatural Wisdom. 1999, 2002, 2006.
This is the most complete prophetic guide with amazing revelation. Many subjects, no other book that I have seen, has.

Eric L. Warren
THE SEVEN SPIRITS OF GOD
LEARNING TO WALK IN THE DOMINION AND AUTHORITY OF CHRIST
2010.
This essential resource is full of revelation on this vital teaching.